Awakening Cheops

Awakening Cheops

*Energy of the Great Pyramid –
Avoiding Global Cataclysms*

ANDRZEJ WOJCIKIEWICZ

Library of Congress Control Number: 2019914380

HARDBACK: 978-1-951461-74-4
PAPERBACK: 978-1-951461-73-7
EBOOK: 978-1-951461-75-1

Original title: Przebudzenie Cheopsa

Translated by: Mariusz Wloczyszak
Corrected by: Joseph Nowosielski

Ordering Information:

For orders and inquiries, please contact:
1-888-404-1388
www.goldtouchpress.com
book.orders@goldtouchpress.com

CONTENTS

INTRODUCTION

Dear Reader,

I believe that it is not a coincidence that this particular book found it way into your hands. So-called "coincidences" are often the way life leads us, and so when you finish reading this book, your life may also change its direction in some aspect.

The book describes the stories of people, who experienced such an enormous number of coincidences and events within a few years, that at a certain moment, they understood that all this could not be accidental.

The main character of the book, Lucyna, lives in the Polish city of Wroclaw. She is referred to here as the **Lady Called Life**. Her real name is Lucyna Lobos. It was she who started the story related here as "awakening the Cheops." Lucyna has unique abilities that started to develop within her after her clinical death and "her return from the other side." The book includes excerpts of authentic communications resulting from hypnotic age regression and telepathic channeling sessions conducted with her between May of 2001 and July of 2005.

Hypnosis is referred to in the book as "dreaming" and telepathic channeling as "waking dreaming." During the hypnotic regressions, Lucyna was taken back to the time of the building of the Great Pyramid, and related what she saw through the eyes of an Egyptian priestess. During some sessions she was also capable of traveling in time and space. The telepathic channeling did not require Lucyna to enter an altered state of consciousness. After a brief period of concentration, she was able to "connect" with her spiritual guide, to telepathically hear his voice and repeat what she had heard. The sessions were recorded on audiocassettes and, with Lucyna's permission, I could use them in writing this book.

The metaphors "dreaming" and "waking dreaming" (instead of hypnosis and channeling) were used in order to facilitate understanding of these unusual phenomena by the reader. This allowed communication of many shocking items of information in a simpler way, less "esoteric" and easier to comprehend, especially for those who do not know, understand, or simply accept the reality of such phenomena.

The purpose of Lucyna's communications is to reach the place of burial of the pharaoh who built the Great Pyramid. We call him Cheops in this book, although his real name was Khufu. In context of this book the name "Cheops" should be taken rather symbolically, since there is a lot modern research that suggest, that he Great Pyramid was not build by this pharaoh, but much... much earlier. However finding his tomb of its builder may be the most exciting archaeological event of all times, compared to which, the discovery of Tutankhamen's tomb will become only a pale shadow. The most important objective of the entire project, however, is to save the Earth and humanity from the threats of possible cataclysms predicted by so many prophecies in the past.

All the persons referred to in the book are authentic and are participants in the "Cheops Project." Some are called by their surnames, some only by their given names, while a few remain concealed by pseudonyms.

The source of the information flowing through Lucyna is referred to in the book as the *Universe*. It is the *Universe* leading her and other people, and it is the *Universe* talking directly or indirectly to them. In fact, the *Universe* of this book is the symbol of a specific Spiritual Entity who communicates through Lucyna with our level of matter and provides information through her. The name of this Spiritual Entity is given toward the end of the book.

The events described here are really happening. Step by step, in the following chapters, the reader can follow the circumstances that have led to the archaeological excavations on Mount Sleza near Wroclaw. Since August 2004, until the time of writing (August 2005), these excavations have been conducted by the *Institute of Archaeology of the University of Wroclaw*. This stage of our work has given credibility to the information received with Lucyna's help. It has also made many scientists and archaeologists realize that the sessions with Lucyna are not only a projection of her imagination or a desire to gain publicity, but a verifiable reality. Research in Egypt constitutes the next stage of the project, which was initiated with a trip to Cairo in June 2005.

The book is a metaphor and a warning. Its purpose is to draw attention to the current situation on the Earth, to problems related to global warming, to the external danger of the fluctuating activity of the sun, and of the so-called *Planet X*, about which scientists are writing reports to the Pentagon. It is also a warning about the dangers of the year 2012 that was mentioned in the writings of the Mayas and of the ancient Egyptians.

The final chapters offer a "projection into the future." They have not happened yet but were forecast in Lucyna's sessions ("dreams"). Will they come true? Life will tell…

Andrzej Wójcikiewicz

1

IT ALL STARTED WITH A SMILE

For many years, for as long as I remember, I have been a *Wanderer*. I wandered from city to city and taught people to recognize their Own Voice within themselves and to find the Best Way. I taught them to talk to it and learn from it. Many envied me, because I could travel all around the country, all around the world; I was not committed to one place and it seemed to me that this was my *Best Way*. Everyone seeks his or her own Way, and there are moments when it seems that he or she has found That Which Was Sought, only to find out after a while that That Was Not Yet It. I thought that That Was Already It...

And then, on a March afternoon in 1997, I met along my Way the **Girl to Whom Every Morning Smiles** and gradually, my entire, carefully planned world started to change. From the very first meeting, the smile accompanied her. Even when she was not smiling, when sadness came to her face, she had an inner smile, hidden and visible only to the initiated. It was this smile that made me invite her to dinner. And so it began. Like in the story of the Little Prince, I became responsible for what I tamed, although there were moments when I did not quite know what to do with this responsibility.

Our becoming acquainted with one another took a very long time, although in reality, we knew each other since the origin of existence (though we were not aware of this in this lifetime). We met from time to time. She smiled and I wandered on. It took some years before Time came to visit us...

Time knocked on her door and asked, "Are you ready for change?"

"I don't know," she said, "but if you have come, then I must be ready."

And then Time sent us a kiss, not even asking me for permission. Since then, smiles have started leading us along a Way completely different from that which we had thought to be the only one possible.

I did not yet know then that her kisses would be unlike the kisses of all other Women Who Wanted to Be Kissed. That they would mark the beginning of the Way of the New Awareness, of the Way to Awakening the **Pharaoh ...**

This way began, in fact, on a day when my wanderings once again led me to the neighborhood where the *Girl to Whom Every Morning Smiles* lived. When she saw me, she said mysteriously, "Come with me, I will introduce you to a Very Extraordinary Person. Do you want to meet her?"

"Your friends are my friends. If it is important to you, I will be happy to meet her."

"Yes, it is important, because she asked me about it and I always do my best to fulfill the requests of my friends."

And this is how, with the help of the *Girl to Whom Every Morning Smiles*, I met the **Lady Called Life**. It was a strange meeting. Initially, the new acquaintance did not seem promising. The *Lady Called Life* was timid, distant, and cautious. She was afraid of everything and everybody. And although her Way was clearly designated, at that time, she was not yet sure if she was proceeding the way she should. She had, however, a huge advantage over All Others Who Walked Their Own Ways. She heard the Universe leading her.

She talked to it every day, and was assured every day that she was proceeding along the Right Way, though somewhere deep within her lay a fear of the Unknown; a fear of herself. She did not yet know how far to go or whether she would reach where she wanted to be. Moreover, she could not get there all by herself. This could be the reason why the Universe placed in her Way the *Girl to Whom Every Morning Smiles*. The energy of a smile reinforces the goal, gives a feeling of enhanced confidence, and brightens life, just as the sun brightens the land. The Universe decided to offer such a smile to the *Lady Called Life*, to help her proceed along the designated Way.

One day, the Way itself told her that she should ask me, the *Wanderer,* for help.

Initially, I did not want to help. Indeed, how could I know where she wanted to go, and why we should travel somewhere together? I did not know her. Till now, my wanderings had involved only the place where the *Girl to Whom Every Morning Smiles* lived. Soon, however, it became obvious that it was not by accident that the Universe had placed her smile in my Way.

"Why do you want me to help you?" I asked the Lady Called Life. "We hardly know one other."

"The *Universe* told me that we, together, are to awaken the Pharaoh," she replied.

This request surprised me. I had no idea what the *Lady Called Life* was talking about. What universe and what pharaoh? I knew that all the pharaohs had died a long time ago. At most, some of their mummies remained, but one cannot wake up a mummy.

"I can see no sense in your words," I said, "Please explain."

"There is a level of existence," the *Lady Called Life* started to explain, "which I call the *Universe*. I talk to It every day in my thoughts, and It leads me through life and helps me to meet different people. It helped me meet the *Girl to Whom Every Morning Smiles*, It helped me meet you, and It gave me my present name. Earlier, I had the name of the **One Who Is Afraid of Her Own Shadow.**

I come across many people in my wanderings and it does not surprise me when they speak unusual things. This time this was uniquely unusual… so unique that I started listening to her words attentively.

I asked her, "Why does the *Universe* talk to you in particular? Does It also talk to others?"

The thought crossed my mind that psychologists have multitudes of patients, who state that they converse with various exceptional dead persons or that they are those persons themselves. However, there was something fascinating and normal in the behavior of the *Lady Called Life*. A feeling that cannot be explained by reason.

"It talks to every human being on the Earth," she replied to my question. "It is also talking to you, but you don't hear It now. We together are to awaken the Pharaoh Cheops, the One Who Built the Great Pyramid."

"But we are in the twenty-first century," I tried to remain on the side of rational thought. "Cheops lived a long, long time ago. How can we awaken him?"

"Cheops is only sleeping. He is waiting to be woken. He must see the sun, before things go wrong on the Earth… This means that we have to find his body, his mummy, and excavate it.

"Why should *we* look for his mummy?" I asked, surprised. "There are so many people on Earth who could do it better."

"I don't know why it is up to us. I only know that you are to help in this. You and the *Girl to Whom Every Morning Smiles*."

"I am a *Wanderer*," I smiled unconvincingly. "I know nothing about pharaohs, nothing about archaeology, and I have seen pyramids of Egypt only in pictures."

For a while, I considered what to do, but what I had heard seemed to me so inconceivable that I leisurely wandered along to another city, to stop thinking about the Pharaoh and about the notion that somewhere there was something that I could not understand.

It was March of the year 2001.

2

HOW THE LADY CALLED LIFE VISITED THE UNIVERSE

The *Girl to Whom Every Morning Smiles* has the given name Iwona. Her smile was as extraordinary as she was, and so I bestowed on her that very special name. When you encounter someone along your way, you do not know what this encounter signifies for you, where it will lead you, what changes will entail, or how it will change your future. And I did not know what her smile really meant. Why did this happen?

Its true significance was explained by the *Lady Called Life*. Her real name is Lucyna. It was she who began to make sense of successive events; she explained to me why one smile may change one's whole destiny. Her life was initially as normal as the life of every "normal" person on Earth. Her Destiny was changed only after her encounter with the *Universe*. It appeared to her many years ago, at the time when she survived her clinical death, and asked her to pay It a visit.

"Tell me about this meeting," I asked her when we met during my wandering.

"I will tell you," she replied, "but you must open your mind to things that you may not understand."

"My mind is open. In my wanderings, I also tell strange things to people, so you go ahead. If I do not understand something, I do want to understand."

"What you will hear is also strange," Lucyna started her story. "Twelve years ago, during an operation in a hospital, I crossed over to 'the other side' and I was 'sent back' here."

We both laughed at this "sending back," although I could not imagine how anyone could be "sent back" from a place existing only in the imagination, because that is how I understood her mention of "the other side."

"Tell me more," I asked. "What kind of operation was it that treated you with such a trip?"

"I had cancer. During the operation, the doctors made a mistake and overdosed my anesthesia, so I flew away into the beyond. I paid a visit to the *Universe*, in Its home, and this was the 'other side.'"

Recollections came to my mind of books written by doctors who described clinical death and the stories of "traveling through a tunnel" told by the patients who came back from there. Could Lucyna also have made such a trip?

"Tell me: what did this 'home' look like? How did the 'visit' start?"

"At a certain moment during my operation, I started to wonder how these doctors had put me to sleep, since I could see what they were doing. I was aware that I was on the operating table, and that I was being operated on; I could hear the doctors, their shouting and their swearing. I wanted to let them know that I was not asleep, but my body did not give any reaction. I continued to try to made contact with the doctors and then suddenly, I could see nothing at all. Total darkness. A small light started to emerge from this darkness. I did not know what it could be, but I was intrigued. The light started to grow and revolve. This light started to draw me in; I felt I was soaring through a tunnel of light. I did not see my body any more. It was as if only my spirit existed, but I did not understand this at all. Together with the light, music began to pull me in. It was so beautiful that I have never, to this day, to this moment, heard anything like it — a combination of flute and tiny church bells. All this was becoming more and more intense, and the light was so warm, it wrapped itself soothingly around me. I don't remember how long this lasted. I know that the music continued, and I felt so good within all of this, that nothing else was required, other than just being within this."

"Did you know then that it was the *Universe* asking you to visit?" I asked.

"How could I know? I did not know where I was, at whose place, nor in what form I existed. I had no idea that it was the *Universe* inviting me to Its home. I felt so good that I wanted to stay where I was forever."

"So, how did it happen that you returned?"

"It told me to. I suddenly heard a voice… the voice ordering me to return."

"What did it tell you?"

"The voice that I heard there told me I had to return. It said something remarkable: 'Go back! We will call on you.' I will remember this till the end of my days."

"What happened next?"

"I was forced out. It was as if a vacuum cleaner had been switched on, but the direction was reversed. I was shoved very quickly back into that tunnel of light and again, I heard the voices of the doctors saying, 'Well, we have her back.' The point of light disappeared and I saw the clock, which indicated ten o'clock. When I was awakened back in the recovery room, I told the doctors that they were swearing too much, and that using such scurrilous words in the presence of a woman was not appropriate. They only looked at each other in silence. Then I remarked that the operation took a long time, starting at eight o'clock and finishing at ten, because I saw the clock. The doctor asked, 'What clock? There are no clocks in the operating room.' It turned out that at ten, I was dying."

For a while, Lucyna and I remained silent. I could see that she was reliving that extraordinary trip to the place from which few return. I allowed her to remain silent, since I also needed a moment of reflection on what is really present "on the other side."

"What a great trip I had," she said after a while, "but evidently, I had to return here."

"What happened to you after your 'return?'"

"From the time of my 'return,' strange things started happening to me. I had some visions. I started to 'see' apparitions. It frightened me very much, because this generally happened at night. When it began to intensify, I thought I had gone mad. I went to a psychiatrist, who examined me thoroughly and found no pathology, no clinical changes. But I continued to have these nightly visits."

"What visits are you talking about? Did someone come to you during the night?"

"Well, now I know that it was the *Universe* letting me know that back then, It started to prepare me for my role on the stage of a life different from what I used to have. At that time, I was not really aware of who was visiting me. In my imagination, I saw figures and I heard voices. One day, I told a friend about all this, and he took me to the **Man Who Could Make People Fall Asleep**. Stanislaw (for this was the given name of this specialist) asked me why I had come to see him. 'I don't know,' I replied, 'but please put me to sleep, then something should become clearer.'

"He looked at me as if I were mad, and shrugged his shoulders. He then asked me, just in case, if I was on drugs and commenced his procedure. After a few moments, I was gone. And then, as if I were a ventriloquist, a male voice spoke through me, greeting Stanislaw very graciously, and said, 'My name is the **Universe**; I am Lucyna's spirit guide. Tell her that I am now calling her, that the time has come to start working for me.' It spoke for a long time, but Stanislaw was unable to pose even a single question. When I was awoken, I saw that both Stanislaw and my friend were pale as chalk and severely shaken. They told me, with details, what had happened. And this was how the *Universe* 'officially' became part of my life."

"Did you stop being afraid?"

"Yes, I stopped being afraid, because I felt the *Universe* as a very good energy. From that time, I have been guided and taught."

"What did that 'teaching' consist of? Did you enter an altered state of consciousness, in which the *Universe* taught you?"

"No, it was not like that," Lucyna replied. "I would hear something that could be called an 'inner voice' telling me, 'You will do this or that; you will start learning; I will show you new things; I will prepare you for the mission.' It was as if somebody was teaching a small child. I learned 'to walk.' I learned to dream. At that time, I did not yet know what the mission was to be. I often asked the *Universe,* 'Why did you pick me? Could you not find someone else? There are so many clairvoyants all over the world, waiting only to talk to you.' Sometimes, It said, 'Because you are the priestess.' I did not question this but I did not know what this meant. One day, It told me, 'You will be guided to the Great Pyramid, the Pyramid of Cheops.'"

"Were you very surprised by this?"

"Of course. Previously, I used to see the pyramids, especially the Pyramid of Cheops, as a pile of stones, and I would ask myself what various fools could see in these stones. However, sometime around 1997, something happened, which I can call a turning point. A photograph of the Great Pyramid fell into my hands. When I picked it up, I felt as if an electric current had penetrated me. When I asked about it, the *Universe* told me that the mission had begun."

Then it came into my mind that this was the same time in which the *Universe* had placed in my way the smile of the *Girl to Whom Every Morning Smiles*. What an interesting coincidence, I thought.

"Did you read any books about the Pyramid?" I continued my questioning.

"I have read only one of the books about the Pyramid. It was written by some German scholar. Frequently in bookshops, I would pick up a book about the **Pyramid of Cheops**, and then, leave with a different book. To this day, I cannot read anything on this subject. When I pick up such a book, it is as if it was burning me. Tears come into my eyes, I cannot see anything and I feel sleepy. It is as if the *Universe* was 'taking' it out of my hands. I asked It about this, and It said, 'You will not clutter your mind with rubbish that people make up. You need to have a clear mind.'"

"What else did the *Universe* say?"

"*The Universe* said that I was a priestess when the Pyramids were built and that, at the proper time, It would put in my way people who will help me and who would lead me, and I would become only a tool. Those people will not be accidental. They will be selected."

"What happened then?"

"For a long time it was tranquil. *The Universe* talked to me, taught me automatic writing, taught me to listen to Its voice, taught me to understand. Initially, when I started to write automatically, this produced rubbish. Slowly, I managed better and better, allowing my hand to be guided."

"How did people react to you? Did you tell them about your conversations with the *Universe*?"

"During the course of those years of learning, many people were around, but they disappeared fast. They left, as if I pushed them away. *The Universe* explained to me that my uniqueness scared them. I do not consider myself to be 'unique' and I know that I am only a tool, a link. I am glad it was so, as I did not have to waste my time on human stupidity, which saw only that I was 'different.'"

"What do you do to make contact with the *Universe*? Do you close your eyes and relax?"

"I have to focus on something. I concentrate best by looking at flowers. When I am focused, the *Universe* contacts me. It helps me to see images, It helps me to dream. When I am asleep, It takes care of my dreams."

"Have you talked to any priest? Surely, the *Universe* is a world of spirituality, a world about which priests should know a lot. Did they help you?"

"Oh, *Wanderer*, you know that priests usually stay away from people like me. Yes, along my way, I met a priest. His name was Stanislaw and he was a specialist in exorcism. At first, he accused me of making it all up or engaging in spiritualism. Once, I met with him and asked the

Universe to talk to him through me. I talked at length and when the priest heard this, he said to me, 'I don't know how you have done this, but you spoke in the language of priests. That this was an authentic communication leaves not the slightest doubt. I do not know how, but you have managed to pass through the gate to the other world.' In conclusion, he added, 'You have my blessings. Continue doing this, for this is good. Do not allow yourself to be distracted by insinuations of people. There is a purpose in this, since the *Universe* called on you. You must not retreat now. You have to continue going along this road, because this is the road of truth.'"

"That must have been quite an experience for him," I remarked.

"He was so moved, he had tears in his eyes. I also burst into tears then. This is how our meeting ended, and I was assured that I was on a good road, not one of illusions or hallucinations."

And so, toward the end of the twentieth century, when the Pisces was about to pass power on to Aquarius, the *Lady Called Life* was reborn. *The Universe* started to live in her imagination; she talked to It, argued and disputed, although in her private life, it was still difficult for her to tell anyone that she was having such conversations. When someone says that he or she "hears the voice of the Universe" and converses with It, the so-called "normal person" is sure that the former must be mentally disturbed and tries to keep away. For a "normal person," this is how schizophrenia looks. Time passed and Lucyna continued working in her profession, therapeutic massage. The "other dimension" was gradually becoming a more and more clear, more reliable, and more significant element of her life.

Looking at all of this from the perspective of time, I know that the *Universe* planned all the events very precisely. It guided each of us, adjusting everything in turn in such a way so that the *Girl to Whom Every Morning Smiles* smiled at the appropriate moment for me, the *Wanderer.* So that at exactly the proper time I would meet the *Lady Called Life.* So that, for each of us involved in this project, and for those who will become involved, the road toward Egypt and the tomb started right at the beginning of the Age of Aquarius.

3

THE FIRST DREAM OF THE PRIESTESS. THE CONSTRUCTION OF THE GREAT PYRAMID

I meet many people along my way, but striking up a friendship with them is something that rarely happens. Like every *Wanderer,* I meet them, share my knowledge, and leave. With Lucyna, it was different. There was an immediate awareness of her unusual and exceptional being. How did this come about? A coincidence? It may be that I simply like people who express their emotions and opinions directly, without wrapping them in beautified words that really mean nothing. Lucyna openly expressed her opinions about daily life in Poland. She talked to me honestly, although initially with some considerable reservation. Well, I was a *Wanderer,* a globetrotter, who had already seen a lot in his life, while she was a *Masseuse Repairing* the *Spines of Strangers* and the *Person to Whom* the *Universe had Conferred* the *Name of Life.*

For me, her world was something unknown. She called it the World of Spiritual Entities, the World of Energy. This was for her the *Universe,* which guided and taught her. For me, themes "from the other side" were just fairy tales. Spirits were always associated in my mind with something that haunts. A subconscious fear had been within me, even as an adult. I always admired people who said that they were "talking to spirits," but I was wary of such people and avoided them.

In Lucyna, I met a person who not only behaves quite normally. Like any other she swears normally like any other Pole, but also declares that she talks with the *Universe* and quarrels with It, and this was just part of her daily routine (like eating scrambled eggs or drinking coffee).Not only was I not afraid of her, but I was fascinated by this.

I listened to her stories with some degree of incredulity, but, after all, every one of us has a Guardian Angel. For Lucyna, the *Universe* was her Angel. For her, this was a world of Guardians of People, of Guardians of the Earth, a world representing the highest Spiritual Entities guiding our life as humanity and the life of every single person. This was a world guided by the will of the Supreme Being, the Almighty Being, the Supreme Intelligence, the entity which we humans call "God." This is why Lucyna was not afraid of contacts with the *Universe*. For her, It was the embodiment of the Supreme Good, the Guardian of All That Existed, who, through Its Angels, had selected her to communicate important information to people.

"Is the *Universe* your Guardian Angel?" I once asked her.

"A Guardian Angel is something else," she replied. "It comes at the moment of birth and remains with you all the time. *The Universe* takes care of me through Special Guardians, who help me in the mission, who guide me. It speaks not only to me, but also to all people. To you, also."

Yes, the *Universe* spoke to me with Its own voice, but I listened only to what I wanted to hear.

"Can you help me fall asleep?" Lucyna asked me one day.

"I know nothing about putting people to sleep," I replied, surprised.

"*The Universe* states that you do know," she said. "I want you to help me go back in my dream to the time when the pyramids were built."

This theme was strange and very remote to me. I could not imagine how I could help somebody dream about something about which I knew nothing.

My reluctance led to the **Lady Who Can Move Back in Time** appearing along the way of Lucyna. Her name was Łucja. Even psychologists have spines that need special attention from time to time. Since Lucyna was a *Person Who Can Repair Spines in Pain*, Łucja was repaired. Maybe out of gratefulness, maybe by accident, she agreed to become the *Psychologist Who Would Make Lucyna Go Back In Time for the First Time and Allow Her to Have a Dream about the Pyramid*. This was how the first Important Conversation with the *Universe* was conducted with Łucja's help. It occurred in Iwona's home.

One day, in May of 2001, Lucyna comfortably arranged herself to sleep and started listening to the voice of the **Lady Who Can Move Back in Time**.

"I want you to fall asleep," Łucja spoke in a quiet, soothing voice. "I want you to start your dream of a time long ago. I want you to leave the gates of your current existence, to pass through them and start anew a dream, which you may have dreamt before. This will be the dream about the Pyramid, about Cheops, about what nobody has yet really dreamed, about what no living person has ever seen. Can you dream such a dream?"

"I can," replied Lucyna and opened the gate of time, merging her thoughts with the unity of time and space, with the field of information where the past, the present, and the future exist simultaneously. She became the **Priestess Ki**. She became the *Lady Called Life*.

The dream was clear and full of colors. Łucja had no doubts that this was an authentic dream of the Priestess prepared to travel in time.

"I am in a temple in Egypt," the Priestess dreamt. "In the temple of the Goddess Isis. I have been given the name Ki, which means Life. I am the Priestess, the servant of the **Priest Juno**. He is building the Pyramid together with Cheops. He is the Chief Builder."

"Dream on," Łucja pleaded, "and tell us, are they building the Pyramid now?"

"No," Ki spoke slowly and sleepily. "The preparations start with building the facilities. People need to have a place to live. Tents are being put up, a very large number of tents. As far as the eye can see, one can see tents. They are setting up more and more of them. The Tent of the Temple is also being erected. It will serve Cheops and **Juno**. This is a strange tent. Everything takes some time."

"What year is it?" Łucja asked.

"I do not see time. I am with the priest. He is very good."

"What does the **Priest Juno** do?"

"He is the chief priest, he serves the Pharaoh."

"Are you with him?"

"I am with him always, I help him, I carry out his instructions. The construction of the facilities for the people and animals is almost finished. The settlement is almost finished. Cheops himself is arriving. He is a man 35 to 40 years of age. He is very beautiful and possesses such dignity. He tells the people that the work on the construction has begun. Cheops and Juno are preparing the people only to assist in the construction and do auxiliary work. The work will not be hard and so there is even more joy among the people. They have come from all parts of Egypt and from the whole world."

"Go on," Łucja encouraged her. "Tell us everything you see and experience, everything your eyes can see, because you are talking about what no one has ever seen. If you are telling the truth and you are the Priestess Ki, live that life and dream about it, because you are dreaming a dream that nobody has yet dreamt. So many people dearly want to have such dreams, but do not know how. Dream and tell what you see."

"I see how they are building the Pyramid," Ki continued her story. "It is being built not by people, but by the **White Winged Brethren**, who have come from the **Other Earth**... From a great distance... They are beautiful, and their base is behind the Earth's Moon. Cheops told me about all this. He is very good to me. I believe him, although people cannot understand. I can see the vehicles used by them. This construction will take twenty years."

"Continue telling your dream," Łucja whispered. "Anyone can dream, but your dream is so exceptional that time becomes one with that which was and that which is now. You may be seeing the gate of time which no one has ever passed through just like you. Do you know why you dream this?"

"I know. I know my Way. I have found it. I am to help find the Tomb. Now I can see the building of the Pyramid, because Cheops is still alive. He is directing the construction… him and Juno. They direct the people helping in the construction work… they are good for them… Cheops and Juno are friends of the White Brethren. In fact, it is the White Brethren who are building the Pyramid. They have come from Orion, from the planet Ashun. They are very tall and beautiful. They wear one-piece garments, closely covering their bodies. On their heads, they have helmets. I see them; they have such good eyes. I would like to dream like this all my life. I feel so much warmth and love… Will you allow me to remain in this dream forever?"

"Please, continue your dream. Your dream is extraordinary," Łucja assured her. "I will allow you to dream as long as you want, but you will come back to me, because you have said that you have a mission to fulfill. This is an important mission."

"The Pyramid is being built at night," Ki continued her dream, "because in Egypt, the nights are cooler, and the stone building blocks are so hot that this cannot be done during the day. They are transported to the construction site. Airships bring them, the airships of the White Brethren. These airships are rectangular; some also have the shape of a corncob. Each stone block is lifted by means of some strange rays. These rays emerge from the airship and thus the blocks are placed each one on top of the others. I see how the airship lifts the block, which is first polished. The cutting of the blocks is done with a sword that looks like lightning, which also emerges from the airship. Then a streak of light lifts the block, moves it through the air, and places the block on the pyramid like a brick, without any equipment, without workers, without effort, and without suffering. This is a marvelous, wonderful sight; something that we Egyptians do not understand, but we are happy because we feel we are being cared for. The Pharaoh is being cared for, Juno, and all of us…"

"I know that you are dreaming your dream more and more deeply, that you see your dreams more and more clearly," Łucja whispered to the Priestess, "but Pharaoh and Juno are human beings, like yourself. You are a human being from the future, a human being of this Earth and from this Earth. Does your dream show you what these people do? There must be very many people there, beside the Pyramid. Dream on and tell us what you see."

"Yes, I see people," Ki dreamt. "Working people. The people pour water onto the stones that were placed by the airships. So much water is needed... water cools... water binds... every consecutive block is watered... In the future, nobody will guess how much water was needed... People will wonder how the Pyramid was built, how the blocks were joined together... It was water... so simple... The White Brethren devised this..."

"Ki," Łucja whispered, "I will need to wake you up soon. You must return from your dream and become the *Lady Called Life* in the distant future. You have to become Lucyna again. Your future is beautiful... just dream about your mission. Tell me why you have to find the Tomb."

Ki curled up in her dream and began to weep.

"I don't want to dream about it," she said. "I don't want to... The Pharaoh has died."

There was a moment of silence, during which the Priestess experienced something. This was her tragedy, her grief, her despair. Finally, she tilted her head and continued talking about her dream.

"I am to find the tomb of Cheops," she said quietly. "I am to come back to the Earth in the distant future and meet people who will help me in this. Now I see the burial of the Pharaoh. They do not bury him in the Pyramid. Cheops purposefully did not allow himself to be buried in the Pyramid. The strangers who built the Pyramid did whatever they could to remove all traces, foreseeing that people may plunder the pyramids. They will be looking for treasures and that was why the Pharaoh chose a site nearby, and at the same time, distant. Nearby, because no scholar will think that it could be so close. Within the tomb are stone tablets, all covered with inscriptions; many of them. They are made of a stone that looks like granite, but is lustrous. Throughout the whole period of the construction of the Pyramid, the priests inscribed the information. On the tablets is inscribed who built the Pyramid and what it conceals. It is inscribed that the Pyramid is the central point for connection with the Other Earth. Within the Pyramid is a device that runs all the time on the basis of magnetic fields flowing in both directions."

"Your dream will come to an end soon," Łucja whispered quietly, "so tell only why the Pharaoh has to be found in the future."

"The tomb has to be found," Ki dreamed on, "because the secret has to be revealed, in order to create for people the same Earth as the other one. When this happens, those who built it will come, they will teach us everything, they will repair what has been destroyed by people. They will teach love and they will give love. Everything was precisely planned, designed, and discussed at the time of construction. So it must happen, so Juno told me, so decided the White Brethren. I must find the tomb because I know exactly where it is... and I will know it in the future, when I return to the Earth."

Łucja was listening, fascinated with this extraordinary dream, this extraordinary description. For some time, there was silence, broken only by Ki's more and more restless breathing. Łucja knew that the time had come for the return, for the awakening. Ki had to carry out the return journey in time.

"Don't wake me," Ki pleaded, "I want to be with the Pharaoh."

"You are needed in my time," Łucja said. "Your body and your dream have to be brought to the future. You will pass through the Gate of Time again many times, but now, you are on your way back."

Ki returned from her dream very slowly. She was moving in time through thousands of years of the Old and New Age to Time Zero. The time when the *Universe* chose Lucyna from the Polish city of Wroclaw as Its link. As the one who would awaken Cheops, so that people would understand love...

And to save the Earth.

4

LISTENING TO THE UNIVERSE

The way along which I walked with the *Girl to Whom Every Morning Smiles* was winding, turbulent, and uneven. At times, it was a narrow path, and one had to clamber up with great effort. At times, it was a broad highway with beautiful views and experiences so wonderful that it appeared to be the Only Way to the Omnipresent Goal. This goal was always with us, although now and then, it slipped out of sight. There were moments when it seemed to us that we knew where we were heading, only to notice later that we were going uphill with no end in view. As a *Wanderer*, I was used to various complexities of the terrain, since I have been wandering around for so many years. Despite my experience, it was difficult for me to focus on where I was going and to take care not to go astray and take the Path Which Leads Not to the Place that It Should. At first, we did not have any road signs along our way. There were moments when we walked hand in hand along the sea shore, with warm, soft sand under our feet. At other times, I felt sharp stones and traps, which had to be avoided.

The *Lady Called Life* was our road sign. She once looked at me, and said, "You are going along the proper road, but not necessarily in the proper direction."

"I don't understand," I replied. "If the road is good, it must lead me where I want to go."

"Not necessarily," she persisted. "Your eyes reach only as far as the horizon. That which is really important is hidden to your eyes."

"How am I to see what is hidden?"

"Do not look with your eyes nor with your mind. Look with your heart, with the Breath of the Universe, which enters your lungs every day. *The Universe* breathes in every action of yours and in the words of the *Girl to Whom Every Morning Smiles*. You both are Its United Breath. You only have to learn to listen to that which It is passing on to you, what It is saying to you. You have to make many changes."

"Of late, I do not feel the *Universe* talking to me at all," I said. "It may be that the *Girl to Whom Every Morning Smiles* is more sensitive in this respect. After all, she is a woman and women are more sensitive to all universes. I am normal. I do not occupy myself with the universe. I occupy myself with my wanderings."

"And I hear everything that the *Universe* says about you and about her," persisted the *Lady Called Life*. "She also has to make many changes in her life, though she does not know this yet."

"How do you know that what you are hearing is really the voice of the *Universe*? It may be only the Voice of Your Imagination."

"I know, because the *Universe* speaks to me about what will be. Its words are then confirmed by life. That was why I know that It speaks the truth and that It is the True Voice. If you want, I can teach you to listen."

I hesitated, because in fact, in the depth of my soul, I did not believe that anything (besides people) could talk to me. People use words, which are understandable. How can the *Universe* talk to me?

"But the *Universe* does not know the language of people," I objected

"It knows," replied the Lady Called Life. "People can easily cheat you. Spoken words may seem credible and conceal the real intentions. You cannot cheat the *Universe*. It reads your mind, feels your emotions, and connects itself to your mind. It is with you and It can guide you, if you ask It. It can show you the way far beyond the horizon, which is inaccessible to your eyes. It talks to everyone, but very few are able to hear It."

"In that case, what is the *Universe*?"

"It is energy. It unites everything that is. When you think, you send out energy. When you feel emotions, you send out energy. When you take action, you show your energy. All this unites you with the *Universe*. When you ask It for something, It responds, because your thought is composed of the same energy that It uses. When good emotions embrace you, you link up with It; when bad emotions embrace you, you move apart, separate yourself. You are alone."

"What is this energy called?"

"Love..."

"What is love?"

"Ask It; It will give you an answer."

"Good," I said, "teach me to listen."

"When you are ready, I will teach you," she said. "For the time being, try to hear It by yourself."

I left on another wandering and I still did not know how to talk to the *Universe*. I tried to listen in the morning and in the evening; I tried to listen to It in my dreams, but how could I know whether my thoughts and dreams were the Voice of the *Universe* — or only my longing for It? *The Girl to Whom Every Morning Smiles* walked with me along the uneven way and also was not sure whether she was traveling along the right way. Every now and then, she looked back, wondering whether to turn back or go ahead. I did not know how to help her or even whether I should help. Surely, everyone has to find his or her own path.

One day, she said to me, "The *Lady Called Life* wants to meet you. *The Universe* told her that you are ready. You are to help her talk with the Pharaoh Cheops."

I was surprised, "What did It tell her?"

"That you are to help her meet with Cheops." The *Girl to Whom Every Morning Smiles* was somewhat embarrassed.

I thought that I, personally, did not know Cheops, so how could I introduce these two and help them to talk with one another? Furthermore, this was a Pharaoh who lived quite a long time ago and I had no opportunity to meet him. This request, therefore, was not only strange but also completely preposterous.

"What are we to do at this meeting?" I asked just to keep the conversation going.

"She wants you to put her to sleep. She wants to return to the Pyramid once more."

"But Łucja has already done that," I replied. "I do not know how to do this. Besides, talking through a dream is not for me a reliable method of communication, especially with such an important person as Cheops."

"She says you will do it well. *The Universe* told her so."

The thought crossed my mind that even the *Universe* may have really weird notions, and I dropped the subject.

One day, a strange thought came into my head: "In my wanderings, I help so many people to fall asleep and I teach them how to talk with their dreams, and how to understand their innermost hopes and desires. Could this be the same as talking with the *Universe*? Perhaps, I could do the same with the *Lady Called Life*." If the *Universe* says I can, It could be right. If I am to help her meet the Pharaoh in her dream, then everything is possible in dreams. So what that I don't know Cheops, that I have not drunk wine or beer with him, or that he is a few thousand years old, while I am still far away from one hundred? Apparently, the *Universe* does not recognize the notion of time if It proposes such things.

I phoned the *Girl to Whom Every Morning Smiles* and told her I was willing. She was delighted and promised that she would pass this on to Lucyna. At that moment, I felt the smile of the whole universe, which suddenly also became *my Universe*.

When my wandering led me again to the place where the *Lady Called Life* lived, I met her and helped her fall asleep, so that she could see Cheops.

"Who are you?" I asked her when she fell asleep.

"I am the Priestess devoted to the god Ra. My name is Ki, which means Life."

"What do you do?"

"I serve the priests, mainly the priest Juno, who supervises and manages the construction of the Pyramid."

"Do you talk to him often?"

"Yes, since I am always with him."

"What year is it?"

"I do not see time... This is the time of the building of the Pyramid, the time of the life of Cheops."

"Is the *Universe* with you?"

"It is. It is always with me."

I thought it was a good moment to talk directly to the *Universe*. After all, It had asked for the dream for the Priestess, It had provoked the conversation, and so I felt entitled to ask It some questions.

"May I ask the *Universe* a question?" I asked.

"Yes," Ki replied sleepily, "ask. It will give you an answer."

"Who are you really?" I asked the *Universe*.

"I am the **Guardian of the Earth**," It replied through the Priestess.

"Why did you want to talk to me?"

"Because you do not hear me in any other way."

"Why should I hear you?"

"Because in front of you there is another road than the one that seems the best to you. You have been traveling this other road for a long time now, but till now you did not know this. You are not walking alone, the *Girl to Whom Every Morning Smiles* is with you, and there will be others. Together, you must help the *Lady Who Is Now Sleeping*. She needs your help."

"Where is this road to lead us?"

"To Egypt, to awaken Cheops... The Pharaoh must see the sun."

"Is the Pharaoh sleeping?" I asked in surprise. "He has been dead for a long time, for sure, and no one really knows where he is."

"I will tell you where he is and how to reach him... and how to awaken him," the *Universe* assured us calmly. "You only need to listen carefully and let yourself be guided there. Along your way, I will place many *People Who Will Help Find the Tomb*."

"So tell me: where is this tomb?" I asked, intrigued by these words.

"It is close to the Pyramid. You have to make a triangle with one corner in the middle of the Great Pyramid from the side of Nile, the second corner lies between paws of the Sphinx, and on the third corner will be the tomb of the Pharaoh. "

"Can you ask the Priestess Ki to explain this more precisely?"

"Ask, and I will guide her."

"Where is the tomb of the Pharaoh?" I asked Ki.

"It is outside of the Pyramid. I can show you the place."

"Please, do this."

"I have to stand in the middle of the Pyramid on the side of Sphinx," said the Priestess. "With my face to the sun. It is noon and the sun shines directly onto me."

"Please move forward toward the tomb," I requested.

"I am now walking forward toward the tomb, toward the Nile. I have the sun more to my left, not directly onto me."

"Walk ahead and tell me how long you are walking."

"I do not see time. I am walking...," Ki repeated. "I am still walking... at this moment, I can feel vibrations of immense power. At this moment, I am standing on the tomb."

"Is it finished already?"

"The tomb... I have moved in time... I am standing on the tomb already covered with soil."

"How far away are you from the Pyramid? Count the steps."

"About six hundred."

"When will be the time to find the tomb?"

"When the Pisces transfers power to Aquarius. It has to be the time of Aquarius."

"Ask the *Universe* if It has something important to communicate."

"Yes. It says that the most important thing is that people believe that the Great Pyramid was built only in part by human hands. Whereas, in fact, all the hard work was done by Entities from Another Planet, the *White Brethren*, and they wanted to leave this enigma to future generations when they come and are willing to believe."

I wanted to ask the Priestess more about the details of the building, but I thought that this did not have to be her last dream. I had a hunch that, if we are to find the tomb, there would be many more dreams about Egypt, the Pyramid, the Pharaoh, and the Priest Juno. I was curious now about the tomb.

"Could you describe more precisely where Cheops is buried? How to reach him? How to dig him up?"

"I will tell you more precisely when the time comes for the trip to Egypt and the awakening of the Pharaoh," the *Universe* answered. "Then I will indicate the place through the Priestess."

"Why not now?" I was surprised.

"You see, Wanderer, there are people in the world for whom only one thing is important – gold, treasures, fame and they would do anything to win these things, without heed to the consequences. The "Pharaoh" mission is my mission. Only people with pure hearts and pure intentions will reach the Pharaoh. I will not allow others. This is why my information now is such as it is. When your group is ready, when I have selected the proper people, then the time will come for the details."

"Why arc we to do this, when there are so many people in the world?" I asked after a moment of silence.

"You have been selected for this." *The Universe* seemed somewhat irritated. "Do not ask silly questions."

That was not a silly question at all, I thought. There are some billions of people on Earth and here the *Universe* is striving to make me believe that I, the *Wanderer,* was appointed for something like this. It is true that I am a Wanderer, but I have never been in Egypt and I have seen the pyramids only in photographs, and the Pharaoh is ancient history to me.

"What kind of people will you place along my way?" I continued.

"Various kinds. Some who think that they are important, and some who are very humble and will truly become important. All will lead you in one direction, because the road you are now walking leads only one way."

"You are speaking with the voice of the Priestess, so you are with her."

"Yes, I am, but in her dream, she is living in times which are not remembered by a single living person. Then she was the Priestess Ki; then, her name was Life. When she wakes up, she will again be Lucyna of the year 2001. But in your time, Lucyna is not alone on the Earth. The priest, Juno, is with her, the builder of the Great Pyramid, her guardian. He also lives in your time."

"Where does he live? How do we find him?"

"He is a shaman in Peru, the **Guardian of the Sacred Mountain**."

"What is his name? How is he called?"

"Wanderer, I am the *Universe*, I am of different matter than you, I am spiritual energy and in my dimension, there are no names. There is only energy. Do not overestimate my capacity and do not ask about names."

"I thought that you are omniscient," I remarked.

"Only the Owner of the Earth is omniscient, the Entity which you on Earth call God. I also belong to Him," the *Universe* replied,

"Why don't you ask Him about this?"

"He guides me, and I ask questions only in exceptional cases. It is your task to find Juno in the time of Aquarius."

I became somewhat worried by this answer. It seemed to me that if the Universe is the *Universe*, It must know everything. I could not imagine how I could find a guardian of a mountain in Peru, which is sacred, since I do not know either the name of the mountain or the name of the shaman. "Perhaps there is only one sacred mountain in Peru," I thought and this calmed me down somewhat. However, just in case, I asked, "How can I find this shaman?"

"Science knows his name. Trust me. My energy is immense and I will help you."

"What do we need this shaman for?" I asked.

"To confirm credibility of the words of the Priestess," the *Universe* replied.

This was logical. If the shaman has the same dream as that of the Priestess Ki, the information becomes credible. Then, scientists may become interested in this; even those who do not believe in dreams.

"Why is Cheops to be awakened?" I continued asking.

"In order to open the Great Pyramid."

"How is that to open? It is just a pile of stones put one on top of the other, you can't just open it."

"The Pyramid of Cheops was built to become a key or **Gate** to me," the *Universe* explained. "It was built for a specific purpose, to serve as a message, as a contact with me, and especially, as a contact with the Other Earth."

I wondered for a while what the Other Earth was. I knew only one Earth, the one I walked on during my wanderings. If there was another Earth, it had to be very far away, all the more so because the *Universe* seemed to me to be very far away, even though It was apparently talking to me through the mouth of the *Lady Called Life*.

"Where does this **Gate** lead to?" I asked, after a moment of hesitation.

"The Gate leads to the Other World."

"What is the Other World?"

"It is a Perfect World, where there is no animosity, no anger; a World which can teach the people on Earth how to be perfect. There are also Wanderers and those *Who Can Teach Beauty*. They want to come to the Earth, so as to enlighten people's minds and prove their existence. They have been here already. It was they who built the Pyramid and helped Cheops fall asleep. The main purpose of this visit then and now is that humanity should become perfect."

"What is this perfection all about?"

"It is about understanding what **love** is, Wanderer."

"And what is love?"

I was gladdened, as I had been waiting for the opportunity to ask this question, and now the *Universe* itself had raised the subject.

"Love is to see yourself in another person, and to want to receive from the other what is best and to give to the other what is best. Love is when you always feel safe. Love is like a sensitive photographic film, capturing in moments of great illumination what is beyond time and space. Love is also when each day you faithfully ask God to take care of you, when you desire to provide inspiration drawn from the depth of your spirit, when you want to enter the realm of experience of the world, and you want to help those who do not understand love. This is love. Only such love can save people and the Earth."

Strong words. I did not expect that the Universe would so beautifully and with such passion start to talk about matters that philosophers for so many centuries had been trying to fathom, writing hundreds of volumes of wise treatises. And here, with just a few sentences, It comprised the essence, the nature of love. I thought to myself that what the Universe has just said I would digest later I felt that within these couple of sentences there was immense wisdom. I just did not understand why love would save the Earth?

"What do you have in mind, when you speak of saving the Earth?" I asked.

"You will understand later. It is not yet the time for it now."

"Here on Earth, there is also love. There are *People Who Walk This Path*. I think that I also am walking along this way."

"You do, but you still vacillate. There are only few such people," the *Universe* replied. "Far too few. That is why the Pharaoh has to be awakened as soon as possible. This is Your New Way of Wandering, onto which you already stepped out long ago, without knowing it. You are walking it now, as is the *Girl to Whom Every Morning Smiles* and the *Lady Called Life*. That was why you met. That was why I speak your language."

"What is your language?"

"My language is the **language of accidental occurrences**, of coincidences which you all experience. That is why you do not hear me, you do not see the way along which I guide you, you and *All the Persons Who Appear on Your Way*. These are not coincidences. This is My Speech, the language in which I talk to you. When you learn how to listen to it, you will be able to talk to me every day. In your life, there have been no accidental occurrences for a long time."

I stood there at my crossroads, fascinated, not sure whether this was still a crossroads or a path, along which I walked with the *Girl to Whom Every Morning Smiles* and in order to meet the *Lady Called Life*. The road has now become a highway directing me toward the Great Pyramid, Egypt, the real treasure linked by alchemy of coincidences with me and with those *Who Have Stood and Will Stand on My Way*.

"How interesting this is," I thought. I woke up the Priestess and at the same moment, I myself began to awaken from the dream.

5

THE SHAMAN FROM MARKAHUASI

S ometimes, as one walks along and watches the world, one is forced to make adjustments along one's way. Sometimes it appears that you are walking well, that you are on the right road, and suddenly, the whole world begins to tell you: "Not there. Not that way." How good it is to be able to hear the whisperings of the *Universe...* but few people are able to do this.

Both I, the *Wanderer,* and the *Girl to Whom Every Morning Smiles* were slowly learning to listen to the *Universe* and to trust It. We were learning to listen to our intuition, imagination, and to understand Its words. Often, when thoughts of the *Universe* or the Pharaoh were coming into my mind, when images from the Priestess's dreams appeared, I asked myself the question: "How does imagination differ from intuition?" I knew one thing: that intuition is a function of imagination and is part of our reasoning. Only that reasoning so often prevented me from accepting unreservedly what I heard from Ki, and what my own dreams were starting to tell me.

When I shared my doubts with the *Lady Called Life,* she smiled and said, "You see, *Wanderer,* besides this physical world, there is another world – the spiritual world. *The Universe* is such a world; so feel It, make friends with It, and when you have doubts, ask It for help. Ask honestly and It will help you, because It always helps. Not right away, but always."

"How could I have a friend I cannot see?" I complained.

"You cannot see, but you can feel. Besides, you surely have noticed that your life has changed since we met and since my dreams started, as has the life of the *Girl to Whom Every Morning Smiles*, not to speak of myself. *The Universe* is affecting the physical level of your existence; It is guiding you."

The *Lady Called Life* spoke wisely. I wondered how this simple woman could be so wise, so knowledgeable. I considered during my wanderings, how to tell people, how to convey the notion that I have made friends with and talk with the Universe. I knew well enough where they send those poor fellows who claim to speak about other dimensions.

When I shared my doubts with Lucyna, she said, "Do not worry. *The Universe* will help you to select your earthly friends carefully. It will place on your path only those who will help you walk along the way to Your Destiny. This is a very important way. It is important for you, for me, and for the *Universe*. For indeed, it is important to It that we arrive at the goal, which is Cheops."

I admitted that Lucyna was right and decided to stop worrying about the meaning of all this, for myself, for Iwona, and for my wanderings. I came to like Ki all the more, as she was becoming more and more clearly a part of my life. For me and for the *Girl to Whom Every Morning Smile,* the strange behavior of the Priestess was something normal – we began to like her rough nature and admired her uniqueness. She dreamed unusual dreams and Iwona, Łucja, and I were becoming an integral part of her dreams.

There were four of us and, looking at this with sober eyes, finding the tomb of Pharaoh Cheops and digging it up by our small group seemed to be a "mission impossible" and so incompatible with the everyday life that I was living, that it lay somewhere on the border of the absurd. Indeed, what sane person would start any serious activity on the basis only of the dreams of an unknown woman? I decided, therefore, to wait for the promised coincidences. "Since the *Universe from Lucyna's dreams* states that Iwona and I are to do something together, let It put those promised people onto her way or onto my way," I thought.

And suddenly, things started happening, which some would describe as normal occurrences, while others would say, "Surely, there is an invisible hand guiding this." One day, my wanderings led me to Polish town, Gdansk. There I met the **Man Who Thinks Rationally and Has Been to Peru**. His name was Roman. He was a very well-known journalist, writer, and traveler. He used to wander, like myself, around various countries and described what he saw. For no reason, he started telling me about Peru and about the books he had written about this unusual country. I told him about Egypt and the Pharaoh.

Then I remembered something, "Listen, the Priestess Ki during her dream said that there was living in Peru a priest, the *Man Who Built the Great Pyramid,* the Priest Juno."

"Wow, he must be very old," Roman joked.

"I mean his reincarnation, which is living again now."

Roman was shocked and asked, "What words did she use?"

"She said, "The *Man Who Built the Pyramid* lives now and can be contacted. He is a shaman in Peru and the Guardian of the Sacred Mountain. He can confirm the credibility of the words of the Priestess."

"In Peru, every second mountain is sacred," Roman remarked, "but my wanderings once led me to a mountain called Markahuasi. It is a very strange mountain, mysterious, engulfed in a multitude of tales. The natives call it 'the Forge of the Gods,' They believe that this was the place where the gods created the human species. I know a shaman there, he is called **Don Severiano**. I will show you his photograph."

And here occurred the First Very Strange Coincidence. The Universe indicated Don Severiano as the *One Who Built the Pyramid of Cheops in Egypt,* who was the Priest Juno, the friend of the Pharaoh, and the guardian of Priestess Ki. He was the *One Who Could Confirm the Words of the Priestess,* make her story credible, and make her dreams credible. *The Universe* said so to Lucyna, when It looked through her eyes at his photograph.

There was only one problem. Don Severiano did not know who he had been in the past. In his everyday life, he was a simple peasant, cultivating his field, and also a shaman, a healer, who treated the local peasants. He was a guide for the tourists, who from time to time visited his district, attracted by the strangeness of the mountain, and he was the *Guardian of the Sacred Mountain,* whose secrets he knew like nobody else.

We also were not sure whether this was indeed the right person, although the *Universe* itself assured us of this, but... again... this could be just a dream. How can one believe without reservation in someone's dreams? It is not hard science, nothing tangible, nothing verified in many experiments.

"How could he confirm it?" Roman wondered.

"He must also fall asleep and go back in time," I said. "But I do not know how to help him fall asleep."

"That is simple," Roman was sure of himself. "Every shaman in Peru knows how to do this. There is a brew called **ayauasca** that may be used for this."

"What is ayauasca?"

"It is a liquid, a brew made from Peruvian herbs, that helps shamans to wander wherever their physical body cannot go. It helps them to wander in time, in space without limits. Ayauasca is a liquid of the imagination, derived from plants. Where the imagination wants to go, ayauasca will lead it, if you know how to use it."

"So do we go to Peru?" Roman asked.

"We are going to Peru," I replied. "After all, I am a Wanderer."

So, along with the *Girl to Whom Every Morning Smiles* and the *Man Who Has Already Been to Peru*, we decided to go there to meet Don Severiano and ask him to fall asleep and use ayauasca to go back to the time of the building of the Great Pyramid. The preparations were under way and we were getting ready to leave in January of 2002. At a certain moment, I noticed that Roman was hesitating.

"Perhaps all this is untrue?" he pondered.

"It could be... But at this time, we have only one method to test it, and that is by going to Peru."

"What if everything turns out to be untrue?" Roman started to express his thoughts aloud.

"Perhaps you would like to listen to the dream of Priestess Ki? Perhaps you would like to talk to the *Lady Called Life*?" I suggested.

"Yes," he answered. "I don't believe in dreams, but I will listen to her dream."

The dreams of the *Lady Called Life* require a certain ritual, a procedure for falling asleep and a procedure for waking up. I knew that Roman was very curious about how one could talk in one's dream, and talk sensibly. So I let him see this with his own eyes. I did not pay attention to his lack of trust and this was a mistake. I already had some proficiency in making people fall asleep. After all, I was doing this for the second time, so I was sure of myself, and even proud that I, the *Wanderer*, was able to facilitate dreams for the Priestess. I could make her travel in time.

We met in Wroclaw, in the apartment of the *Girl to Whom Every Morning Smiles*, in Iwona's apartment.

"Fall asleep," I started to whisper in Lucyna's ear... and after a while, she was sleeping.

"Where are you?" I asked.

"I am sitting on the bank of a river. The weather is beautiful and I am waiting... waiting for the voice," she spoke sleepily and slowly. "It will speak... The voice has something to communicate... It is strange... I feel very strange... since the images that I see in the distance, look like a movie... as if there was a barrier... a screen through which I cannot pass. I am waiting for the voice... There is a voice, which will communicate... will facilitate communication."

I did not know what this voice was and what this voice had to communicate, but I waited patiently. After all, dreaming is a world of fantasy. So we all waited for the voice.

"The voice says," Lucyna spoke slowly, "that we will move in time by the signs... By the signs of the map of the heavens. These will be the signs of the Zodiac and we will move along this road all the way to the Pyramid. The voice says that everything began from Pisces… that, at the time of Pisces, the Pyramid was already there, but not in Egypt. The first Pyramid-Temple was in **Atlantis**. Then, on this island ruled a Great Leader, the Prince of Peace. Already then on the island, there was talk of annihilation, of the order which would roll on through all eras. 'In Atlantis,' the voice says, 'there lived four colors of people,' The colors were white, red, yellow, and black. All these colors were taught and schooled and when the annihilation of the island was to ensue, all four colors were sent out to the four corners of the world: to the east, to the west, to the north, and to the south. At the moment of the annihilation, the Great Prince and Leader departed, but he said that he will come again... when Pisces will rule."

Up to now, none of us knew what the Voice was talking about. Who was the Great Leader, the **Prince of Peace**? We all patiently waited what would happen next.

"The Voice is speaking again," the Priestess said, continuing her story. "The next significant occurrence for the Earth, for people, takes place in the cycle of Libra. Then the **Council of the Gods** assembled and established the order, the sequence of events for the Earth... and the countdown. The next occurrence follows when Libra gives way to Pisces, and then the construction of Sphinx commenced. It is a forerunner of the Pyramid, which is to arise. After the construction of the Sphinx, the Guardian of the Pyramid, the decision was made on the Other Earth to build the **Sign of Time**."

Here once again, the Priestess Ki made mention of the "Other Earth." I was very curious as to what planet she was talking about.

"Where is the Other Earth?" I asked.

"Orion," the Priestess spoke sleepily. "The first star in the belt of Orion; the planet is there. Those who came, say that it is called *Ashun*. This is the name they give me."

"Dream on," I encouraged her, "We are surrounding you with our warmth. Your dream is important to us. What is your Voice saying?"

Lucyna hesitated for a while and then quietly continued her dream. "The Voice says that we will move between cycles in the construction of the pyramid, which was built in the age of **Scorpio**. We will move to the age of Pisces, when the Great Leader, the Prince of Peace, returned to the Earth. Just as he said, he will return again in the age of Pisces and then already, the great countdown will commence. The inhabitants of Atlantis knew about all of this and they knew that something had to be done for the Earth, in order to save both the Earth and the people."

"Who is this voice?" I asked.

"I do not know... I do not know... I do not have a picture..."

I still wanted to ask who the Great Leader was; the one Ki had called the Prince of Peace. I knew, however, that Roman very much wanted to talk in person with the dream of the Priestess. He was listening to her words, watching her dream, and waiting for my permission.

"It's your turn," I said to him. "Ask about anything you want. We are here for you."

"Was the Pyramid built from the foundations?" he asked, with a slight hesitation.

"Not from the foundations," Ki replied quietly. "After the Sphinx, there was nothing for a long time... There was only the project... the selection of the site... the designation of the central point. The foundations are very deep. The pyramid stands on foundations... There are underground chambers."

"Are these foundations older than the pyramid itself?" Roman's voice started to sound more assured.

"Much older... Cheops's father had the task of building the foundations... the underground chambers. Only when the roofing was already closed did the actual construction commence. Cheops himself began this."

"What sort of a ruler was Cheops? Was he a good king?"

"Magnificent," Ki dreamed on, "He was a beloved ruler... All loved him... People came from various corners of the country and even of the world. Everybody wanted to have a share in the message that is the Pyramid."

"Was the pyramid painted in some way?" Roman asked.

"Not during the construction..." the voice of the Priestess was calm, "only after it was completed... I do not understand this... I will speak of what I see... that which I know... what I understand... Something was poured over it that looked like liquid gold... It was poured over from above... It was beautiful... lustrous."

"Did you see Cheops's wife?"

"This was a bad woman.... She hated the pyramid. I saw her only once. She did not come to the construction site. She hated everything that was connected with the Pyramid. She hated Cheops himself, because he devoted all of his time to the Pyramid. Cheops himself did not speak about the queen."

"What did this queen look like?"

"She had dark skin, strongly tanned; she was slim; she had black, fairly long hair, and always an ill-natured look... The picture of the queen is fading away... She hated the pyramid so much."

"Did Cheops have only one wife?" In Roman's voice, I began to detect some mistrust.

It was not difficult to guess that before Roman came to the meeting, he had read various stories about Cheops and the Pyramid, and that he was now confronting his book knowledge with that which the Priestess Ki said.

"I don't know... One wife... but he also had... they were not slaves... they served Cheops voluntarily... They were wives to him... Yes... There were several of them... They loved Cheops very much..."

"As regards the tomb of Cheops, is this a large chamber or a small one?"

"I don't know if it is large... It is, it seems to me, of the size of a royal chamber... of the one located in the Pyramid... It will not be larger... The sarcophagus with the king is located there... There are tablets..."

"What must happen now so that we can find the tomb of Cheops?" Roman suddenly changed the subject.

"The people must believe the words of the Priestess."

"Where is the Priest Juno now? Where is the one, whom you call the person who built the pyramid?"

"Juno came to the Earth again in the Age of Pisces... meaning when Pisces was approaching the point of handing over power to Aquarius. Then Juno came to the Earth. His objective... or message is to awaken the sleeping Pharaoh; to awaken Cheops. Juno now, in the Age of Aquarius, is a shaman. He is waiting in order that he can awake. To help the Pharaoh — who is the key to this gate — to arise. The Pyramid is the gate."

Roman stopped his questioning and, with an indifferent expression, only looked at the Priestess Ki, who continued sleeping with her strange dream, and dreamt about the voice which said strange things. I grasped that Roman already knew what he wanted to know. I knew that I myself had to guide Ki along her dreamy paths to the Pharaoh.

"What has to be done," I repeated Roman's question, "to awaken the Pharaoh?"

"The words have to be joined up. The words of the priestess and the words of Juno have to be communicated to people with hearts of stone. There is no other way."

"Who are these people with hearts of stone?"

"Those who must consent to the digging and those who must pay for it, who have gold. The predictions about the Earth, which speak about humanity, are becoming fulfilled, and rescue for the Earth may come only from the Other Earth. If this warning this extended hand is pushed aside, within a short time, people will be decimated. There will be a cleansing, and it is from this that the newcomers, the friends from Orion, want to save the Earth and the people."

Ki dreamt on about Cheops for a long time, about his life and about her love of the Pharaoh. For so long, that again she did not want to wake up and come back to the present. We tried to wake her several times, till at last she opened her eyes tearfully. Back there, in the past, she felt good. She felt loved and was cared for. She came back, because back then she already knew that she had a mission to fulfill. She had already been told then that she would return. Cheops had told her this, Juno had told her this. She returned and again became Lucyna, the masseuse, the *Lady Called Life*.

"I do not believe Ki," Roman said when Lucyna left, "She made it up."

At this moment, he became the *Man Who Prefers to Doubt*.

The shaman from Mount Markahuasi still does not know that once he was the Great Priest Juno, the Builder of the Pyramid, the Friend of Cheops, and the trip to Peru became just a dream. Will somebody help him fall asleep, so that he would recall who he used to be, help him to dream a dream about the Pyramid and the Pharaoh? At that time, I did not know the answer.

My head was full of questions. Will the Priestess Ki nevertheless meet the Priest Juno now, in the age of the Aquarius? Who is living on the Other Earth? Why would anyone from Orion come to us, in order to help us? What does it mean that people are to be decimated? Why does the Great Pyramid have to be opened now, in particular, and why is the tomb the key? At times, the thought would come into my mind that Roman may be right. After all, he was the *Man Who Thinks Rationally*. And then, I thought that sooner or later, my wanderings will lead me to a path where I will find the answer. So Ki had promised me. So the Universe had promised...

6

A DREAM ABOUT THE PRIEST JUNO

In the dreams of Priestess Ki, Juno was her guardian, her guide, and her master. When, as a priestess, she dreamed about the future, she asked him for help and dreamed together with him. I wondered who Juno, in those times long ago, really was; as a person and as a priest.

The Priestess Ki talked about him in her dreams with great respect and love, so I decided to ask Lucyna to have a special dream; a dream about the Priest Juno. She willingly agreed. She herself, as Lucyna, was curious to know who Juno really was.

I asked the *Girl to Whom Every Morning Smiles* so that together we could help Lucyna fall asleep and dream of the past. Lucyna felt better and slept deeper when she was calmed by a smile that reached into her heart.

"Sleep deeply," I said, when she was ready. "Listen only to my voice and that of Iwona. In a while, you will be with the Priest Juno; as Ki you will greet him. Your dream will be as clear and true, as is true your life as a priestess in Egypt. Tell us where you are."

"I am beside the Sphinx," Ki started her dream. "It is very hot."

"Is the Priest Juno with you?"

"Yes, he is now with me. He is looking at me with great concern."

"Ask him," I started to say, "ask him to talk about himself, about his life, to tell you where he came from. Can you have this dream?"

"Yes," Ki said, "Juno is with me, he is smiling. He says that he will be happy to talk about his life, he will tell everything he knows about himself."

"Tell us what Juno is saying about himself."

"He says that he was born on Earth, but that his ancestors came from a Planet called Nibiru. He says that this was a planet that perished and became dead. When it was clear", the Priestess continued, "that there were no chances to save Nibiru, it was necessary to evacuate the human beings living there to a previously selected planet. This planet, where the previous inhabitants of Nibiru now live, is the Other Earth in the belt of Orion. This is their new homeland. Juno's ancestors settled on the Other Earth. Juno says that he was born for the first time on the Other Earth. He came from a princely lineage, and he was taught and was educated in many and various fields."

I surmised that Juno had had several incarnations before he became a priest on Earth and the Guardian to Ki. I was curious why he came to the Earth. Before I had time to ask, the Priestess continued her dream.

"Many beings from the Other Earth," she spoke slowly, "were preparing to go on a mission here, to the Earth, because it was already known that the message would be built the code in the central point of the Earth's axis — that the Pyramid would be built. When his time came, Juno was born in Egypt. He had an Earthly mother and an Earthly father."

"What was he like when he was a young boy?" I asked.

Ki smiled and continued her extraordinary dream.

"Juno says that in the times when the father of Cheops ruled, he was given as a young boy to be taught and to serve the priests and he acquired his schooling there. He was more or less of the same age as Cheops, and so they managed to become friends quickly. They played together as boys, they took their lessons together, and were both distinguished by their outstanding abilities. Juno says that he was linked to the Pharaoh by a great friendship, so great that he never let his friend feel that he possessed greater knowledge, although he did not know then from where this knowledge came."

"How did it happen that he became the Chief Builder of the Pyramid?"

"When the time came for building the Pyramid, Cheops's father chose Juno to supervise the construction, on the basis of the abilities which he possessed."

"When did he learn where his abilities came from?"

"Juno says," Ki smiled again, "that he also was amazed that learning was so easy for him. He understood this when the White Brethren came to the Earth, those who were responsible for building the Pyramid of Cheops. They came from the Other Earth. He says that he had a vision and found out then from where he had come and who he really was."

The dreamy smiles of the Priestess made me happy. In her dreaming, she rarely smiled but often wept, so that I wondered why she wept, why it was so difficult for her to come back to the present. Now I knew why. I saw how happy the dream about Juno made her, how she admired her master, and discovered even more reasons for this admiration in her dream.

"Was Juno able to directly contact the White Brethren, the Pyramid builders?" I asked.

"Yes, conversation proceeded directly in the Special Tent, in the presence of the Pharaoh and Juno, or by means of **telepathic speech**."

"What do you mean by telepathic speech?"

"Juno says that this is a language known now and it will be known in the future. He says that it is possible to activate the layers of the brain and to talk only by means of thoughts. When the White Brethren, wearing their close-fitting one-piece garments, were on the construction site, then Juno and the Pharaoh talked with them by means of telepathic speech. He also says that sometime in the future, all people will talk to each other like that."

I thought that it would indeed make everything very much easier, if we all could talk by means of thoughts. I wondered only if such communication would require some knowledge of foreign languages. Can a Pole, for example, talk telepathically, without an interpreter, with a Chinese person? And then Iwona joined in to the conversation.

"What did Juno look like? What was his day-to-day life like?" she asked the Priestess.

The thought crossed my mind that this was a typical question from a woman.

"His life was simple," Ki dreamt, "like that of everyone who worked on the Pyramid. He dressed as befitted a priest, in long, white robes. He was very modest and he did not want to stand out. He even ate his meals together with the workers. That was Juno: simple and loved by everyone. There was no pride or conceit in him. He was love and solicitude."

"Can you describe his appearance, his figure?" Iwona continued.

"He was tall. His body was not white, since his parents were Egyptians. His skin was the color of a beautiful dusky tan."

"Did he appeal to you as a man?" Iwona could not hold back her feminine curiosity.

"Yes, he had beautiful facial features and was distinguished by his appearance. Dignified, beautiful, always engaging."

"What was his hair like? How did he comb it?" Iwona did not let go.

"He was bald, but all priests were like that. Shaving the head was dictated by the religion and the need for maintaining hygiene. Black, beautiful eyes - that was Juno."

I interrupted the flow of feminine curiosity, "How did Juno become a priest?"

"I am asking Juno and he is a bit embarrassed by my question. He does not like to boast," Ki answered sleepily.

"I understand his modesty, but please, ask him to answer." I repeated the question.

"He became a priest because of his knowledge. This was what made him stand out among all those who came to learn, he was the most skilled of all. He learned quickly and often surpassed his teachers. He even taught the teachers and this resulted in him being appointed as the supervisor of the Pyramid, the main supervisor, because there were many more priest- supervisors. Juno says that he could not be responsible for everything. There were priests who were responsible for medical matters, others for delivery of food, still others for animal care, for cultivation of plants and for gardens. Each had his role in the construction of the Pyramid."

I wondered if I could ask another question which came to my mind — a question which would surely make Iwona glad and also satisfy her curiosity. I wanted to ask about the relationship between Juno and Priestess Ki, but I hesitated as to whether it was proper to ask the holy Priestess about such not-so-holy things as male-female relationships. I did not know how Ki would react to such a question, whether she would feel offended. I decided to risk it.

"Tell me Ki if there were between the two of you... well... some sort of closer relationships... If... if..." I did not know quite how to formulate the question, so that she would not feel offended.

"You want to know if we were lovers?" she interrupted my efforts.

"That is what I wanted to ask." I was surprised by her openness.

"Yes," Ki answered with no trace of surprise or embarrassment, "I was with Juno all the time. I did whatever he wanted; I was there to serve him and to meet his needs. All the priests had priestesses with them. This is normal. Juno says that physical love is an immense energy which multiplies strength, provides incentive to work, and gives joy to life. It was only later that people made a taboo of this, as something shameful. Every stone of the Pyramid speaks about our great love."

The Priestess suddenly became silent. Her smile was warm and a bit playful. Perhaps she was dreaming about Juno, about times that were very pleasant and beautiful for her. I did not interrupt her recollections. After a long period, Iwona broke the silence.

"Did you have offspring? Did you have children?" she asked.

"No. We did not have offspring. The purposeful intent of the White Brotherhood was that there be no offspring from our relationship. Juno and I had to consume special herbs, which prevented progeny."

"Why was it so important to the White Brethren that you would not have children?" Iwona was surprised.

"I do not know," Ki dreamed on, "I cannot answer this. It appears that Juno came in a straight line from another planet, but was only born as an earthly being. I am an Earth woman and some circumstances did not allow children being born from such a relationship."

This was a surprise to me and to Iwona, but Juno apparently had reasons, which he did not want to explain in detail regarding the reasons for such a situation.

"How did the Pharaoh and Juno behave?" I continued my questioning.

"The Pharaoh often came to the construction site, to the Pyramid. He often stayed for many months, among the common people. He did not require any tributes for himself. On the contrary, he behaved in such a way that, if any stranger had came here, he would not know who among the workers was the Pharaoh. They were both like that."

"Now some people say that Cheops was a tyrant, that he was a king who was inaccessible, and that the work on the pyramids was that of slaves."

The Priestess was silent for a while; she may have been talking with Juno in her dream, asking him what to answer. After a while, she started talking very slowly and very clearly.

"The reality was completely different. Both of them, Cheops and Juno, knew what sort of a mission they had undertaken and who had told them to carry it out. They were both devoted to this with their whole hearts. Both of them loved what they were doing and both of them knew that they would leave when the work was completed. I do not know from where came such stories of slave labor, of a tyrant. Everyone loved Cheops. People from all over the world came to build the Pyramid. Not a single person was a slave. Juno says that the truth will be evident when Pharaoh sees the sun again, because everything, the whole history of the construction is written on the tablets."

"Was Juno honored in any way after his death, by those who remained on the Earth?" I asked.

"With a city," Ki answered. "He was honored with a city. He received a city, which was named after him, Juno. That is all."

I did not know that there was a city named Juno in Egypt, but I thought that geography and history were never my strong points. I was happy that I was finding out so many interesting things about her and her Great Friend. More and more fascinating for me was the thought that the two would meet again at some time in the near or not so near future. What Ki dreamt was happening many thousands of years ago. In this lifetime, she also has a chance to meet her Juno, but will it happen? I wanted to wake her up, but a question came to my mind about the present time, the current Juno.

"Ask Juno," I asked Ki, "if he can look into the future. Can he move in time to the start of the age of Aquarius, when he will appear again on the Earth?"

"Juno says that you can ask. He is already in his future."

I was surprised with the speed of this progression. I was not sure if I was now to address the Priest Juno directly or to continue making use of the Priestess's dream. It was her dream, so I turned to her again.

"Ask Juno who he is," I asked.

"A shaman in Peru," came the answer.

"What is his mission?"

"The same as that of the Priestess..." It seemed as if Juno was answering directly, without Ki's intervention, "to reach the Pharaoh. To break open the safeguards and to participate in the funeral procession when the Pharaoh is moved to the sarcophagus in the Pyramid. With this, our role comes to an end. If everything goes well and the work is crowned with success, we will complete it."

"Who is your spiritual energy?" I posed the last question.

"My father was Anu. Anu was created to settle in the planet Nibiru and to produce progeny. The origin of my spirit is Nibirian. I proceed directly from a princely, royal line. I am a relative of En-Ki."

This information was astonishing. En-Ki, the *One Who Created the Human Race,* was a Sumerian legend. This topic, however, was too extensive and difficult, so I decided to ask no more questions and terminate the session.

"Is there anything else that you would like to tell me, before you wake from the dream?" I asked Ki.

To my surprise, the Priestess answered in the affirmative.

"Yes. Juno says that he already exists in another matter, in another time. He is a shaman whose consciousness does not yet know who he was in the past."

"How can the shaman learn who he is and what his mission is?" I asked.

"He must release himself from his consciousness and then before him will appear the unknown areas of his life, the former life. He will be able to see the Pyramid, to see Atlantis."

"In what way can he enter the state of altered consciousness?"

"Every shaman knows how to do this. He has done this more than once, when entering the Sacred City under the Sacred Mountain."

I surmised that the Priestess was dreaming about the **Sacred Mountain Markahuasi** where Severiano lives. In the book of the *Man Who Preferred to Doubt,* I had read about the legends and the mysterious city, which is said to be located under this mountain, under the ground. Don Severiano wandered there in his dreams, with the help of the ayauasca brew."

"Is there anything that one can tell him, any question that should be posed to him, to direct his attention to Ki?" I asked.

I was thinking about what could interest the shaman from Peru in the *Lady Called Life.* Like showing him that the knowledge which the present-day Lucyna possesses is immense and comes from the *Universe,* the same source from which he draws his knowledge. If contact is made, something will be needed to convince him and make him understand that the world extends beyond Markahuasi and that he has another mission, beyond that of healing the local people.

"You can ask him how the Sacred Mountain behaves when the full moon commences," was the answer.

"How does the Sacred Mountain behave when the full moon comes? Can you tell me?"

"I can. When the full moon commences, the Sacred Mountain starts to give signals, to shake slightly. At this same time, all places of special power give similar signals."

"Is there anything else that you can tell me about the shaman?"

"He is very sensitive to energy that he receives," the Priestess dreamt, "both that from Space and that from people. Juno says that it is this energy that will indicate the place where the Pharaoh rests. Energy — not hardware and equipment."

It was late and I decided to wake the Priestess. She looked tired and spoke more and more slowly. I was afraid that she would start weeping again, because of her longing for the time when she had lived surrounded by happiness. I asked her to recall Juno's kiss... A smile immediately appeared on Ki's face.

"Take the vision of this kiss with you," I asked Ki, "and bring it into your present life... What is most beautiful will remain with you forever. It will facilitate your mission, will help you and Juno... He is living in another time... His soul is still asleep... He is waiting for you to awaken it..."

"Yes... I will awaken..." whispered the Priestess and started her return journey.

Lucyna stretched and lay for a few minutes in silence.

"How are you feeling?" Iwona asked anxiously, when the eyes of the *Lady Called Life* were open.

"I am feeling perfect. What did I dream about?"

"You dreamt about Juno, the one of the old times and the one of the present."

"I want very much to meet him," she sighed.

I thought that since the *Universe* had arranged everything, so that these two were to awaken Cheops, then sooner or later they will look into each other's eyes, so that their souls could recognize each other.

I did not know whether this will happen in Egypt or in Poland or in Peru. I left this puzzle for the *Universe* to resolve.

7

DREAMS

Dreams are a window to another world. They can look into the future or the past. The *Girl to Whom Every Morning Smiles* could dream beautiful dreams. Dreams which spoke to her about the future. They showed the way. She was able to ask the dream whether something was true or only an illusion.

"Ask the dream," I smiled to her smile, "to tell you what It thinks about Cheops? What It thinks about the Pyramid? Is that, which Lucyna dreams about, which she tells us about, the truth? Or is it only her imagination, as the *Man Who Prefers to Doubt* said?"

"Why don't you get advice from your own dream?" she asked.

"I believe in your dreams and in mine. Let's do this together. We have been dreaming together for so long," I replied.

The dreams, which the *Girl to Whom Every Morning Smiles* dreamt and which I dreamt, were not like those which Lucyna dreamt. For our dreams we did not need external help. Nobody had to make us fall asleep. Our dreams whispered to us at night, they talked to us in images and they did not allow anybody except us to listen to or view their contents. During our dreams, we were in deep sleep and only our imagination saw them. Nobody else had access to them. Some of these dreams were dreamed by us the way dreams are dreamed by everybody on Earth, who wakes up during the night and knows, that he or she had a dream that he or she still remembered.

Every human being dreams. Some dreams are beautiful, colorful, and full of joy. Some are nightmares from which you want to escape, which you fear. Some are a jumble of images and symbols, as incomprehensible as life itself is on occasion. Some dreams show your fears, others, your desires. There are dreams which can show your future — or one of your possible futures. You may dream of something that happens in your life later, although at the time when you dream it, you do not know that what you are dreaming is to happen. Sometimes you have dreams that ask, "Do not do this..." or that suggest, "Do this..." Sometimes, they warn you of danger or show you the best way.

When you fall asleep, you have access to all the possible futures and to all the pasts which have ever happened. You begin to have access to mysteries of the Universe, to Its Unlimited Intelligence. You can wander around It without end, learning Its Great Secret. When you are dreaming, the Universe may show you your Way; you only have to ask for this and to take notice of Its answer. When you are dreaming, the Universe may present you the Best of the Possible Futures, which life has assigned for you, so that you could fulfill your Destiny, your Legend. When you are dreaming, you make contact with another world; a world which is beyond your understanding. This world also speaks to you. It talks to you through your dreams. A world that can help you...

There are people who can ask a dream, "Is the way along which I walk? a good one?," or "What should I do to find My Best Way?" Then their mind wanders at night through the existing universes seeking an answer and, if an answer exists, it is communicated in the form of symbols, metaphors, images, feelings, or words... What you do with this information is up to you.

It was through such dreams that we learned to dream with the *Girl to Whom Every Morning Smiles*. We learned to program our dreams, and to ask what is true and what is not. What is good and what we are to avoid? We learned to believe in images, symbols, and feelings that indicated our way. These dreams were not spontaneous. They were created for us at our request. They were a gift of intuition, which in this manner responded to our request for directions, answers, signs, and assistance.

We now both wanted to ask the dream for an answer to our most pressing question: were the dreams of Lucyna/Priestess Ki dreams about the Pyramid, Cheops and his tomb a way to nowhere or a way to the Very Important Destination. Is the Pharaoh really there? Can finding Cheops help people? We both knew that if Cheops is our Most Important Destiny, dreams will clearly show us this way and intuition will feel it.

In the evening of a day we agreed on, before falling asleep, each of us asked our intuition a question: "Is what Lucyna says about the Pharaoh's tomb true? Is it the right way and a safe way for us?"

The dream of the *Girl to Whom Every Morning Smiles*

"I dreamt," she said, "that I was wandering over the Earth and seeking a truth which was hidden somewhere. I did not know what truth this was or what it looked like. At last, I noticed that I was in some southern Arab country, walking along a street with many large, beautiful, and rich shops. Each of these shops overflowed with gold and diamonds in their windows. Some shops were closed, while others, one could enter and buy something. I knew that this street was very important and I was happy that I was walking along it, but I was aware that I had no money for all these precious things — the gold and the diamonds — which sparkled in the windows. I felt regret that this was so close and at the same time, so far away. I walked on, however, because I knew that I should. I was alone, but it was a safe aloneness. I looked in the windows, admiring the beauty and the richness of the items exhibited there.

"At a certain moment I found myself beside a shop, which was the most beautiful, the most splendid of all. It had a huge display, in the form of something that I might call a recess. I knew that this was a very important shop. Suddenly, I noticed that the display of this shop had no window; it was completely unsecured. One could reach in and remove anything in the recess of this display. With astonishment, I looked inside and noticed there were small figurines there. On each figurine was written a price so huge, it took one's breath away. I realized that these figurines were absolutely priceless, that they were of the highest value that could be, that this was something that none other of these splendid, unique shops had.

"How is it possible that such a priceless item is not protected? The thought came into my mind that anyone could take it. I looked around. People were walking by me indifferently and no one took any notice of the shop, of me or of the recess. I reached into the display and took a priceless figurine into my hand, admiring its uniqueness and beauty. I knew that I could walk away with it and nobody would stop me. I replaced it and entered the shop. The owner looked at me with a gentle expression and smiled very warmly, sincerely, very encouragingly.

"'Why is so precious an item there in the display not protected?' I asked him immediately. 'Anybody can take it. Anybody can steal it.'

"'The most precious things are invisible to the eye.' he replied calmly. 'Only those can see, whom we allow to see. No one, who has not been called, will take it.'

"He smiled again and I awoke with a feeling of peace and safety. It was a very beautiful dream.

"And what was yours like?" she asked, when she had finished her story.

The dream of the Wanderer

"I dreamt about a wandering over the Earth," I started my story, "which was a very dangerous place and bad things were happening all around. Violence, anger, and force prevailed everywhere. Some new and very threatening weapon had been invented. From all sides, there flew in my direction offensive and dangerous missiles. I did not know what was attacking me, where to hide or what to do, surrounded by this indescribable fusillade. I ran along a street, then I left the city and tried to hide in a forest. Wherever I ran, wherever I wanted to hide, there were shots, rockets, and violence everywhere. I was only amazed how it happened that no bullet, no missile, no malevolent energy actually hit me. Everything was flying in my direction. After a while I noticed that, for sure, they were flying in my direction but were missing me.

"Suddenly, I noticed that I was in a safe tunnel. It was a sort of transparent tube, which surrounded me on all sides. The attacking projectiles were passing around me, in some incomprehensible fashion. I noticed that you were beside me. We ran together toward the city, surrounded by an energy which did not allow any danger to come to us. I felt that nothing could happen to us. We reached some courtyard and behind it, I noticed a green hill, which looked very calm and safe to me. We sat down on the grass beside this hill. Immense storms were raging on the outside. Energies attacking the world were flying in from all sides, and I could not determine their source. I knew only one thing: Nothing bad could happen to me or to you. I woke up with this feeling."

"How do you understand your dream?" I asked the *Girl to Whom Every Morning Smiles,* when I finished my story.

"From my dream it is evident that everything that Lucyna passes on to us, as the Priestess Ki, is the truth," she said. "The street is a symbol to me of the road I am now walking. In the context of the question posed, Intuition has given me an unambiguous reply: the existence of the treasure is true. Finding it is easy, but not for everyone. It is easy for us, because so far only we can see it. It is hidden from the eyes of other people. And what do you think about your dream?" she asked.

"My dream was not about the tomb, was not about the treasures. It told me that the Earth and people are in danger, but whatever bad happens around us, whoever is attacking, we will be safe. We are protected, though I do not know where the protection originates. My dream also told me that the road along which we are going is not strewn with roses, but at its end, there is **beauty**, harmony, and peace. That is how I understood it."

"Yes, your dream is very different from mine," quietly said the *Girl to Whom Every Morning Smiles,* "but there is also another, more profound interpretation."

"What?" I was surprised.

"Your dream is a symbol of danger for people all over the Earth. The energy tunnel, which you dreamt about, may be a metaphor meaning that finding the tomb will create an energy protection not only for us, but for all the inhabitants of our planet."

I looked at her with admiration. How interesting that such an interpretation had not come into my head.

"For now, we do know that this is our Way, so let us dream on," I said after pondering her words for a while. "May dreams lead us, where no one before us has been."

8

WHY DOES THE PHARAOH NEED TO SEE THE SUN?

"I would like to fall asleep once more," the *Lady Called Life* said to me. "This time, it is the *Universe* itself requesting this."

"Why?" I asked.

"There is something you have to know, so that you could talk about it in your wanderings, and something else. I like our falling asleep together. I have become used to you and am beginning to trust you."

"But you do not remember your dreams..." I observed.

"When I sleep, I do not remember. You remember and tell me what I dreamt. I like listening to these stories."

Her trust made me glad. After all, not every woman allows herself to be put to sleep from time to time by someone who wanders around all the time. I was also curious as to what new thing the *Universe* had prepared for me and what It wanted to tell me.

"Moreover," she added, "you have to learn why we are to find this tomb. When you know why, your consciousness will cooperate better with you and your intuition will show you how to get there. Your free will, will also help you and you will pose fewer silly questions both to yourself and to the *Universe*."

In my soul, I admitted she was right. If one does something, one should know the purpose the action serves. The more thorough one's knowledge is, the higher motivation one has, the more energy one dedicates to reach the goal and the more actions one undertakes. Up till now, the awaking of the Pharaoh was an undefined dream to me. For the dream to become a goal, I needed to know not only what I wanted to achieve but also why I wanted to achieve it.

"You speak wisely," I remarked. "How do you know all this?"

"*The Universe* prompts me." She pointed her finger to the ceiling.

"Then ask the *Universe* to be with you in your dreams all the time," I said.

"But *It* always is," Lucyna huffed, "Do you think that a single image or word which I dream is produced without *Its* knowledge? Without *Its* control? Without *Its* prompting? *It* speaks through me to you, *It* directs me, and *It* suggests thoughts to you. Indeed, *It* has already told you that in your life there are no coincidences, that *It* is guiding you. I am only *Its* tool when I dream, but it is the *Universe* speaking the words of Priestess Ki."

Once again, I had to admit she was right. The events of everyday life confirmed the information from her dreams, and Lucyna, Iwona, and I were living examples of this.

"You fall asleep again," I said to the *Lady Called Life* and she fell asleep obediently. "Sleep deeply," I asked, "listen to my words and travel with me. You are the Priestess Ki and you are beside the Pyramid. The year is 2002 and before you move back in time, I want to talk directly to the *Universe*. Can *It* talk to me in my time?"

"Time is an unknown notion," Ki replied. "I can travel in your time at will. *The Universe* is with me. *It* sometimes assumes some names, that might bring It closer to people, and sometimes *It* remains nameless. *It* is ready to talk to you."

"Who are you truly?" I asked the *Universe*.

"I am a **Spiritual Entity**," *It* answered in Lucyna's voice.

Lucyna spoke calmly, a little more slowly than in her everyday speech. I was glad, because in films I had seen that, when spiritual entities talk through people, these people speak somewhat differently, with a voice as if from beyond the grave. Somewhere in my subconscious, I feared that at some moment there would emerge from Ki some weird, unearthly baritone or base. Ki spoke somewhat sleepily, but normally.

"What is your role?" I continued to ask.

"I have already told you about this, Wanderer," Ki's voice was very indulgent and patient. "Open yourself up to my energy and receive the information which I send you. I received the Earth to take care of it. I received the Earth to lead humanity to perfection. I received permission to warn you that if the human species does not understand life, it will have to leave the Earth."

"What is your true name?" I ventured to ask.

"The time will come when you will understand me and then I will disclose to you who I am," the *Universe* replied.

Well, I thought, if *It* is taking care of the Earth, *It* must be close to the Almighty. For a moment, I felt pride, that so important a Spiritual Entity was coming down to my level, but I quickly suppressed this. Pride is not something that I need for anything.

"In what way will finding Cheops's tomb help?" I asked.

"Finding the tomb is of immense meaning, since the cleansing of the Earth, which was planned and has already started, will continue smoothly for the simple reason that Cheops comes in straight line from **Orion**. Cheops will break the code, which opens the gate to the Other World, the perfect world. The entities who helped build the Pyramid, who came from Orion, will come to the Earth and help people to understand the meaning of existence, to understand life. The Pyramid is this gate. If Cheops is not awoken, if human beings ignore the warning that flows from me, from us, the purification will occur anyway, but it will be horrible for people, since then all will perish, both the good and the bad. Then, either human beings will come to understand life — or all of them will leave the Earth."

I did not really understand what "cleansing" the *Universe* has in mind. Is some apocalypse awaiting us? What does Orion have to do with this? I wondered if I should ask about such a trifling thing as

"What is this gate to the Other World?" but I did not want to appear as an ignoramus at this meeting, as one with no knowledge of the cosmos, so I kept silent. *The Universe* continued talking through Ki.

"The important thing, the most important thing is to save the Earth and those who will believe. This was said by the **Owner of the Earth**. Now I want to explain this to you: I am not the owner. I only supervise. I watch. The *Owner of the Earth* is the one you call God. Wanderer, pass on this message to people. Everything has its appointed time. Human beings have also received theirs. Time... You are now the only ones, the last beings, who are subject to the law of purification. This purification does not, at all, need to be painful, but everything depends on you, and on how you approach this mission that I have received."

For a moment, I was once more filled with pride that I was talking with *That Part of the* Universe *Which Personally Knows God*. It is true that Neale Walsch declares in his *Conversation with God* that he converses daily with the Almighty, but I am not Walsch. Not everybody on Earth happens to have such opportunities.

"Does this mean that you are an Angel?" I asked.

For a while I felt foolish. Of course, the *Universe* is an Angel. Who else could It be, if not an Angel, since It wants to help people and in so important a matter as saving the Earth? "I wonder if spirits can be offended?" I thought. I recollected the definition of angels in the catechism, which I learned as a small boy in religion lessons in church. "Angels are pure spirits, who have reason and free will, but they have no bodies," the priest told us.

The Universe was not offended and replied very specifically.

"Wanderer, I am the very powerful Universe, the son of the God Yahweh. He is the *Owner of the Earth,* He is the Supreme Energy. As His Son, I am on the highest rung of the spiritual ladder. In your wanderings, you will find people who will abuse me, say bad things about me, but my true name is not terrible."

"So what is Your True Name?" the question immediately came to my mind, but before I managed to pose it, the *Universe* continued:

"My aim is to save people from annihilation, so that the Earth becomes a pure planet, at least partly similar to the Other Earth. The key to the Other Earth is the Great Pyramid. The key to opening the Pyramid is the 'awakening' of the Pharaoh, digging up his tomb and placing the mummy into the sarcophagus in the Pyramid. Cheops must see the sun and then the gate will be opened."

I thought to myself that surely many people, many archaeologists have been searching for the tomb and, if they have not found it by now, then how can they believe me, a Wanderer, when I say that I know where it is? At that moment, I imagined talking to some well-known Polish businessman, and asking for funds for the Cheops Project. Such a *Very Rich Man* will inevitably ask, "How do you know?" So what do I answer? If I say that there is living in Poland the Priestess Ki, who saw the Pyramid being built, that in a Lucyna from Wroclaw is this Priestess, who dreamt of the place where Cheops is buried, then any *Very Rich Man of Sound Mind* will smile with compassion and direct me to a psychiatrist, who very willingly, for an appropriate fee, will listen to my story and prescribe the appropriate medication for my common sense. Moreover, I did not quite understand how finding the tomb can 'open' the Pyramid."

The Universe was reading my thoughts.

"I am sure that you are wondering," It continued talking in Ki's voice, "why nobody has dug up the tomb yet. It is not easy to reach our key, that is to say – the Pharaoh. It has been said: the Pyramid, the Sphinx and the Tomb have their security systems. The security flows from Orion and, if unauthorized human beings make use of all this truly precise information for iniquitous purpose, we will let them reach the tomb, but then the security will be activated and that will be the demise for those who reach that point. The Purification of the Earth will then be very difficult, because all will leave the Earth, both the good and those with hardened hearts. I will add, Wanderer — pass on my words — that human beings be not so sure of themselves nor so blind in their conduct. The *Owner of the Earth*, your God, will not allow people to destroy his house. There is too much evil on the Earth already."

I was shocked. The *Universe*, speaking about purification, clearly had in mind the killing of people. Removing them from the Earth. "It declares that It represents the forces of good," I thought, "that It wants to help, and yet, It threatens with killing."

Ki slept on, with her peaceful sleep of the Priestess, unaware of the prophecies being communicated with her mouth. Iwona was present at this dream; the *Girl to Whom Every Morning Smiles* was listening, frowning, and was without a smile. The atmosphere became uneasy. I did not know what to ask. Nothing wise came to my mind.

"Explain 'purification' once more," Iwona saved the situation. "What is all this for? Why are you frightening us?"

"I do not want to frighten you," the *Universe* answered. "I want only to warn you. This may happen, if nothing changes. Just look around, Iwona, look around. Wanderer, look at the world. Is this a planet of dreams, an ideal planet, such as was intended by the Creator? This planet is already so very polluted that a change is needed. Your 'time zero' has come. We want to save what good there remains, and so we have been talking loudly for a long time through selected people: 'Open up to one another,' 'Communicate what is warmest in your hearts, what is most beautiful.' Love is the medicine; it is salvation for the Earth. Who has a pure heart and transmits the energy of love into the cosmos has nothing to fear."

We were silent for a while, allowing Priestess Ki to continue dreaming her strange, prophetic dream, which allowed us to talk with... Well, indeed, with whom were we really talking? I thought about this for a while. Is this really the *Universe*, the *One Who Guards the Earth*, guided by the will of the Almighty Creator, and who wants to help people to understand the laws ruling the cosmos, or is it simply the imagination and improvisation of Lucyna, who in her dreams, plays the role of the Priestess Ki? Can one improvise such things?

My hesitation lasted only for a while. I knew that only life could answer these questions.

"Cheops is the **key** to the Pyramid," Ki repeated sleepily, "The Pyramid is the gate to Orion."

I looked at Ki, at the *Girl to Whom Every Morning Smiles*, and I felt warmth in my heart. I felt as if some unknown person had put there several warm, golden sunrays. "What a person feels is invisible to the eyes," I thought. Perhaps this strange, invisible world is talking to us in just such a way. Through our emotions, feelings, the impulses of our heart, the inner warmth which suddenly arises in the solar plexus. Perhaps it is God talking to us in this way. Perhaps people should look for this warmth, when looking at others, because when the time comes to pass into another dimension, no bank account will matter, nor whether one has a house, a car, an airplane, or even an entire island, whether one is *President of a Very Important State* or a *Housemaid*. What will matter is the warmth experienced in life and that given to others. Perhaps this is the crux of the message of Orion, the message of the tomb, the message of the Pyramid.

"Your dream has told us a lot," I whispered into Ki's ear. "I do not want you to continue sleeping. Your dreams are beautiful but sometimes difficult. They help one to feel the goodness but they also show the fear. Before you wake up, do you want to say anything more to me?"

"Yes," Ki answered, "I want to say that the time will come when the Earth will be a perfect planet and finding the tomb will help good people to stay here, to enjoy this perfection."

"What about me?" I asked.

"You, Wanderer, you now have to learn love," Ki answered and slowly returned to Earth. Once again, she became the *Lady Called Life*, the everyday Lucyna.

After the session, I was thinking about her message, about what the *Universe* said through the Priestess. There were many questions in my head, for which I could not find answers. I could not understand how placing the Pharaoh's mummy in the sarcophagus could "open" the Great Pyramid. What does "open" mean? What is this "opening the gate" about? What will happen then? Will some spaceships start coming to us? Will space visitors start walking along the streets of our cities, teaching people how to live? I thought that perhaps, with time, the *Universe* will start answering these questions, but at this moment, it was still very complicated and unclear to me. I understood one thing — digging up the tomb will save the Earth and the people from something that was described as "purification." I also understood that if you have love in your heart, and if you share it with other people, you are safe.

9

THE WANDERER'S HESITATION

Every day that was spent in wandering brought me new thoughts, new events, and new adventures. There were moments of hesitation when I was still not sure whether I was moving along the right road and what meaning all of this had. I met many "wise people," who nodded their heads sadly as they listened to my story about Cheops. I saw compassion in their eyes, as if they were saying, "Oh, and he seemed to be such a normal guy."

Furthermore, when in my wanderings I again met the *Girl to Whom Every Morning Smiles,* it became apparent that we were starting to walk along different paths. I was sad, because it was thanks to her that my adventure with the Pharaoh started; she was the cause of so many coincidences and through her, I met the Priestess Ki. Suddenly, my thoughts became thoughts of grief and discouragement, and the Pharaoh became something less important, distant. No more daily, morning, sincere smiles. Instead, uncertainty took up residence in my thoughts. Finally, the *Girl to Whom Every Morning Smiles* went off along a different road, leaving me alone. Or so it seemed to me at that time.

At times, anger engulfed me and I welcomed this anger with true relief. It was medicine, as it allowed me to feel myself. I asked my dreams what I should do, but they were silent. I asked the signs in the heavens, but they showed me emptiness. I asked my imagination, but it had already misled me more than once, so I let Destiny have a free choice. Let it come to me on its own accord.

I waited for many weeks and nothing happened which could assure me that I was still moving in the Right Direction. Everything seemed of little importance, and the road to Cheops was becoming less and less clear. Nothing was happening along it. One day, I wandered to the place where the *Lady Called Life* lived.

"You are not yourself," she remarked, when we met. "Come, let us ask the *Universe* for advice."

I thought that the *Universe* surely knows what was happening to me. Being the *Universe*, It sees us all, our emotions and our actions, although I did not know how It could help me. I had lost the support of the Smile, and without this, it was hard for me to continue my way. However, I agreed to a conversation, because I wanted to share with someone my worries and hesitation. I needed new energy and I wanted to tear myself away from various, unnecessary thoughts.

"You have your way," the *Universe* said, "Why are you hesitating?"

"*The Girl Who Helped Me*, the *Girl to Whom Every Morning Smiles*, is not with me any more. I see only my sadness."

"Wanderer," the *Universe* answered calmly, "things are not always as they seem to be. Keep your faith in me and remember one thing: what you do, you do it not for the *Girl Who Should Smile in the Morning*. You do it for the Earth, which needs your wisdom. You do it for the people, who have lost their hearts. You do it for those who are afraid to open their hearts, because their gaze is fixed on the Delusion of Success. You do it for all those who want to live, but are now slowly dying in their lives. Stop looking back. Look at the world, which is killing itself. Look at time, which is shrinking."

I felt ashamed at my silliness and the thoughts that I had allowed to dominate in my head. During my wanderings, I teach people to look into the future, to control their thoughts, and yet I cannot do this myself at the time when it is so important. I teach people how to find their Most Important Way, I explain how to walk it safely, and I myself have allowed my reason to fall asleep. "Evidently, I need a lesson in humility," I thought.

"My hesitation had no force," I said to the *Universe*, "and was only a temporary regret for flights of fancy, with thoughts that I could not drop or change. I understand my error. I know that I cannot be sorry for myself, when the whole world is waiting for my action. I will not turn my back again. I will not turn aside from the road."

"Good," *The Universe* was pleased. "Anyway, Wanderer, when you met Lucyna, when you awoke the Priestess Ki, you stepped onto a one-way road. No step back is possible on this road. You can only go forward. I will plant thoughts in your mind and put in your path *Those Who Will Help*, and I will teach you. There are many lessons ahead for you, many tests, but I ask one thing of you: do not lose faith even when it will seem to you that all this is pointless, or that I am letting you down. Do not lose faith when others laugh at you and at those who go along with you. Do not lose faith even when you are angry with me, when it seems to you that I have left you. I need your faith, because without it, it is more difficult for me to act and to help. Remember, Wanderer, faith is most important, faith and trust."

"Advise me what am I to do with the *Girl to Whom Once Every Morning Smiled?*" I asked hesitantly. "She helped me very much. Thanks to her, I met the *Lady Called Life*, she accompanied me in every meeting with you, and now, she cannot understand herself."

"The heart does not change from day to day," the *Universe* said, "The soul always remains the same. Her heart is surrounded by a cloud but inside, it remains pure and beautiful. It has not changed. When the clouds disappear, she herself will find the Right Way. Wait. This is the only way for you to help her understand herself. Her free will must itself find the direction, in order to reach the place where harmony and love reside."

Priestess Ki opened her eyes, and I looked once more at the senselessness of my previous thoughts. After all, My Way had never changed, only my circumstances had changed. Emotions had changed, but the dream remains the same. I know the direction and whether I will be alone on my road or with the *Girl to Whom Every Morning Smiles*, the direction will not change.

"Thank you," I said to Lucyna. "You are and you will be for **me the Lady Who Helped in Difficult Moments**. Thanks to your mediation, the *Universe* has given new life to my thoughts and power to my choices."

"*The Universe* will always secretly favor your best choices," she replied. "Follow Its whisper. Observe what It says, because you know that It talks to you every day. Learn to understand what It says, to hear Its words."

All this time, it seemed to me that I was listening to the *Universe*, that I was hearing Its words. But was it really Its voice or simply my beliefs, my conscious mind talking to me?

"How do I differentiate Its voice from the thoughts which I create myself?" I looked at Lucyna.

"Do you have a brain?" she asked.

"Sometimes I think I have."

"So use it sometimes."

"Easy for her to say," I thought. Emotions often cloud the mind and it is difficult to see through their intensity. How does one use the logic of thought when one is dominated by resentment, anger, sorrow, or other similar emotions? Free will then seems to be engulfed in a dense cloud, through which the sun of reason cannot penetrate.

Because I knew that in spells of emotion, it helps to quiet down inside oneself, calming the mind and relaxing the body, I often entered a state of special meditation, the so-called "**alpha state**." I had an impression that in such moments, I get in touch with the *Universe* myself, that I talk with It in my thoughts, and this calmed me down. During one such "conversation," the *Universe* advised me: "Talk to the *Girl to Whom Every Morning Smiles*. She is already starting to understand her emotions better."

I decided to talk to her and tell her about the conversation with the *Universe*. I knew that it was not easy for her and also, that she too was searching within herself for the Best Way.

"Within us, there is sadness and happiness, there is certainty and uncertainty of tomorrow," I said when we met again along my path. "The Lord God has given us a mind; the *Universe* is helping us to use this mind in important moments. That is why It linked up you and me, so that we could reach the place where Cheops is resting. That was why you appeared on my way, you and the Priestess. Although you are now walking along a different path, we are together, whether we want it or not."

"My path," she answered without a smile, "is to get to know emotions that I have not known before. New emotions. I want to experience in my imagination the evil that I have not experienced in life. Only then will I know what is good. Only then will I have a choice."

"If you choose my way," I said, "it will not be an easy path. Sometimes we will stumble, you will have to negate yourself, but this way will lead you to something that no one in the world has ever accomplished. It is difficult, because it is new, uncharted."

"I do not know yet which way I want to go." Hesitation and uncertainty colored her voice. "My heart does not talk to me. It does not show me the direction."

"Sometimes, my eyes were looking," I said to her, "but I did not see the tomorrow, because they were looking but not where they should. Although it seemed to me that I was walking, I was not moving forward, because I had a weight tied to my leg, a weight I did not know existed. Although I felt that I was living, I was dreaming dreams which led to a sand-covered steppe, while the sand was pouring into my home. You opened for me a door with a view to the ocean. This ocean is a vastness of possible futures, a constantly undulating sensation that has no boundaries, always exists and never ends. This is the future, which can be such as will be created by Free Will and Reason. Happiness is a choice, a decision, a way of using the Free Will given to us by the Creator. This is his greatest gift to mankind. Look at how many people play in the lottery of life, where the chance of winning is less than one in a million, without knowing that all that they need is the decision to win. How few people there are who can undertake such a decision. There are many doors ahead of us. They are the gates to the future. It is our choice which of these gates we decide to open."

"I know this," she said, "but my heart needs time. Give me this time, so that I can find in myself that which, it seemed to me, I had lost."

"*The Universe* told me the same thing," I thought.

"I will give you time to find within yourself the smile that you have lost," I said quietly. "If you find it, we will continue our journey together. If not, it may indeed be that your Way is different from mine."

I paid my greetings to the *Universe* in my thoughts and set out again on my wanderings. I decided that this journey will lead me to the Pharaoh , regardless of the route I will have to take and who will be going with me. I surmised that my Legend has already been written by the *Universe*. I must only allow it to come to life.

10

A RETURN TO THE PYRAMID: ANOTHER DREAM OF THE PRIESTESS

When I talked about the tomb and the Pyramid, many people requested, "We want more details. It is not enough to say where the tomb is. This is too little. What does contemporary archaeology say about this?"

"Finding the tomb is the sole authentication," I answered.

"We need something more than dreams," I heard again and again.

They were right. Dreams do not fit into accepted scientific methodology. People need evidence, verifiable and replicable proof. It is not enough to be convinced once by somebody. Our logical hemisphere of the brain will find some contrary arguments. I decided, therefore, to read some articles on the construction of the Great Pyramid, and to compare them with the dreams of the Priestess.

It turned out that scientists and official archaeology affirm to this day that the Great Pyramid was built by the hands of ancient Egyptians, who had no knowledge at that time of the wheel. Its construction took twenty years and one hundred thousand people participated in it. The lightest blocks used for building the Pyramid weighted about two and a half tons, and the heaviest, about seventy tons. Thus, over a period of twenty years, two million three hundred thousand stone blocks were set up with incredible precision. The official version for the construction of the Great Pyramid calls for pulling successive stone blocks along ramps specially built for this purpose. According to the latest calculations, such a ramp would have to be 1,450 meters long to reach to the top of the Pyramid. The cubic volume of such a ramp would be three-point-seven times larger than the cubic volume of the entire Pyramid of Cheops.

Even for a layman with meager knowledge of Egyptology, these theories give rise to many unanswered questions. One engineer has calculated that, if the construction took twenty years and people worked for ten hours every day (with no breaks for holidays), then the builders of that time would have had barely two minutes for the positioning, fitting, and incorporation of one block into the structure. One must keep in mind that we are talking about a society that had no knowledge as yet of the wheel. Stonework was based on cracking and chipping stones by hitting one stone with another, and the only metals known then were gold, silver, and copper.

Even with the use of contemporary technologies, with the application of the most modern and largest self-propelled cranes, it would be very difficult to position a block with such precision every two minutes. Added to this is the preparation of the stones for the construction of the Pyramid and the organization of the work of so huge a number of people.

The famous Greek traveler and chronicler, Herodotus, who lived in the fifth century BC, left a description that was well-known in his time, of the building of the Great Pyramid. According to him, thousands of people dragged the blocks for the building, one after another, with the aid of special machines, for a hundred days every year over a period of twenty years. This provides an even less probable version of the building process, according to which placing one block would take only thirty-one seconds.

Having become familiar with these details, I asked the *Lady Called Life* for another dream about the Great Pyramid and Cheops. I wanted to hear once again her description of the construction, of the way she saw it at that time. Science affirms that the Great Pyramid is a Great Tomb, that Cheops built it for his own glory and that he was to be buried there. Herodotus described him as a bad king, a tyrant, who oppressed his subjects and forced them into slave labor, in order to build this tomb for him. I thought that in fact Herodotus did not know what sort of a king Cheops really was, how he ruled, and whom he loved. In the time of Herodotus (that is, at least two thousand years after the completion of the building of the Pyramid), many untrue stories could have arisen.

The dreams of the Priestess and her travels in time are indeed "unscientific," but they provide an opportunity for looking into this unknown past. Real or imagined, but a past such as she can see in her dreams.

Lucyna agreed without the slightest hesitation. She liked to dream about the Pharaoh.

"Fall asleep," I asked, "and dream your dream about the Great Pyramid and Cheops. Tell me what you see. Tell me about the life about which you are dreaming now, about the Priestess you are."

"I am a Priestess of the Pharaoh, I serve the priest, Juno, and my name is Ki," the *Lady Called Life* started her dream.

"What time is this, what year?" I asked this question once again.

"It is the time of the building of the Pyramid."

Once again, Ki was unable to specify when she lived. I decided not to ask her any more about time. I thought that I might be able to establish when the Great Pyramid was built in some other way. Official science designates the time of the construction to 2,500 years before the birth of Christ.

"Tell me what you see," I asked. "Is the Pyramid ready? Can you see how it is being built?"

"They are not building it yet. The preparations are still underway."

"Have you seen the construction plan?"

"No, the plans are secret. They are known to Cheops and the priest, Juno. They are bringing in the animals for the work. The work is proceeding very quickly; joy can be seen in every face, there is no coercion."

"Dream on," I encouraged her, "your dreams open the eyes of many people. In the future, you will no longer be a priestess, but you will be able to dream what you see now. You will be able to help people understand the secret of the Great Pyramid. See the Pyramid and the chambers? What do you dream?"

"At the base of the pyramid, there is one room, or rather a chamber," Ki dreamt on. This chamber is on the side of the queen's chamber. A further one is on the side of Cheops's chamber, while the third and the last two are located above the king's chamber. The chambers are positioned one on top of the other. I do not see any more hidden chambers. The last one is at the top of the pyramid and is very large."

"Is there an entrance to these chambers?"

"Yes. The connection with all the chambers is located in the King's Chamber. It is hidden."

"How long did the construction take?"

"Twenty years, including the corridors located around the Pyramid."

I thought, "Here is further confirmation of the time for the construction of the Great Pyramid. If it was so, simple mathematics excludes the theory of its being built by a primitive civilization..."

"Go on... tell me more, Ki. Was the Pyramid to be a tomb for Cheops?" I asked.

"No. The Great Pyramid is being built to become the key or gate to the universe. It was built for a specific purpose. It was to be a message, a contact with the universe, and especially, a connection with the Other Earth. It is connection by means of the waves, which flow in both directions, from the Pyramid toward the Other Earth and back here from there. The Pyramid is a sign of time and was built to become a code in the future."

I was happy with what she was saying, that she was confirming what she had dreamed previously. I only wondered how an Egyptian priestess could have knowledge of the meaning of such a symbol as the Pyramid.

"How do you know all this?" I asked.

"Juno says so," she answered. "He says that the Pyramid stands in the central point of the axis of the Earth. All the energy fields converge on this point. The Pyramid was the beginning and the Pyramid will be the end. That is why it is so important."

"Does everything you know come from Juno?"

"Sometimes, I say what I see. Sometimes, Juno speaks to me and then I know. Sometimes, one of the White Brethren speaks to me."

"What language do you use to talk to Juno, to the White Brethren?"

"What a question! The one we all speak. I do not know any other."

I wondered how the Egyptian Priestess Ki talked to me in her sleep in Polish, while back there in Egypt, some thousands of years ago, she understood the language used at the time of the building of the Great Pyramid. Does she have some "internal interpreter," who recreates, in some way understandable only to her, within the mind of the present Lucyna, the information from those times so that she can communicate it in the only language available to her now? For a while, I wanted to ask Ki to speak to me in that ancient language, but after a short hesitation, I gave up the idea. Even if she started speaking some strange words, none of us could understand them. Seeking out someone who could understand the language used in Egypt many thousands of years ago seemed to me to be a task too difficult and completely unnecessary at that time.

I also thought that the *Universe* was probably fulfilling for her the role of such an "interpreter." It helps her to communicate in a way, which is understandable to her, irrespective of how far in time and to what country the dreams take her. With such help, Lucyna does not need to know the language of the country about which she dreams. In her dreams, Juno, Cheops, and all other entities talk to her in her own language. If she could not understand the words dreamt, she would not be able to repeat or communicate anything.

I smiled to my thoughts and returned to the main issue.

"What is the name of the man who speaks to you?" I continued.

"His name is Oliver, but for them, names have no meaning... They ask to addressed as "Friend...""

"Ask where the Other Earth is."

"The Other Earth is located in the belt of Orion. This is the first star and around it is the planet Ashun."

I wondered about one thing. If this planet is inhabited by beings similar to us, made of flesh and bone, how did they fly to us? What kind of space-traveling technology must there have been on that planet, if traveling over such distances was possible? At present, man can only go to the moon, a probe was sent to Mars, but the belt of Orion is much, much farther away. I left this issue for a later time.

"Can you see those who are the builders, the ones who came from the Other Earth?" I asked. "What do they look like?"

"I can see them, but from a distance. Direct contact with the Earth is dangerous for them. The Earth is contaminated. Their organisms are not immune to earthly bacteria. They have protective clothing."

"Tell me what they look like," I requested.

"They are beautiful men. They have strange coveralls and helmets on their heads," the Priestess dreamt on, "and when they are on Earth, they do not take them off. This is to protect them against earthly bacteria."

"Why did they come here?"

"They have come to teach people, to enlighten our minds, and to prove their existence. The main purpose of this presence, previously and now, is to make mankind perfect."

"Yes," I thought, "this had already been said in previous dreams of the Priestess Ki. It seems that, in order to become perfect, one must feel love. But... love for everyone? Even those who harm us?"

"Do you know Cheops personally?" my curiosity prevailed over philosophy.

"Yes, we meet often. I often go to his place with Juno, but I was not present during the more important talks and communications. None of us were allowed to participate in the meetings in the Special

Tent. Only Juno and Cheops have the right to enter this tent. Within it are held the meetings with the White Brotherhood, with the visitors from Orion."

It followed from the dream of the Priestess, that the Special Tent was the place where Cheops and the priest Juno met eye to eye, without coveralls, with the visitors from the Other Earth. It was a place of consultation, where Cheops and Juno received further "guidelines" on the construction.

"Continue dreaming and tell me what the Special Tent looks like," I requested.

"It is built of wood and covered with cloth, like other tents. The difference is that it has three compartments. The first is for cleansing. The second had a similar function, also for cleansing. The third is for the consultations."

"What is this cleansing for?"

"To cleanse the Pharaoh and Juno of earthly bacteria, which is dangerous to the visitors, so that the White Brethren could talk to them without their coveralls."

"How does this cleansing take place?"

"Cheops and Juno must prepare for the meeting with the White Brethren for three days. On the first day, in the first compartment, they must drink a special liquid prepared by the White Brethren. On the second day, they move into the second compartment. There, onto a stone table is placed a globe, which emits blue-violet rays, and there, their cleansing from earthly bacteria is completed."

"What was done in the first compartment?"

"All the internal organs were cleansed. They had to drink a specially prepared liquid."

"Was the composition of this liquid known?"

"No, no one knew it, not even Juno and Cheops, but they trusted the White Brethren without reservation and subjected themselves to cleansing with no objection. Only on the third day could they enter the third compartment, where the consultations were held, where they received instructions concerning further construction. No one was allowed to enter this tent and this was respected without objection."

I thought that Herodotus could not have written about this, because he had no one who could tell him about it. I was curious whether Ki knew the Pharaoh well, so I changed the subject.

"What did you call Cheops?" I asked.

"**Khufu**."

"Why is that?"

"I don't know. That is how the chosen addressed him."

Interesting words. This is how history refers to Cheops, how his name is written: Khufu. I thought that perhaps this was not a name only for the chosen, and perhaps everyone called him by this name, but at this time, this was not important. I asked Ki to continue dreaming.

"Where are you now?" I asked.

"I am beside the **Sphinx**. People are helping with the construction... There is a road and scaffolding. Every newly laid level has sand poured onto it. This is how the construction looks... The Pyramid was located in the center... One level... they are building scaffolding, pouring on sand. Then the next level..."

"What are the people doing?"

"The people are helping in the construction. The builders are not people. This means... yes... people, but not from our Earth. They are those from the Other Earth."

"I know, you have already dreamt about this. Tell me what you see. How are they building the Pyramid? What material was used for the construction?"

"Stone blocks. They were brought here from quarries, transported by their ships. Only the wood for constructing the scaffolding came by the Nile, while the stone blocks were transported by the ships. That was why the stone blocks could be brought from far away."

"Do you mean airships? How was it happening?"

"It was strange. Now I can say only that, which I see, which I understand. The ships for transporting the stones were quite large. There were no ropes, no protective devices. The stone block simply floated in the air. From what Juno tells me, this is energy. Juno does not want to explain to me what this is, what sort of energy. I only know that it is very powerful. The suspended stone was brought into the construction site. There, another airship, much smaller from the former, cut and prepared the stone. The stone, prepared in this way, was then placed on the Pyramid with mathematical precision. Stone after stone. The construction was always done at night. During the day, the people did other work, also related to the construction."

"What did they use to provide light, so one could see?" I continued my questioning. "Now, in the time of Aquarius, people have something called electricity. Was it known then?"

"No, this concept is unknown to me. The construction site was illuminated by the ships. I do not know what this illumination was, but it was so bright that one could see every detail."

"The Pharaoh? Cheops? What did he do in the construction?" I asked.

"The Pharaoh is often on the construction site. This is his mission, his vocation. From beginning to end, he is present at the construction. He supervises, he manages, but he does not rush the people. The construction has to proceed in its own rhythm."

Ki spoke more and more slowly, more and more sleepily... I did not know if she was tired, or if I should wake her up or ask more questions. My curiosity prevailed.

"Please, move on in time now," I asked. "The construction of the Pyramid is completed. See the moment when the Pyramid is ready? What is happening?"

"Yes... the construction is finished," the Priestess dreamt. They are now disassembling the scaffolding. Section by section, slowly, they remove the sand, they remove the wood. Everything is stored to one side, since the material will be needed for the construction of the next pyramid, which will start soon. The second pyramid is to be located precisely in line with the second star in the belt of Orion."

"Is Cheops alive now, when you are looking at the finished pyramid?" I asked.

"Yes, he is alive," Ki started to be uneasy in her dream.

"And when did he die?"

Ki became silent and tears came to the eyes of the sleeping Priestess. She started to weep, and after a while, her weeping turned into sobbing. I did not know whether I should wake her or let her weep herself out. I decided to wait a while and then she gradually began to calm down.

"He died in a strange way," her breaking voice betrayed her immense sadness. "One day, he went to the temple and his body was found without life. He left his body and departed. This was a shock for everybody. He was still very young. I only know that he departed at his own request, after the completion of the construction. Thus also it had been said that when the construction was completed, Cheops would leave."

"Tell me: How are they burying him?" I asked.

Ki started sobbing again. She could not calm down, so I asked whether she wanted to wake from her dream.

"I don't want to," she said, weeping. "I want to bid him farewell."

This lasted a while and then she continued her dream through her tears.

"A special funeral procession is carrying Cheops from the Sphinx to the place of his rest. It is a long procession. They are carrying his embalmed body, to lay it in the place which he himself chose before his death. A place which will not be accessible to people for the next 6500 years. After Cheops was laid in his tomb, special priestly servants cover up the entrances with sand. I am standing to one side and..."

She burst into such tears, that I did not know whether to console her or try again to wake her up. I decided to wait. (After all, she is a woman, and sometimes, women must have a good cry to feel better.) Her tears continued, so I decided to try to help her in her grief. "Perhaps I should express my condolences?" I thought, but on the other hand, the customs in those times might have been completely different. I wanted to stem the flow of her tears, but I did not know how. To be sure, it was only a dream but I did not want it to be unpleasant.

"Did you love Cheops? Did his death affect you very greatly?" I asked.

"What a silly question," I thought. "If she had not loved him, there would not have been such a fountain of tears." However, I could not think of anything wiser to say. I was also glad that she had provided a specific time period. If the tomb was to be opened in 6,500 years time, that means that the Great Pyramid was built **6,500 years** ago from the present time, or 4,500 years before Christ, and not in 2500 BC, as affirmed by the official version.

"Juno... is holding me in his arms... We are all weeping, but everyone has to go away, to leave him," Ki continued through her tears, ignoring my question. "Cheops is in the tomb now. A ship is flying in and placing a slab to cover the tomb. We all go back along the same way that the procession came. Behind us, other servants cover up our track with sand. When we are back beside the Sphinx, the road to the tomb is cut off. The other road, the canal, which was empty until now, will be flooded with water... Now they are opening the dam... the water is flooding in..."

I wanted to ask her how she felt, but this question seemed to me to be out of place. How can a woman feel, when her beloved ruler is laid in his tomb and covered by sand? Miserable, obviously. Ki started talking again, through her tears.

"Somebody we loved has left. Our Pharaoh... Khufu... He was an excellent king. He was loving, good... and he knew that we all loved him. He loved us as we loved him. He left early, but said that we will meet. We will meet in the future, when he returns. Juno said to wait patiently. Our meeting will happen."

Her breathing slowly began to calm down again. This took some minutes, so I waited for her dream to continue. "To wake her or not to wake her? That is the question." I noticed that her calm and even breathing was returning.

"Sleep on," I said quietly, "dream your dream, because I do not know when you will be able to dream it again. It may be that this is the most important of all dreams dreamt by anybody. Your dream will help to awaken the Pharaoh. Can you dream on? Do you want to?"

"Yes," she replied. "You can ask me. I am calm now."

"Please describe, in more detail, how the Pharaoh's funeral appeared. What do you see?"

"There are stairs not far from the Sphinx, on the side where his head is. The entrance is there, through which the funeral procession is entering."

"How deep do they go down?"

"One level, perhaps two. It is quite deep. They go down below the ground. They carry Cheops to the place of rest. The prepared tomb is there, enclosed on all sides by stones."

"How does it look inside?"

"It is empty. There stands only a rectangular sarcophagus made of the same stone as the Pyramid. It stands almost in the middle of this chamber. They are laying the Pharaoh there."

"And what then?"

"The ship of the White Brethren is flying in above us; it covers the sarcophagus with a stone. No one has to die with Pharaoh; all leave the tomb."

This was for me a fascinating part of the dream. She spoke as if there was taking place before her eyes the unusual scene of the burial of a man, who has been sought for thousands of years by scholars, archaeologists, treasure hunters, and adventurers.

"Sleep on," I asked Ki. "Tell me what you see. Where are they going?"

"They are coming out," Ki dreamt, "by the same way that they went in."

"Were there some riches or utensils left in this chamber?"

"No," she answered, "there is only the body of the Pharaoh there."

"Nothing more?" I was surprised. "I heard that various precious items, gold and ornaments, were buried together with famous kings."

"Yes," she answered, "there is some gold, his personal things, but this gold is not what is most important. Most important are the information tablets."

"What sort of tablets? What is on them?"

"These are the **tablets** on which priests wrote during the whole time when the Pyramid was being built. There are many of them, very many. They are in the sarcophagus, beside Cheops, and also in other places. They are made of stone similar to granite, but lustrous. On the tablets is reported who built the Pyramid and what is hidden in it. They hold the history of mankind, the history of Atlantis, the history of the Earth. The *Brethren from the Other Earth* said that the tablets must remain intact until the time of the Aquarius."

I saw that the Priestess's breath was normal, her eyes were closed and her body relaxed, so I decided to continue the questions.

"So the Great Pyramid was built not for Cheops, but for the future?"

"Juno says... Cheops says... The message... the code, which is the Great Pyramid, is to serve human beings in the future, in a specific time in the future, when the Pisces hands power over to Aquarius. The prophets will speak about this, it will be foretold. The Pyramid is to be the gate, which will open, and the entities from the Other Earth, those who are with us now, will translocate through an energy and magnetic channel. In order to open this gate, this code, one needs to have the cipher or key. The Pharaoh is the key."

I thought that at the present time someone could come up with the idea of dismantling the Great Pyramid. Researchers continue to speculate that there are treasures inside, that the Pyramid has some special energy, which is widely discussed in the world.

"Can this gate be opened without the key?" I asked.

"One can force the gate without the key, but then there is danger. Beings in the future will not know what is hidden behind the gate. Juno says that it will be very dangerous, if they force the gate without the key."

"Why dangerous? What can happen then?"

The Priestess Ki hesitated and was silent for a while, breathing again at a slightly accelerated rate. I thought once again she was reliving the death of Cheops, but after a while, her breath became calmer again.

"Here I must say," she started to talk slowly in a calm but very assertive voice, "what I have been told, what Cheops and Juno tell me. As I said, the Council took place before the Sphinx, a meeting of the Council of the Gods, since human beings began to inhabit the Earth, not in the manner as the gods had planned. That was why at this historic Council, about which Juno speaks, a time was designated for the Earth and its inhabitants. This time was to come to an end when the Pisces relinquishes its power to Aquarius. Then the purification of the Earth will commence, the purification of people. Nature will help the energies of the gods in this purification. The tomb must be found, because its opening and the opening the Pyramid will help to lessen the severity of the purification. Juno said that after the passage of 6500 years, after the opening of the Pyramid with the key, the gods will return to the Earth, to help people once again. Just like now."

I began to understand why, for so many centuries, no one had found the tomb. No one had even guessed where it is located. The majority of archaeologists assumed that the tomb is in the Pyramid, though no one knew where, because all the chambers found in the Pyramid of Cheops were empty. "So the safeguards worked," I thought. "It is to be found only now."

"The tomb has safeguards. The key must be found in order to open the gate. The safeguards were put in place, because, as the White Brethren said, human rapacity will grow. The greed for gold will increase from generation to generation. That was why Cheops is so carefully protected. The protection flows from Orion and woe to those who, exploiting this information, will try to reach him. They will find the tomb, but all of them will die. Only those people can be safe, who come to the Earth in the age of the PISCES and find themselves in the age of AQUARIUS. These will be the chosen, selected individuals. This could not be done earlier, as the appointed time had to pass."

"From this," I thought, "it follows that the *Universe* had chosen us, Lucyna, Iwona, Łucja and me, as 'selected individuals.' This had better not go to our heads," I immediately thought. It is but human nature to always seek exceptionality.

I noticed how little of what Ki dreamt corresponded with the official theories of scientists and archaeologists. There was no agreement on either the date of the construction or on the manner of the building of the Great Pyramid, as well as on the theory about the cruelty of Cheops. The only point of agreement was the duration of the construction of the Pyramid: twenty years, and the fact that it was built by the Pharaoh who was called Cheops (or Khufu) by Lucyna. On the other hand, the date given by Ki for the construction of the Great Pyramid differed by 2000 years from the official date of the reign of this Pharaoh. These were details which did not fit at all into the mosaic arranged by modern science.

I felt that the dream of the Priestess would have to come to an end, but I was curious what will happen when we dig up this tomb, so I asked another question...

"When the tomb is found and opened, are there any rituals to be performed, so that everything proceeds as it should?"

"When the Pharaoh sees the sun, when the tomb is opened, the Pharaoh has to be carried to the Sphinx, to the Guardian," Ki answered. "There homage should be paid to the Guardian and then the Pharaoh's body should be taken to the Pyramid and placed in the sarcophagus prepared in the King's Chamber. It was built specially for him, but now it is empty. The Pharaoh has to lie there only till the full moon. Then his body, as it is written, is to be given up to science. This will suffice to disengage the safeguards and open the hidden entrances, since the Pyramid conceals other chambers which will be opened only after the tomb is dug up. There is a special procedure for removing the safeguards. The selected individuals will come to know it, when the time is ripe."

Ki fell silent, as if she had dropped into a deeper sleep. I also said nothing. I waited for her words, but the silence continued.

"Do you want to wake up?" I asked.

"No, I don't want to. Let me stay here a while. I feel so well here. There is so much love around me."

"You have a task to fulfill, a very important task. I will transfer you soon to a time when you can meet the Pharaoh again. You will be able to awaken him."

"Let me stay," Ki whispered and started to cry.

"I cannot, you are needed here, so wake up," I decided to be more firm. Ki cannot sleep indefinitely, for she would sleep through finding the tomb.

"Wake up!" I repeated. "Move on in time into another dream. The dream which you have in the future."

She curled up, but I saw that her return was starting.

"Wake up!" I repeated once more. "You are the *Lady Called Life*. You are Lucyna. Your dream is the dream of life today. In a while you will stop dreaming."

The *Lady Called Life* slowly opened her eyes. She lay there for a long time, unable to regain full consciousness, before she again became Lucyna.

11

THE BUSINESSMAN

He introduced himself as a Businessman but I called him the *Man Who Says That He Can Earn Money*. We met in a shop and it was another coincidence. He knew a thing or two about computers, women, and earning money. I hesitated whether to tell him about Cheops, because in the eyes of such a businessman, I did not want to appear as a dreamer or a nutcase who tells unbelievable stories about Egypt, the Pharaoh, and the Tomb.

Since such meetings are rare, the *Businessman* invited me to his home. He talked a lot about his businesses and about money, which attracts more money, and so on. I thought that even businessmen occasionally like to dream and wander in their imagination beyond percentage accrual of capital, securities, bonds, and the exploitation of man by man, although the last, a communist slogan, was something that the *Businessman* would relate mainly to female-male relationships. He gave the impression that he was open to various strange things in the world, so I decided to take a risk and to admit him into the Egyptian secrets...

"I will tell you about Cheops," I said to him one day.

And here occurred another chance event, or coincidence. The *Businessman*, the *Man Who Says That He Can Earn Money*, turned out to be an architect, passionate about archaeology, and immediately offered his help in the search for the *Greatest Secret of the Universe.*

"I have been in Egypt," he said, "and have dug up various things from the sand. I know people, I know how to arrange things. We'll do a good business on this."

"How?" I asked, no longer surprised by anything.

Coincidences and unexpected meetings with people, it would seem, are so far away from things Egyptian, have suddenly become the norm. People sleeping the deep sleep of just citizens of a normal country — whose dreams were about going to work, earning a living, eating, coming home from work, watching television, and going to bed — have suddenly changed into extraordinary people. They no longer wanted to dream their normal dreams of normal reality. They have started to dream about a different reality, the "abnormal," exceptional reality that is hidden somewhere deep down in the subconscious.

Suddenly, in front on me, there started to open a world of people who were the same but different. People who now dreamed not only about gold and treasures, but about *All Human Beings Living on the Earth. The Businessman* seemed to me to be such an unusual person, and suddenly, I believed profoundly in his financial wisdom.

"One deals with this just as with everything in the world," he said, when I asked him about the Pharaoh. "First, one has to find money for this expedition. When this is done, we will talk to the Polish Archaeological Mission and we will hire them to arrange the permit and carry out the excavations. We have in Poland *a Very Renowned Professor of Archaeology.* The Egyptians will not turn him down because he is there all the time and finds things."

"Do you think it will be easy?" I asked.

"No sweat."

His not-inconsiderable dimensions even seemed to swell up somewhat with a feeling of pride and importance. "Just a piece of cake to me. We need half a million dollars at most."

I imagined myself approaching somebody and asking for five hundred thousand dollars, telling that person that I know where the

Tomb of Cheops is, the one that has been sought for thousands of years by archaeologists, clairvoyants, and businessmen, wanting to find gold and fame there. I say that I know how the Pyramid was built and who built it. What happens next is easy to imagine.

The dreams of the *Priestess* Ki? What sort of science is this? Where are the facts? Where is the research? Where is the ground-penetrating radar? Today's scientists and businessmen do not believe in dreams, in conversations with the *Universe*, in Its spirituality, or in the existence of extraterrestrial civilizations.

I shared my doubts with the *Businessman.*

"That is why I am a businessman, to dream such a dream that may appeal to many *Very Rich People.*"

And this was how the *Businessman* started to create with me dreams about Egypt, about riches, fame, and above all, business. Well, he was indeed a businessman. He did not say how much money he had himself, but I surmised that he was a bit short of the half million, for otherwise he would immediately have invested it, if he had had it. I therefore waited for some interesting proposals on his part.

Time passed and what he dreamt did not always prove to be the best way to go. The first salvo was directed at telephone companies, whose advertising budget is pretty hefty. Advertising that "With us, you will get through even to Cheops" seemed to be a good idea, but time was passing and the money was not there.

The Girl to Whom Every Morning Smiles suggested, "We should include the dreams of the Priestess in our search. It was the *Universe* who placed the *Businessman* in your way, so perhaps, we may learn what way has been prepared for him."

"If the *Universe* will be willing to show it to us," I remarked.

We went to meet Lucyna with the request for help from the *Universe.*

"Talk to it yourself," she said, when I came.

I did not understand her suggestion. How am I to talk to the *Universe* by myself? It was she who had daily contact with It. I only had brief encounters, thanks to the dreams, which I helped her to dream.

"You can start talking to the *Universe* directly, not just through the Priestess Ki," Lucyna continued. "Initially, if I had told you about such contact, you would have been too shocked to believe me. Now, you have your own experience, you are beginning to understand what is happening in your life. You are starting to see the higher meanings in things. You are beginning to understand that your coincidences are not accidental, that they are the quiet whispering of the *Universe*, which is talking to you all the time. I, as the Priestess Ki, had to teach you to listen, to open your ears and your eyes. You have already started to hear, and the veil over your eyes is slowly becoming transparent. You are ready to experience the conversations."

"What is such a conversation like?" I asked in wonder.

"It's very simple: you ask, the *Universe* answers," she said. "I will be only an intermediary, a connection between the two of you."

I arranged another meeting with Lucyna... a new adventure... a new experience... She sat at the table, looked at me, smiled and said, "Ask away, I am ready."

I was shocked. What is this? No formalities? So simply, without any ceremonies, without any rituals? Without a black cat or a crystal ball in dim light? This was too normal for me.

Seeing my surprise and embarrassment, Lucyna said, "*The Universe* is normal. It is speaking, so you should ask. This also is a dream, but a WAKING DREAM."

"Perhaps It should say something to me first?" I mumbled, somewhat disconcerted. I did not know how to start.

"Welcome, Wanderer!" spoke the *Universe*, suddenly, in the voice of the Connection. "It is I, the *Universe*. We will converse today in a manner unusual to you. This is the manner that I most frequently use to talk with the Connection. I am the *Universe*. I am the energy which takes care of you, which guides you. I know your worries, I feel your confusion, I feel every emotion of yours. I know your thoughts, and I understand them perfectly. We can start our conversation."

For a while, I was silent, not knowing what to say. I wanted to ask about Egypt, money, the *Businessman*, but everything seemed to be too simple to be true.

"My world," the *Universe* continued, feeling my hesitation, "is a world as true as is yours, Wanderer. It is a world of energy, a spiritual world. Contact with me is simple and normal. Just think about me and I can feel it, I perceive it. Ceremonies, rituals, or attributes are unnecessary. Actually, simplicity and sincerity of thought is what reaches me most easily, what I value most in people. You already know that I talk to you through your dreams and through the events happening in your lives. I am an invisible world and I have no other way of communication. You know that you and people chosen by me have started out along a one-way road leading to the Pharaoh and that I will not allow you turn back from this road. That is why I am facilitating this communication. Besides the Priestess Ki, you can now make use of my Connection. It has taken me a long time to teach her to dream while awake, this direct conversation. Now she is proficient in it. I am listening."

"Greetings to you!" I finally stammered.

I did not know what form of address I should use to the *Universe*. I did not want to be judged that I lacked respect, but I intuitively chose the direct form, which was easier because It had addressed me in the second person... Besides, It was difficult to imagine myself speaking to something so vast and undefined as regards to gender, as "Sir" or "Your Lordship." I felt no need to regard It as something remote... It seemed to me to be a good friend...

"Remember, there is strength in simplicity and in sincerity of the heart," the *Universe* spoke to me again, reading my thoughts. "Talk to me as if you were talking to a friend. Here, in my dimension, there are no words such as 'Sir' or 'Your Lordship,'"

"There is a certain person," I spoke out more confidently, "whom I have named the *Businessman*, who is trying to find funds for our expedition to Egypt. Can you help him in finding these funds?"

"His name has no meaning to me," the *Universe* said. "Names are important only to you."

"How am I to call him?" I asked, in my surprise.

"Energy, Wanderer, he is energy to me."

"All right, so do you know the energy of the *Businessman*?"

"Yes, I can feel his energy through you," the *Universe* answered.

I was surprised at this "through you" but, apparently, these are processes that are understandable only there, in the universe, so I did not ask why It feels "through me," rather than directly, as every omniscient Universe should.

"*The Businessman* is the one who states that he can earn money," I said. "In order to go to Egypt, we need our earthly means of 'inducement and persuasion.' Can you help him?"

"If it depended on me and I had such abilities," the *Universe* replied, "I would shower you with gold and give you my blessing. In my world, I do not have the ability to create gold for you. I do not have matter and I cannot create matter. I can only create opportunities for you, placing appropriate people in your path, but the rest you must do yourselves."

"What am I to say to the *Businessman*?" I asked.

"Tell him that I am energy and, in order to reach anybody, I need you, who are matter. Through touch, I can help to influence a person who is of importance to you. Therefore, when the *Businessman* is trying to convince someone who is a potential sponsor, let him, while talking, grasp the hand or touch the arm of the person he is talking to. There has to be a touch. It would be good if the *Businessman* would summon me, at this time or even prior to the meeting. Let him not be ashamed of these emotions. He can do this in the morning on the day when the meeting is arranged. I am the patron of this mission. It is important to me also that Cheops see the light, the sun, so tell the *Businessman* what I have said. Contact must be established and let him ask me for help. Then, I will begin to influence the indicated person. Have I been understood correctly?"

"Yes, I understand," I answered.

In truth, I was not sure if I understood. It had seemed that the *Universe* was omnipotent, and had the power of creation. If so, what was the problem for It in taking care of a matter of a few hundred thousand dollars for our expedition to Egypt? There are so many millionaires in the world. Surely more than one of them would gladly contribute to such an objective as the archaeological discovery of all times, to the excavation of the tomb. I started having doubts as to why the *Universe* had chosen me for the mission, rather than some millionaire, or better still, a millionaire archaeologist and Egyptologist. Such a one would immediately arrange all the permits, pay off whoever should be paid off, and the tomb would be excavated.

I carefully hid these thoughts, so that the *Universe* would not notice them by chance. I said, "I have already talked to the *Businessman* and I asked him to make contact with you; to form a picture of you and to ask you for support. Such a meeting between him and a potential sponsor has already taken place."

"This contact was weak," the *Universe* replied after a moment of silence. "His contact must be sincere. He must believe in this. It is not enough to speak the words, because the words may remain empty, without echo. Complex formulations and flowery sentences are not necessary. It is enough to think with faith, deep faith, 'Universe, help me." Tell him this. He does not have to form a picture of me, because this is difficult. Energy. I am energy."

"I understand. What precisely should he do? Close his eyes and ask you for help?"

"Not necessarily. There are various ways. He may, for example, look at some beautiful flowers and say, 'Help me.' He may look at stars in the night and say with faith, 'Universe, help me,' but this has to come from the depth of his heart, from inside. Remember, faith creates miracles and this miracle will happen when his words flow with faith."

I thought that these words were very important. I also need to strengthen my faith every day, that I am truly dreaming this dream.

"The Bible also says that faith creates miracles," I said.

"Yes, Wanderer. Just so. Even if according to your earthly reasoning, it might appear that nothing is happening, that the case is hopeless, and that this *Universe* is doing nothing, even then, remember the power of faith. If you lose faith, it will be more difficult for me to act. When your faith or the faith of the *Businessman* is strong and you can say to yourself, 'All is well,' these words have immense power. Not 'it will be well' but 'it *is* well,' that is why the solution or answer may come in the most unexpected moment. Even when you do not expect it, the answer comes. And let me repeat once more, that I help when faith is true. I help and I guide. The issue of Cheops is close to me and it is an issue on which I am working, in order to help you."

I did not know what else to ask but I did not yet want to finish this unusual conversation. It was so good and easy to converse with the Universe, that I would gladly continue this conversation without end. *The Universe* broke the silence again.

"As regards the *Businessman*, there is a 'but.'"

"What?" I asked.

"His intentions must be pure. Remember, Wanderer, what I once told you through Ki. I cannot be cheated. I read thoughts, I feel hearts. His heart must be pure."

"What do you mean by 'pure intentions, pure heart?'"

"The issue of Cheops is very important to me and the people I choose for this mission cannot be guided by greed or desire to make a profit. That was why I select my team very carefully and look into their hearts and put them to tests. Some pass these tests, some drop out. There will be people on your way who will fail these tests. This will be their choice, their free will. The *Businessman* must have a pure heart and pure intentions, which means that he must join us in order to help people, and not to enrich himself. If he joins us with such intentions, he will receive all the help I can give. Then he will feel this help, he will feel my energy. If I detect even a shred of greed or of a desire to cheat me, he will not gain my help. Tell him this."

After a while of silence, the *Universe* added, "However you look at this, Wanderer, from my point of view, you are crippled and you need my help very much."

"I know," I answered, thinking in my heart about my own intentions. "I hope they are pure," I thought.

"Till the next time," the *Universe* said.

I understood that for today, our conversation had come to an end.

"Till the next time and thank you," I replied.

Lucyna breathed deeply and looked at me.

"So, how was it?" she asked.

"How was it? Surely, it was you talking to me, you were not asleep, because I did not put you to sleep. You were dreaming but awake. Surely, you know what we were talking about."

"The thing is, I don't," she said. "You see, this is a special kind of dream, which I have been practicing for years, a dream which the *Universe* taught me. He guided me step by step, taught me how to fall asleep, how to hear, how to tell his voice from others, and how to pass his voice on. This took a very long time. First, I learned how to differentiate his voice from all other thoughts, which came into my head. Then I learned how to repeat it."

"So then why did we not start talking like that from the beginning? What was all this putting to sleep for?"

"The special dream is more credible than the waking dream. If I had immediately started... well, simply speaking, you would not have believed me. You would have thought that I am crazy and you would have gone your way. Am I not right?"

"You may be right..."

"She certainly is right," I thought. If Lucyna had come do me and started to say something, telling me that she was speaking with the "voice of the *Universe*," I would probably have sent her to an asylum myself. Now, I was better prepared.

"Why do you say that you *do* not know what we were talking about with the *Universe*?" I asked, not quite believing her. "Your eyes were open."

"The waking dream is a special type of dreaming. My consciousness is altered at this time. I hear you and I hear the *Universe*. It speaks to me and I hear It as clearly as I hear you. In turn, It hears you through me. That is why this dialogue is possible. But when I wake from this dream, I remember nothing, in just the same way that I do not remember the dreams with my traveling in time. It is as if I were waking up from a normal sleep and had no memory of my dreams in that sleep."

"I understand," I said.

I was not sure whether this was really so, whether Lucyna was telling the truth, but this did not matter. Truth or not, the conversation was fascinating to me. I was very proud of this direct contact. I felt exceptional. I felt that I was the Wanderer, with whom the *Universe* converses differently than with others.

The next day, I went to meet the *Businessman* and I told him about the conversation.

"The *Universe* says," I told him, "that your communication with It was weak. It said that It did not hear you, that you did not turn and speak to It."

His face paled slightly and he nodded his head sadly.

"The *Universe* is right. My pride was my downfall. In fact, I did not ask for help, because I thought I could arrange everything all by myself, since I am a *Very Good Businessman*. Next time, I will ask for help."

"It also said that you should take heed of your intentions, and that the main objective should not be to enrich yourself but to find the tomb."

"My intentions are pure," he said, with an offended tone, looking to the side. "For me, this is simply an adventure."

We parted and I waited to see what would happen to the *Businessman*, and how the *Universe* would help him with the task that was most important for us: finding the "gold," — the funds — for the expedition to Egypt.

12

A DIFFERENT MEANING OF EVENTS

Life writes the best scenarios, which even imagination cannot create. My life and the life of the new individuals who joined the project, began writing a more and more interesting scenario about the Road to the Tomb of Cheops.

In order for the expedition to be successful (apart from the money, which was to be taken care of by the *Businessman*), consent was needed for the search from the appropriate authorities in Egypt. The very fact that the excavations concerned so important an issue as the Tomb of Cheops, which archaeologists and treasure hunters have been seeking for centuries, seemed to be a perfect argument for obtaining such a permit. However, when the authorities are approached by a well-known archaeologist, famous throughout the world in the field of excavation, it is one thing, but when the same proposal is submitted by an unknown Wanderer, telling a story about a certain woman in Poland, who just had a dream, it is a completely different thing.

The Priestess Ki described the location of the Pharaoh's tomb with high precision. She did this several times, during different dreams. On each occasion, her dream was more and more clear, and more and more precise. She said what was in the tomb and what the sarcophagus, within which the Pharaoh was laid, looked like.

As long as this was a dream, it did not disturb anybody. However, if the dream were to start taking on the dimension of action, this could alarm many a scientist. What if this proved to be true? What if the tomb really was in the place where Ki had located it? What if, within it, there really were stone tablets describing the history of the world, the history of Atlantis, the history of the building of the Great Pyramid, a history so different from all modern scientific theories? Then, the *Very Wise Archaeologists* and the *Very Learned Historians of the Twenty-First Century* would be forced to verify their beliefs, to begin their studies anew. What would happen, if it turned out that we are not alone in the Universe, and that the Great Pyramid was really built by entities from Orion, from the Other Earth, from Ashun? What would happen if we realized that the other dimension has a message for us and that this message needs to be listened to, admitting our blindness, our narrow-minded thinking, and complete lack of flexibility?

All of science would have to be changed. Authorities would stop being authorities. They would become mere run-of-the-mill mortals. What an upheaval would then impinge on their need to be important, their need to be exceptional, their need for certainty, that everything is as it was. Religion would have to be changed. In the Middle Ages, this would have been simple. I, the Priestess, and the other people in the group would have been burned at the stake and the problem would have been resolved. Today, this is somewhat more complicated, but fanatics from various religions would certainly begin to find ways for igniting some sort of pyre.

Nobody in our group, including myself, felt ready to play the role of a martyr, who, perhaps, might be honored several centuries later by our descendants. A normal, peaceful existence was decidedly closer to our desires. I also thought to myself, that since the *Universe* had started this whole game with Lucyna, Łucja, Iwona, and me, then let *It* worry about how to bring everything safely to a happy end, and how to excavate the Pharaoh.

Looking at our daily reality, I thought that the *Universe* might be right in saying that people do not know how to live. Around us there appear more and more stresses, more and more terrorism, more and more hatred, and more and more conflicts — and less and less understanding and love. People are increasingly more and more stressed, rushing to get a better job, to ensure themselves better living conditions, and to follow the illusion of happiness.

According to the dreams of the Priestess, after the opening of the Great Pyramid (that is after the Pharaoh is found), the White Brethren from Orion will come to the Earth and will begin to teach people a new way of life, they will teach the true meaning of love, based on the complete acceptance of other people and of their exceptional nature.

"What else can the White Brethren teach us?" I asked Ki in her dreams.

"They will teach us to think differently," she responded.

Indeed. If nobody in the world had evil thoughts, there would be no evil in the world. So simple and yet so difficult. Thoughts depend on the emotions which a person experiences. Emotions depend on a variety of situations, in which we find ourselves and upon which we often have little influence. We can only influence the manner in which we interpret these situations and thus control our emotions. Many people need special training for this. This requires an internal serenity, meditation, and relaxation. Few are able to do this, especially at times when the pursuit of riches, money, and survival is of greatest importance.

I started to understand better what "purification" means. Apparently, so much evil has come into the world that our world is no longer visible "from above." It is so polluted with bad energies that entire stretches of the Earth are enveloped by them, as if by a cloud, and the Lord God has decided to stop this pollution. Indeed, in his intent, the Earth was created as a **Paradise Planet**, a model to be followed by others. Our free will has led to such pollution that a cosmic broom, or vacuum cleaner, is needed to bring everything back to a better condition.

When I asked the *Universe* through Lucyna about this, It said, "You cannot be happy, Wanderer, if negative, bad thoughts are predominant in your head. Negative thoughts are bad energy, which is sent out into space and attracts more bad energy. It was not to be like that. The energy of love was meant to be predominant. Love cannot exist if there is animosity, hatred, anger, jealousy, and greed. Then, a dirty cloud is formed around the Earth and this cloud has to be cleaned."

I did not want to ask about anything more. I decided to observe everything that was happening around me and in the world during my wanderings. To see the scenario that life would write, to see what events would start to happen on Earth.

"But what of it, that I see this in this way?" I thought. "What of it that the *Universe* has shown to me another meaning of the tensions that are developing between people, between nations? What of it that terrorism is rampant, that the summer temperatures exceed record readings in England, France, and Germany, or that floods and earthquakes are occurring in different parts of the world? Indeed, I cannot tell people that this is an intentional action of the *Universe,* because even if the pope himself told them so, he would be considered a lunatic."

I believed that the *Universe* would come up with a way to make people understand that the world theater of events being played out around us is not a set of coincidences or whims of nature, but has its own direction. It is a logical activity, guided by Higher Powers, in order to draw the attention of people to the necessity for change, to the necessity of saving the Earth.

I also understood that there will be no **"end of the world,"** about which many religious groups have been trumpeting to the right and to the left for a long time, and which has been predicted so many times. It will rather be a "change of the world," a quality transformation. It may be very painful for many, but the world will not disappear, it will only change.

I also thought that a huge impediment for us was the fact that those in power in this world, the politicians and the people of Big Business, have so great a feeling of security. They have money, they have gold, and they only worry about the votes of the electors or about how to multiply the gold in their bank accounts. Money provides power, influence, importance; it imposes excessive pride... and may make it impossible or difficult to notice the deeper meaning to events. At this time, it does not enter their heads, that everybody, rich or poor, is subject to the eternal cycle of life and death. *The Universe* does not accept money at the deathbed, as payment for life, and gold suddenly ceases to be important. During my wanderings, I met a priest who told me an interesting thing.

"I have assisted many people in the last moments of their lives. Many of them talked to me just before leaving this world. Almost all looked at their life and reflected on it. Not even one of them said 'I regret I did not earn more money' or 'I regret that I did not have more hatred within me,' They all said 'I regret that I did not give more love, that I said **'I love'** too rarely, and that I could have helped so many people and I did not.'"

Many contemporary clergy, priests, and authorities of various religions say, "Let us pray to God, let us send him the energy of love, and the world will be saved." *The Universe* of Lucyna, of the Priestess Ki, says exactly the same, but It adds something very important — physical action. This action is the excavation of the tomb of the Pharaoh, the archaeological discovery of all times, something understandable even to an atheist, who does not even know what prayer is. This is something that places a substantial argument into the hands of a politician, that gives fame to an archaeologist, gold to a businessman, and to the world... Well, in order to see what it will give to the world, one must begin to dig. There is no other way. So little and yet so much.

Theoretically, if strange things start to happen in the world, people should pay attention to them. If this were so, the excavation of the key to the Great Pyramid, the excavation of the Pharaoh, should become an enterprise in which all the governments of the world would try to assist. Every person living on the planet Earth has a personal interest in this. Unfortunately, the difficulty lies in that so many people have a false sense of security. Floods, wars, fires, droughts and other natural disasters that visit the Earth are far away. For the majority, these are accidental and natural events. Apart from a few small groups, it does not enter anybody's mind to connect all of this into a whole.

"Perhaps this was how Atlantis perished," I thought.

I did not expect that I would meet people who think very much like myself so soon.

13

THE MEANING OF LIFE

I f there was a paradise on Earth, why did it not last forever? Why is it not here now? Why did people start having such diverse emotions, and both good and bad thoughts?

Similar questions arose in my mind after the *Lady Called Life* told me about the Council of the Gods and the purification of the Earth. I still did not know what kind of a Council she had in mind and what gods were there. I knew about only one God, our Roman Catholic one, whom we all called the Lord God. He had a beard and, in all of the pictures for children, he was old. Apparently, old age is associated with wisdom, because the Lord God was good and wise for me, ever since my childhood. And now the *Universe* begins to speak about some sort of Council, as if there were more gods than one. Initially, I did not want to go deeper into this topic, because all this seemed quite absurd to me. During the next dream of the Priestess, however, I put the question to the *Universe*.

"Please, tell me something more about God."

"He created the Earth," the Universe replied. "He created everything that exists on it. He created the spiritual entities. He is the Beginning and the End. His name is *Eternity*. His intention was that human beings were to be created in the divine image and likeness, that is, perfect, and that the planet Earth was to be a Paradise Planet; a planet which was to be a model for other beings inhabiting the Universe. This was God's intention until the moment when human beings found themselves on the Earth and, one might say, started adding bad ingredients to a good cake."

"Where did these bad ingredients come from?"

"God gave people **free will** and allowed them to decide their own fate. He gave them the choice between good and evil."

"Sometimes, it seems to me," I remarked, "that this 'free will' of ours is an illusion. We often do things, which we know are not good for us, but, despite everything, we do them."

"You decide about what you do. No one, truly no one has the right to violate this free will. People often wonder how God can allow such iniquities as wars, injustice, unimaginable cruelty, and the atrocities that some people inflict on others. This is **free will**, Wanderer; the free will of people which have led to such pollution of thought that the Paradise Planet is no longer a paradise. On the scale of good and evil, there is now more evil than good. God cannot allow the destruction of his work, and that is why there must be purification. In the Bible, this was described as the Apocalypse. The end of one thing so that there can be something else, better and more beautiful."

"Again, you talk about purification. For you, this is a never-ending issue," I commented.

"People must understand, they must become aware, that they are living in a special time. This is a time of change and how this change is accomplished will depend on them."

"And if we do not find the tomb?"

"Then the purification will be horrifying..."

"It seems that again you raise a frightening threat."

"I do not threaten," the *Universe* said after a moment of silence, "I want help, because I love all people. I would like all to be saved."

"Is this possible?"

"If all people were sending out the energy of love to me and to God, purification would be unnecessary. But look at what is happening around you. You are living in a contemporary Babylon and people have forgotten what is most important for them, why they came onto the Earth."

"You often speak about sending love into space. What does it mean to 'send love?'" I asked.

"This means to look at another person as at a brother or sister, a son or daughter, a father or mother. This means to use Free Will and reason in accordance with the intention, in which God, the Owner of the Earth, gave Free Will and reason to people. This means constantly maintaining the connection with your intuition, with your spiritual guide, and with the spiritual world. This is the true gold, for which one needs only to hold out one's hand in order to find it. One needs only to ask, for it to be given; one needs only to believe, for it is to be. The cosmos feels the energy emanating from the human aura. One needs only to direct a thought to the Creator, to God, and this 'sending' occurs. It is so simple."

"Will it ever happen that majority of people on Earth will begin to send the energy of love into space?"

"When balance is restored on Earth after the purification, and the Earth becomes the Paradise Planet, in accordance with the plan of its Owner, this will happen."

"Yes," I thought, "this energy of love keeps on returning, like an echo. What power this energy must possess, since it alone would be enough to save mankind. It is evident, however, there is too little of it in our imperfect world.

"What will happen after the awakening of the Pharaoh?" I asked.

"The White Brethren will come from Orion and they will help people to understand what it means to live. Those who will understand will survive. They will receive the mark of life. Those whose hearts will be closed will have to depart."

"Again, you raise a frightening threat."

"I give a warning. Tell the people, Wanderer, to start opening their eyes and seeing what is happening around them. So that they understand that I really exist and that I am life. God is not an abstract notion, to be used for raising fear in naughty children, but is true existence, true loving energy."

"And what about religion? There are so many diverse religions in the world, various ways of understanding God. Furthermore, there are so many people who do not believe that God exists at all."

"Here, in my dimension, it is not important what religion a person professes, whether he believes or does not believe, or what he believes in. I see your feelings. I see how much love is in your hearts, and how much hatred, anger, jealousy, and greed. Only how much good you gave away, how many people you helped will be taken into account. Actions, good actions toward another, that is my currency, my money. Only with this, can you pay me for life. What you sow, you will reap, Wanderer, and that is the sacred law of the Cosmos."

"I understand, but life is the highest value of mankind and everyone tries to live it the best way he or she knows."

"Remember, Wanderer, life is just a single moment, one lesson that you have to take on Earth. Before you have time to look around, the other world draws you in and what then? Look deep into yourself and look ahead. See life as a vision of constantly new transformations. As a link of what is with what was and with what will be. Look at it in the way that all people on Earth should see life. Then, before your eyes will arise another, wonderful, larger, much more interesting world, which is not visible today, since for the time being it is closed to you; a world which is an essential part of your existence here on Earth. This existence has to be lived with dignity, so that you do not have to hang your head in shame, when you come to view the film of your life."

I thanked the *Universe* for these words, whose meaning I still did not understand in full. I knew only that there will come a time, when man will be aware of the true meaning of his life on Earth, his past and future incarnations, aware of that "more interesting world" which is "temporarily hidden" to us, aware of his pursuit of perfection and of the lesson which he is learning.

14

THE MOST IMPORTANT ONE

Thrusting a spade into Egyptian sand is a simple and easy movement for everyone. However, in order to make it possible to do this, especially within the area of the Great Pyramid, one needs the benevolence of *Very Important Persons Who Decide Who May Dig and Where.* I do not know how many such persons there are in Egypt, but certainly one of them is the most important one. He is the director. Even if one has super-interesting, absolutely sensational information on the location of the Tomb of Cheops, it is difficult to go to Egypt, enter the office of the *Director of the Pyramids* and say: "I know." Every *Serious Director* will smile with compassion and send the brash visitor out to wander anew.

Assuming, therefore, that someone will turn up — who will believe the *Lady Called Life* and decide to invest appropriate funds in the expedition to Egypt — one must also find a way of communicating this information, so that the director general, the *Guardian of Giza, Director of the Supreme Council of Antiquities in Egypt,* would look at the project with a benevolent eye.

"The only access to the *Director of the Pyramids* exists only through another *Very Important Person Who Is Highly Respected in Egypt,*" the *Businessman* had asserted.

According to the *Businessman*, the only person in Poland who would be able to arrange something like this is the most famous archaeologist — the *Man Who Hunts for Exceptional Discoveries in Egypt* and the only one who could obtain a permit for digging close to the Great Pyramid — Professor Karol Mysliwiec.

"So let us go together to the professor and present to him the whole project," I said naively to the *Businessman*.

He laughed and quickly disabused me.

"You see, it goes like this. Professor Karol is a *Very Important and Famous Professor*. Every *Very Important and Famous Professor* is always very careful about his impeccable scientific reputation. Just imagine that you do go to him and tell him about this matter. What will you say?"

"I will tell him that I know where the Tomb of Cheops is located and that I would like the professor to help me."

"Obviously, the professor will ask you, 'How do you know this?' And then what will you say?"

"Then I will tell him the story of the *Lady Called Life*."

"Good, let us even assume that the professor will believe you for a while and that he will decide to go to the *Director of the Pyramids*, on the basis of the dreams of Priestess Ki, to ask for a permit for research in the indicated place. The whole world of archaeology, Polish and international, will turn their eyes on the professor. And imagine now that the team finds nothing in the place indicated by the Priestess. Do you think that any professor with a sound mind will go to Egypt and start digging only on the basis of somebody's dreams? This is not scientific. If he is not successful, he would become a laughing stock for the whole world of science and he would be finished as the *Most Famous Archaeologist in Poland*. He would become a *Scientist Who Was Once Famous* but no *Most Famous Archaeologist* would risk this."

"Surely so, but we know that failure is out of question."

"We may know, but the difficulty is in communicating this certainty to the professor. We have to find another way."

And then the *Businessman* proposed his crafty plan for convincing the **Pride of Polish Archaeology** to turn his attention to our project and treat it seriously. "It is a simple matter," said the *Businessman*. "First, we have to take care of the funds, then we will go to Egypt and call the professor from there, with the following message: 'We have the money for your trip to Egypt, and for a five-star hotel. Please gather a team of the most famous archaeologists, who would like to earn some money and dig up something interesting. We are waiting for your arrival next week."

"You see," the *Businessman* presented his arguments to persuade me, "Polish archaeology is barely able to keep the wolf from the door, so, when the matter is presented in the way I said, there will be no need to go into details on how we got the information. When the professor comes with his team to Egypt, we will need simply to show him the place and tell him, in outline, what we are looking for. Anyway, most archaeological finds are based on the intuition of archaeologists, that one should dig there and not somewhere else. All that the professor must do is to ask, the *Director of the Pyramids,* to issue a permit for the digging."

"How are you so certain that the professor will take care of this?" I expressed my doubts.

"The two gentlemen know each other well and they greatly respect each other. Besides, when a sponsor is found, we will be able to support our requests with appropriate 'arguments.' At this moment, the *Businessman* supported his arguments with an unmistakable gesture, comprising a rubbing motion of index finger and thumb.

"I understand," I replied. "I am sure that besides, discovering something that would bring fame to Egypt and its people this is an argument of immense influence on the imagination of every archaeologist. Not to mention that finding the tomb will multiply the numbers of television interviews, press conferences, films on issues related to Egypt and the Great Pyramid."

"Assuming that the tomb will be found… " *Businessman* brought me back to Earth.

"But we know that it will be found."

"But what if not?"

"Then the whole matter will grow cold, no one will learn anything, and the *Most Important Archaeologist in Poland* will have had just another failure, not an uncommon fate for every well-known archaeologist, before he finds something interesting."

This scenario was good, but had only one fault. In order to approach the professor and make it possible for him to approach the *Person Who Decides about Everything*, money was needed, and still there was no money in hand nor any prospects that it would suddenly appear in a large quantity. We needed an investor with the soul of Indiana Jones, who was not afraid of risk and who knew how to dream. Someone who would believe in his own dreams and, most of all, in the dreams of the Priestess.

Because nothing new was happening with regard to prospective sponsors on the part of the *Businessman*, I thought that I myself would look for sponsors. This thought stayed with me for a while, but then I drove it away. Surely, that was his role, that of the *Businessman*. He knows more about this. Surely, the *Universe* knew what It was doing, since It had placed him on my way.

I decided to leave guidance in this matter to the *Universe*. It knows that we will not move forward without gold, without money, without someone who has contacts and believes us. So let the *Universe* worry about placing an *Appropriate Person* on the way of the *Businessman*, on my way or on the way of somebody from our group. That *Person* will get us out of this enchanted circle.

15

THE LADY WHO DARES TO SPEAK

Traveling means being in various places of the world. I very much like to wander and my wanderings led me one day to Chicago. Polish Americans are slightly different from American Americans. The average Polish American usually has more money than the average Pole in Poland (that is why he stays in America), but he would like to have even more, because appetite grows with eating. He would be very happy to do something that will differentiate him from other Americans who, complaining about politics, try to figure out how to save more dollars for the next car, the next apartment, the next vacation, the next house... and so on and so forth.

One of the ways of becoming exceptional is to become aware of the existence of the possibilities of controlling one's own life in a way that suits one best. To many people, it seems that their lives are controlled by events and they do not suppose that they themselves create the events through the thoughts that are dominant in their heads and through the energy, which these thoughts generate. That is why one so often sees people walking around the world with sad and stressed expressions, who, like a ship on the waves, with no sails and no rudder, bounce from one disaster only to meet up with another. It appears to them that the whole world is plotting against them, while doom hangs over their heads. They are not aware that the only things that are hanging over them are the shapes of their own imagination. They look with envy upon people in whose lives everything turns out to be a success, who live in happiness and surround themselves with happiness. They are completely unaware that these people decide to choose better thoughts for themselves, to use their free will.

During my wanderings, I teach people self-control of the mind. I teach them how to direct their thoughts and how to control them, in order to lead them to the port called the "best destiny." Among those who come to listen to me, there are some that hear, but do not believe and do nothing. And then, obviously, nothing changes in their lives. Others try and then get discouraged, although the *Universe* whispers to them, talks to them every day... They do not hear this whispering. They do not see the events in their lives that are suggesting to them "Do this...or don't do that...." Finally, there are people who do not try, but simply do what they can, giving one hundred percent of themselves. They begin to cooperate with the universe in creating for themselves the best of the possible futures. They create a new life for themselves; they create the best destiny.

In this fashion, another coincidence brought the **Lady Who Dares to Speak** into the way of my wanderings. Her name was Barbara. She came up to me and asked, smiling, if I could help her become exceptional, admired, and listened to. Her strength was her voice, which spread out into many corners of Chicago, multiplied many times by the marvels of modern technology. Her voice spoke to people in their houses and in their cars, at a time when they turned knobs to tune in to the frequency of her waves. Up till then, she used to talk about strange things, about the secrets of the world, but Cheops and the whole project proved to be the strangest of the strange things that she had heard about till then. It was the biggest mystery, but it was something specific; something that could be seen and touched. One could only dream about a greatness and uniqueness so immense and different that one's imagination could not embrace it. The Pharaoh

Project was both a mission and a destiny for all those who decided to believe and to act.

I looked at her in amazement. I was surprised by her courage and passion. She was brought to me by the **Lady Called Fame**. Now it seems to me that, even before her birth, the *Universe* had entered fame into her destiny. It was an inseparable and unique link in creating more coincidences. If there was no *Lady Called Fame*, my wanderings to Chicago would have been impossible. But for her, the *Lady Who Dares to Speak* would never have heard about me.

One November afternoon in 2002, Slawa and Barbara first heard about Cheops from me. Every piece of information, in order to flourish, must find the appropriate soil. They both proved to be such soil.

"Can I talk about Cheops to all the people who want to listen to me?" immediately asked the *Lady Who Dares to Speak*.

"That is what the *Universe* wishes," I answered. "Talk, if you are not afraid."

"I am not afraid. I cannot be afraid. My profession is the courage to speak," she said.

And so, from the time of my visit, once a week on the Chicago radio waves, there rang out the voice of the *Lady Who Dares to Speak*. She talked about the mission, Cheops, the Earth and its purification, the *Universe*, about the *Lady Called Life,* about the participants in the mission, and about everything that we had learned from the *Universe* up to that time. She was so courageous, that people who listened and heard her voice were fascinated with the fact that the mission to save the Earth was so close and real.

Of course, there were some who listened, while tapping their forehead, and made suggestions about appropriate asylums. There were those who listened and became indignant because this was a Polish woman talking about digging up the Pharaoh and saving the world. What right did she have? So many prominent countries and scientific celebrities had been ignored. This could not be true. There were those who listened but did not hear, they ignored this information, because there are so many absurd ideas in the world.

Fantasies about digging up a Pharaoh will not help to buy a new car, cannot be easily turned into cash, and have no effect on stock ratings in the New York Stock Exchange, so what's the point of paying any attention to this? And there were *Those Who Listened and Heard*. These were the people whose hearts and souls were moved by the courage and passion of the speaker, strengthened by the power of the *Universe*. The *Universe*, seeing her commitment, started helping her with fame, with achieving a uniqueness she could not have dreamed of before. It started creating for her special coincidences and special tests.

I asked the Priestess for another waking dream. I wanted to know whether Chicago would help us with the most important problem. The question of gold. Are there not swarms of millionaires in America? Lucyna agreed without hesitation.

"Will the *Lady Who Dares to Speak* really be able to help us?" I asked the *Universe*. "All of this is so difficult, unusual, and far from routine."

"Yes," It answered, "she can do a lot. Her mission is to reach people, because many people listen to her."

"But will they understand her?"

"There will be followers and antagonists; they will attack her. But remember, that all the people who help me are provided with protection. Barbara also has this."

"What sort of protection? "I was surprised.

I was not aware that the *Universe* can ensure protection for us. "Surely It would not assign to us some 'hulk-like' bodyguards?" I thought. "Some tough guys who will follow us around and guard us. We don't need anything like that as yet?"

"What kind of protection?" I asked.

"The chosen ones, those with allocated tasks, cannot be harmed in any way," It answered. "Even if it seems to you that you have been abandoned, you will still have protection."

"What kind of protection?" I would not let go.

"A protection of energy. I, the *Universe*, have tremendous energy."

I breathed with relief and immediately recalled my programmed dream: the energy tunnel around me and around the *Girl to Whom Every Morning Smiles.*

"How will Barbara's broadcasts help us?" I asked, having in mind future sponsors.

"With her broadcasts," the *Universe* answered, "Barbara will sow the seeds, like a harvester. If the seeds fall on receptive soil, they will sprout. A human being may be saved because his or her heart opens up. When a seed falls on unreceptive soil, it will decay. The choice is with the person listening."

It sounded very nice and esoteric, but I was concerned with the practical aspects of these new coincidences. The concern was money. Without it, we could not move ahead.

"Help us," I pleaded, "help us find the gold needed to dig up Cheops. You are the *Universe.* You can do everything."

"Everything can be done only by the *Supreme,* the *Owner of the Earth,* God. I also am dependent on him."

"What is your concern? Is it not the same as ours?"

"Of course, I am concerned about your finding gold, but also that my message reaches all the corners of the world. So that people, irrespective of the color of their skin, hear about me. Barbara can help in this."

"Various people listen to her," I remarked. "Many are non-believers."

"For me, every human being is equally important. I have said this many times — I look at the heart. The Lord God, your earthly God, in creating human beings, gave you one law, one love, and therefore, I respect all, I mean all."

"What advice do you have for the *Lady Who Dares to Speak?*"

"Let her approach every single person with respect and serenity," the *Universe* replied, "even those who will abuse her after the broadcasts. There will be many who would like to walk over her, saying that she is talking nonsense, that she is sowing confusion in people's minds. Let them think whatever they want. She is to carry out her task. This is my request to her."

This was how the *Lady Who Dares to Speak*, Barbara, created her own dream under the name of the *Orion*–Pharaoh *Mission*. This was a dream about everything I had learned so far through the dreams of the Priestess, about everything the *Universe* had communicated to us through her. She understood that she had been given a chance to be exceptional. She also received a task, and it was not an easy task: to sow the seeds...

I was delighted with her courage and I continuously thought about finding a strategic sponsor. I knew that there are many such in the world, that they are waiting for such an opportunity as this, but have no knowledge of our existence. I understood that even if they found out about it, they would not believe right away. Barbara provided a chance for opening more gates, more hearts, and more minds: a chance for opening the world.

When I met Barbara, it was November of 2002. I set a date for the departure to Egypt as March of 2003 and I decided to wait and see what the *Universe* would do through Barbara, and whom It will send us, whose heart It will help to open...

16

OH, THESE COINCIDENCES

After the last dream of the Priestess, I had troublesome thoughts about the Pyramid and the tomb for a long time. How long are we still to wait for what is to happen? We already know so much. It is indeed so logical, all that which the Priestess says so simply, interprets and explains the unexplained. Why do people listen to this with such indifference?

On the other hand, I wondered what I was to learn from the *Universe* on my way to the Pyramid. I knew that every person I met was a signal, a piece of information, which I must know how to interpret. I started to observe more attentively my surroundings and the people with whom I talked, and I started noticing some interesting things. Some words, sentences, heard from persons encountered even accidentally, began to take on other, more important meanings. This was something of a sort of a "new dictionary of the *Universe*."

One day, during my wanderings to Canada, I met in Ottawa a **Very Wise Man**. His name was Andrzej and he was a scientist, researching clean energies. He seemed to understand the *Universe* and Its ways of communicating with people. We had known each other for a long time and we often talked about inexplicable phenomena. The *Very Wise Man* tried to explain these phenomena scientifically, at the level of quantum physics and scalar energy, and I most frequently listened, fascinated by his wisdom. The dreams of the Priestess belonged to the category of inexplicable phenomena, so I told him about her experiences, I told him about the Pharaoh and about the Pyramid...

"Do you really believe the Priestess?" he asked.

"Yes," I answered. "That, which the *Universe* said would happen, is really happening in my life. I meet people whom I am meant to meet, I receive signals."

"These are all subjective experiences," the *Very Wise Man* nodded his head. "I am a scientist, so I am interested in some objective proof that what she says is true. Something tangible."

"Finding the tomb would be an objective and very specific proof."

"In other words, you do not have the proof, so why do you believe?" he asked again.

"Because I need faith in order to act. I do not see another way."

"There is another way. You can simply stop believing."

"I cannot stop believing. If I did, I would not be able to convince anyone of what I am saying." I was indignant.

"If you believe that, you are no longer free. Besides, the universe is good and bad... How do you know which one of them is talking to you? How do you know whether it is not the bad part that is trying to manipulate you, to disorient you?"

"I know that the one who talks to me is the good universe," I answered calmly.

"Where does this certainty come from?" I felt some irony in his voice.

"You are a *Very Wise Man*," I told him. "Tell me what is wrong with exceptionally important archaeological discoveries? What is wrong with a willingness to help people and to warn them about the possibility of an approaching disaster? What is wrong with the suggestion that people should begin to think in a better way, to send love out into the space?"

"There is nothing wrong with what you are saying, but there is always the possibility that this is not true, until you verify it. And the best method of verification is to stop believing."

I fell silent for a moment. I did not know what to answer. I was surprised that he, such an expert on the phenomena of the universe, was saying such strange things. He noticed my hesitation and explained.

"This does not mean that you should stop your activities, but that you should be objective. A perfect prescription for life is not to believe in anything, until it is physically confirmed, and to have your mind open to everything."

"Explain this in more detail," I asked.

"As regards the dreams of the *Lady Called Life*, my advice is: do not give your faith to anything that the *Universe* communicates, until you confirm some piece of information on the physical level. At the same time, remain open to the possibility that all this is true."

"That's what I do. I regard myself as an observer of events," I was piqued, "but I want to believe. Disbelief would take away my passion, my strength to succeed. Besides, the *Universe* needs my faith and trust, so that It can help me."

"But blind faith will make you dependent on your belief system. You will cease to be free. One moment more, and you will become a fanatic and completely lose the objective view of the matter. Everyone who thinks in a different way to you will become your enemy. Your friends will only be those who will flatter you. This is a very dangerous place."

I silently admitted that he was right. Indeed, it was better to be a Wanderer –Observer than a Wanderer –Fanatic. I will be more credible when I allow the *Universe* to prove that whatever It is saying to me has Its reflection on the level of the physical world. How It will do this — well, that will be for the *Universe* to worry about. In order to excavate the tomb, it would be necessary to link up information from the Priestess with some verifiable reference to this information on Earth. In any form, even the simplest, as long as the one and the other shared the same point of reference. I do not have to dig up the Pharaoh immediately, in order to convince myself that her dreams are true. It would suffice to ask her to dream something else, something easier to verify. I was angry with myself that I did not come up with this idea earlier.

At the next meeting with the *Lady Called Life,* I asked for another conversation with the *Universe.*

"No problem," she answered. "It is always glad to talk to you."

Ki fell into her waking dream and asked me to go ahead.

"Can you prove to me physically, that you are real?" I asked the *Universe.*

"Do you want me to break your leg?" It answered. "You know that I exist."

"No, I do not crave for such proofs," I laughed. "I know that you are here, that you exist, because I am talking to you, because various things are happening in my life. However, in order to convince some businessman with a hefty wallet, you have to think of something else. Something less drastic," I added, just in case.

I thought that it is good that the *Universe* has a sense of humor. Besides, breaking my leg would not convince anybody. Anyone can have an accident and it is nothing special.

"I will think up something, for sure," the *Universe* said. "Give me a little time."

"You said yourself that we do not have much time."

"Be patient... I know that you people need something tangible all the time. It is not enough to show you something once. I have to prove that I exist, time and time again. Even you sometimes have doubts."

"Not any more. I know that your veracity is admirable, that you deliver what you promise. Sometimes, however, you cannot put it into a timeframe. Please try to do this as quickly as possible."

"Well, yes," the *Universe* confirmed, "I do have problems with this time of yours. That is how I was created. But in this case, you will not have to wait long. Time is of the essence to me also. One thing I can tell you. You are linked by my energy with the *Girl to Whom Every Morning Smiles.* You will go to the Pharaoh together."

I parted with the Priestess and decided to wait for what the *Universe* comes up with in the way of tangible proofs. In the meantime, the year 2002 passed and 2003 started.

To my surprise, the *Girl to Whom Every Morning Smiles* started to smile to me again. Her smile was still a bit sad, but it was there. "How did It know about this?" I thought about the *Universe* and Its prediction. This was for me one more proof of the wisdom flowing from the dreams of the Priestess. It was the answer to the doubts of the *Very Wise Man* and a reinforcement of my faith, although still at the subjective level.

To enlighten my wanderings, the *Girl to Whom Every Morning Smiles* gave me a book about Orion. The book had the title *The Orion Prophecy for the Year 2012* and was authored by Patrick Geryl. I read it right away and was surprised that the author had such a black view of the future of the Earth. According to the writings and calendar of the Mayas, the writings of the ancient Egyptian and other documents, which the author had deciphered, on the **twenty-first of December, 2012** the Earth's magnetic polarization will be reversed and a global disaster, similar to that which destroyed Atlantis, will occur. "Well," I thought, "we have some time till 2012." Immediately after this, another thought came to my mind, "Could the tomb of Cheops have something in common with this?" Indeed, the *Universe* affirms that the tomb will help to prevent a catastrophe on Earth.

I did not know who the author was, but from the text it appeared that he was a Belgian. In his book, he also wrote about the Great Labyrinth, which is in Egypt, near Lake Moeris. The Labyrinth is supposed to hold information on the past and future of the Earth, along with suggestions on how to save it.

I thought that it could be worthwhile to contact him and tell him about Cheops, the tomb, and our project. Unfortunately, my search turned out to be fruitless. Discouraged, I left this matter for some undefined time in the future.

And here the next coincidence happened. I received an invitation to Brussels for a special wandering. Some people were waiting for me there, who wanted to learn better control over their thoughts. The trip was sudden, unplanned, and unexpected. I was happy, because just then I had some free time. The trip to Egypt in the previously designated time proved to be impossible. There was no money and no permit, and preparations were underway for the war in Iraq. It was March of 2003.

Before leaving, I asked the *Universe* through the Priestess about the author of the book.

"You wanted proof from me, you will have it," It said. "You are to meet him. He will help you."

"But I don't know where to find him."

"You have to meet him," the *Universe* repeated. "When they throw you out the door, go in through the window."

And with these words, he put an end to the topic.

I was chagrinned because I did not know what It had in mind with this "throwing out." I thought that the *Universe* wanted me to become aggressive, which was definitely not in my style.

After my arrival in Brussels, it turned out that there were thirteen persons at the meeting with me... When I told them about the Cheops Project and about Patrick Geryl and his book, one of participants said with a smile, "My husband is Flemish and a good friend of the author of the book you are talking about."

This was how, with another coincidence, the Universe put Patrick Geryl on my way. I called him the ***Man Who Has a Black View of the Fate of the World.***

17

THE ORION PROPHECY AND THE GOLDEN CHAMBERS

Patrick, the author of *The Orion Prophecy for the Year 2012*, really did have a black view on the fate of this world. Together with his friend Gino, an astro-archaeologist by profession, they calculated that on twenty-third of December, 2012, the stars will have the same alignment as occurred at the time when Atlantis disappeared. They considered its disappearance as a fact. According to them, this was the message in the writings of the Mayas and the ancient Egyptians.

"There will be a global catastrophe, a change in the poles of the Earth," Patrick said a few minutes after we met in Brussels. "We must get ready for this."

"I know," I answered, "I read your book and I know your theory. You state that the North Pole will become the South Pole, and that the South Pole will become the North Pole due to a translocation of the Earth's crust. Do you think that this can be avoided?"

"It is unavoidable." Patrick was extremely self-confident in this respect. "The ancient Mayans and Egyptians knew much more about the world than we think."

"In your book, you write about the Great Labyrinth. If you claim that we all are doomed to die, why are you searching for the Labyrinth?" I asked him.

Patrick's eyes sparkled. It was clear that I had raised a subject very close to his heart.

"Within the Labyrinth, there are places which must be reached," he said with passion in his voice. "There are special chambers and on their walls, there is supposed to be inscribed everything that must be done to prepare for the global cataclysm. Very important information about our times is there also."

I surmised that this was a subject-without-end for Patrick. Just in case, I broke into his talk and told him about Cheops, about the *Lady Called Life,* and about what I learned from the *Universe...* He listened carefully, but I felt that he was not convinced about what I was saying. After a while, he returned to the subject of the **Great Labyrinth** in Egypt. He had been searching for it for a long time, reading everything that he could find on it, and he was convinced that finding the Labyrinth might save people, at least those who will prepare themselves properly for the cataclysm.

"I will tell you briefly about the Labyrinth," he continued his tale. "It is the largest building ever constructed by man, composed of more than 3000 chambers. According to Herodotus, the construction took 365 years, from 4608 to 4243 BC. The diameter from east to west is 48,000 Egyptian ells or 25.152 kilometers! It includes the so-called '**Golden Circle**,' the legendary chamber referred to in the *Book of the Dead.* It is built of granite and covered with gold, applied with a technique provided by a lost civilization, much older than the Egyptian."

"That's incredible!" I was astounded. "Something so huge and nobody knows where it is?"

"Wait, that's not all." Patrick was becoming even more excited. "On the walls is inscribed the astronomical knowledge of the Egyptians. From the hieroglyphs can be read all of their astronomical discoveries. On a gigantic zodiac are displayed the constellations. Many walls are movable. Ancient texts refer to people who died there, not being able to find an exit. They also refer to secret chambers inside the Labyrinth, filled with works of art and documents of a civilization, which flourished on Earth thousands of years ago. There are chambers with documents about the history of Egypt and about the astronomical knowledge of those times."

"How could Herodotus know all this?" I asked.

"He claims that he was there personally and saw most of these things with his own eyes. Furthermore, Herodotus writes that on thirty-six huge tablets, the hieroglyphs present the method for calculating the last reversal of the poles of the Earth. This is knowledge which people today should have as soon as possible, because we are in for exactly the same thing."

"What do archaeologists say on this subject? What does science say?"

"The **Great Labyrinth** is considered by the majority of modern archaeologists as a building that once actually existed, which was destroyed by time or which 'collapsed' under the weight of the desert, and finding it now is very difficult or practically impossible. It is strange, but at the present time nobody is looking for it."

Patrick talked at length about the Labyrinth, while I was thinking about our "accidental" meeting in Brussels. Could the *Man Who Has a Black View of the Fate of the World* help in the Cheops issue? *The Universe* could not give a clearer sign than this "coincidence."

"Are you not intrigued about our meeting in such a strange way?" I asked when he finished his story.

"I am intrigued and that is why I came, in order to see you," he answered. "In general, I am careful, because ever since I wrote the book, various lunatics and prophets of doom apply to see me, so I only meet with selected people."

"I feel honored that you have come to meet me," I remarked somewhat sarcastically, but sincerely.

"When I was writing *The Orion Prophecy*," he said, "various inexplicable events and coincidences were happening to me, coincidences which helped me gain the needed knowledge and information for the book, almost as if an invisible hand was guiding me. You are such a 'coincidence,' That was why I came, although, what you are saying sounds very strange to me."

I knew that the "invisible hand" was the *Universe*, which had decided that at this moment in time and space, the Wanderer was to meet on his way the *Man Who Has a Black View of the Fate of the World*, and that from this time on, they were to go together in the same direction, along the same road.

"It seems that someone up there," I looked up at the sky, "has decided that we are to become acquainted and should start to help one another."

"Okay, that's settled," he agreed without hesitation, speaking in his slightly rough English. "What do you suggest?"

"I suggest a talk with the *Universe,* through the Priestess. On your behalf, I can ask It any questions that you want to pose."

"There are many questions, but three are most important. Does the Labyrinth really exist? How can we dig down to it? Is there important information for us there, which could save people?"

When I came back to Wroclaw, I asked Lucyna for another dream. This one was to be an important dream, this time, about something other than the tomb.

"Ask the *Universe,*" I asked her, "if It can help Patrick?"

"We are helping the *Universe* in fulfilling the task which It received from the Supreme Energy, from God," she answered, "I do not have to ask. It is always available to us. It is enough to ask. When do you want me to fall asleep?"

"Go to sleep now," I requested.

We were in the apartment of the *Girl to Whom Every Morning Smiles*. The sun was shining through the window and smiling as beautifully, as it smiled to all the people in the world. I looked at its golden light, at the Priestess, and wondered if all of this really was to disappear in a few years time. Will we get through with our information to anybody important, who would want to listen to us? What if Patrick was right? Will all these years of morning smiles, with which the *Universe* has treated me and so many people living on the Earth, be in vain? Be blown away by the wind? I did not want to believe that we would all cease to exist.

"Is Patrick right?" I asked the *Universe* when the Priestess started dreaming her waking dream, "In December of 2012, will there really be a reversal of the poles of the Earth and a catastrophe like that in the time of Atlantis? Is this true?"

"Not necessarily," the *Universe* replied. "I do not want to destroy the Earth, as it is too precious. The Earth is linked in one belt of the Solar System with other planets. A disruption of this system could cause a catastrophe in the Cosmos. Other civilizations must move freely in the universe. If the Earth dropped out of the Solar System, a cosmic hole would arise, impossible for other civilizations to jump across. Therefore, as you already know, if people remain obdurate and will not hear what I am saying, if they do not open their hearts to my call, then I would prefer to remove all of them from the Earth. The Earth itself must remain."

"But Patrick thinks — " I started to say.

"I will interrupt you," the *Universe* broke in. "Once more I repeat that what Patrick says is not completely true. Indeed, at this time, with so many negative energies flowing from the Earth, people do not have an influence on what may happen. Patrick is right in this. If indeed something significant does not happen, my intervention or my energy will begin to affect the Earth more strongly and I will make use of the forces of nature. What I can do is to purify the Earth radically. Whether this will occur in the year 2012 is a matter for discussion."

"What will happen to us then?"

"Do not be so scared," the *Universe* reassured me. "This is why I have chosen you and other people, so that you do remain on Earth. All those who help me receive the 'mark of life' from me. I have told this to the *Girl to Whom Every Morning Smiles* in a dream, a normal dream. She knows this."

I felt a pleasant warmth in my heart.

The Universe had called Iwona the *Girl to Whom Every Morning Smiles*, the name that I had given her. I thought that perhaps It was starting to learn the techniques of human communication, which say, "If you want the person with whom you are talking to feel good in your presence, use the same expressions that he/she is using."

"Does this mean that there will be no polar reversal?" I asked again.

"If Pharaoh sees the sun, there will be no polar reversal," the *Universe* repeated.

"And if not?"

"Then the Earth will not have protection against what will happen. People will perish, but the planet will remain."

"What protection?"

"You will learn later..."

"So why did you arrange our meeting with Patrick? What help can he provide?"

"But it was you who asked me for this."

"I asked you for this?" I called out, astounded. "A month ago, I did not even know that he existed."

"You asked me to give you a specific proof that I, the *Universe*, really exist," It answered, "that what I say through the Priestess is true."

"So Patrick is to be this proof?" I was surprised. "For everybody, this is just an ordinary coincidence, in no way a tangible proof."

"Your meeting is not a proof," the *Universe* agreed with me, "but the Labyrinth is."

"Patrick is sure that the Labyrinth really exists, but he does not know how to find it." I commented.

"The Labyrinth exists but now I have to expand the subject, so that you would understand the heart of the matter. I wanted to explain to you why the Labyrinth was built. Well, the existence of Atlantis is a fact and, when human beings were relocating from Atlantis to the rest of the Earth, they also brought with them their skills, beliefs, and traditions. There was also a Labyrinth on Atlantis and when the people evacuated to Egypt, they decided to build something similar there."

"The Greek traveler, Herodotus, wrote that there are 3,000 rooms there."

"Are there 3,000?" the *Universe* pondered. "I have some doubts about that. Perhaps with the corridors? However, my calculations do not support this number. Nevertheless, I can tell you that the labyrinth is connected with the pyramids in Giza, as if earthworms had made tunnels in the Earth. One can get to the Pyramid and to the Sphinx itself by way of the Labyrinth. This whole underground network has connections with the pyramids, mainly with the Pyramid of Cheops."

I was surprised that the *Universe* hesitated in giving the exact number of rooms. I still thought that It knows everything, but it appears that It has difficulties with counting rooms. I dropped this thought and I continued asking.

"From what you said, I understand that the Labyrinth covers quite an area? Where is it?"

"The Labyrinth starts at the city once called the **City of Crocodiles**," the *Universe* spoke with the voice of Lucyna, "and includes a lake called Lake Moeris. Farther on, circling around the lake, it extends toward the Pyramids. Here is where the Labyrinth is located. It has several quite simple entrances. One is by the third Pyramid built in Giza. The three Pyramids are connected with one another. The third Pyramid is connected with the Labyrinth. That is why it is not difficult to enter the Labyrinth. It is a more difficult matter to walk around in it. Whoever enters it without knowing it will simply perish."

"What was its purpose and when was the Labyrinth built?" I asked.

"The construction of the Labyrinth started even before the Sphinx was built. This construction commenced about 500 years before the Sphinx."

"For what purpose?" I repeated my question.

"The objective was to transfer everything from Atlantis to another place on the Earth. The preservation of the same history, as it was in Atlantis. As you know, they all had to leave this island, but the people who lived there could not reconcile themselves to losing everything.

They wanted to reconstruct the same island and the same history that they had had there."

I felt as if the *Universe* was not telling me everything. There must have been some other objective than history... For the time being, I put aside this subject, so as not to create the impression that I did not believe the *Universe*. I thought that I could ask about this on some other occasion.

"Of what use to us is this Labyrinth?" I continued asking.

"At last, you have asked the question for which I was waiting," the *Universe* was pleased. "You asked for proof of my existence and for physical confirmation of my words. A proof more easily found than the tomb of Cheops. There is such proof in the Labyrinth. Within it is the 'Golden Circle,' a series of rooms filled with gold up to their ceilings."

I was speechless with emotion. This is what Patrick spoke about during our meeting, what he wrote about in his book. I did not think that the *Universe* would refer to this subject...

"This is that earthly, tangible proof that you asked for," the *Universe* continued. "It is true that **gold** means nothing when compared with history. You cannot feed people with gold, but in your times, it is a huge magnet. I will tell you and Patrick how to get into these chambers and this will make it easier for you to find sponsors, because those who have money want to have more of it."

"Yes, you are right. Only how do we find these Golden Chambers?"

"If you want to know the entrance to the Labyrinth and the shortest way to the Golden Chambers, I will show them to you. There are articles made of gold, there are coins used in Atlantis and many other valuable items. One percent of what you find there is enough to dig up fourteen pharaohs."

"So where is this entrance?"

"It is between the third pyramid in Giza and Lake Moeris."

I thought that these bearings were not very precise. True, I have not been in Egypt yet, but Patrick was there and surely he would better understand what this was about and where to search.

"Can you give us more precise bearings to the Golden Chambers?" I asked. "What would be the best way to get there?"

"I will try to do this, Wanderer. When you are beside the Pyramids in Giza, go to the last Pyramid. You need to stand on the side of the sun at noon. Stand in the middle of the Pyramid. When you do this, wait for exactly noon. The angle of the sun's rays will indicate to you precisely the place where one should dig."

"I do not understand. What do you mean by the angle of the sun's rays? What angle? How can the angle indicate a place?"

"You will understand this at the appropriate time, but now I will make your life easier," the *Universe* continued talking in the voice of Priestess. "Divide the distance between Lake Moeris and the last Pyramid by two and there will be the entrance to which I am referring. That is where you should dig but I emphasize that it is not shallow. You need to dig down to several stories below the surface, since it is as deep as the height of the Sphinx. Remember this. Halve the distance between the last Pyramid and Lake Moeris and there, you will enter the Golden Chamber. The access to it and the excavation is much easier than the access to the tomb. When you find the gold, the tomb of Cheops will be an easy enterprise."

This news was sensational. To be sure, I had a question rattling round my mind about which point on Lake Moeris I was to draw the line to: the middle of the lake or the shore, but I decided that I would always have time to ask this question. Besides, I thought that this lack of precision was perhaps a tactical move on the part of the *Universe*. That which we are seeking should be found by those whom It had selected, who will be seeking not for the gold, but to save people. Not for fame, but to help Mother Earth.

Lucyna waited for more questions. I recalled that Patrick wrote in his book about important information that is said to be hidden in the Labyrinth, in the Golden Chambers. Herodotus also mentioned this in his writings.

"Will the knowledge located in the Labyrinth," I continued asking, "help to save mankind from the catastrophe?"

"Not only the knowledge or the excavation of the Labyrinth may save people," the *Universe* replied. "Opening a channel of communication between Orion and the Earth can save the Earth and the people, that is, opening up the Pyramid. Not without a reason was all this built and located in one place, Egypt and the area of today's Giza. The one is closely related to the other and when you start opening the channel connecting the Earth and Orion, all the other secrets will start to be revealed."

"I understand, but Patrick claims that in the Labyrinth can be found thirty-six hieroglyphs, inscribed on a wide wall, and that there is described the method by which the civilization of that time calculated the date of the previous cataclysm."

"The previous civilizations, Wanderer, cooperated with me very rigorously and conscientiously. Throughout all these centuries, I helped in the recording of this knowledge, making use of human hands for this purpose."

"Do you know where this is? Where these inscriptions are?"

"Everything that is significant and needed to provide proof of my existence is located in the submerged Pyramid in Lake Moeris. This lake is not a natural lake. It is an artificially constructed lake, with water brought in from the Nile. When the time comes, you will reach there also."

"How many pyramids are there around Lake Moeris?"

"Two. Only two and both are submerged. There was a third but it was destroyed by time. It was the least significant."

I remembered that, in the course of our conversation, Patrick spoke only about one pyramid beside the lake.

"Patrick has the impression that there is only one pyramid there, made of mud bricks, in the place called Hawara. Is this the one that was destroyed?" I asked the *Universe*.

"This is the one that no longer exists. The submerged ones are of stone. They are in the middle of the lake. I will continue to stick stubbornly to this information." the *Universe* became very firm at this moment.

"How is the knowledge, that is in the Labyrinth, related to the knowledge in the Tomb of Cheops?" I posed the next question.

"I had to create several ways that would lead to the same point. When the Great Labyrinth was built, and then the Sphinx, it was said, 'After a certain time, we will build the message,' The Great Pyramid was to be this message."

"Is excavating the Labyrinth or part of it as important as excavating the mummy of Cheops?"

"Less so. It is important to history, since excavation of even a part of the Labyrinth will give scientists something, at which they now laugh, believing that there was no Atlantis and many other things. In this way, the eyes of the scientists will be opened and they will have proof that they were wrong, and that human civilization goes back many, many thousands of years. That is why digging in the place I told you is important. You have to open the eyes of these 'blockheads.'"

The *Lady Called Life* looked tired, so I thanked the *Universe* and I asked her to wake up. Lucyna breathed deeply, looked at us, and smiled...

"What did I dream about? Will my dream be of any use to you?" she asked.

She dreamt so many things, she said so many things, that both I and the *Girl to Whom Every Morning Smiles* were stunned. A new way, a new perspective was opening up before us. At this moment, I did not know yet whether we must first strive to excavate the tomb or to find the Labyrinth. It seemed to me that the Labyrinth would delay the matter of the tomb, but it also appeared that the *Universe* was guiding us in that direction. Apparently, It had Its reasons... and these reasons became clear much later.

I was full of admiration for the *Universe* for Its "constructive abilities." Some exceptional energies were needed to create so many coincidences in such a short time. It was a truly intricate masterpiece, that allowed me to go to Belgium and draw my attention to the Labyrinth in Giza.

I placed all these "coincidences" in a chronological series of events. March of the year 2003 was the introduction or prelude to this symphony.

First the *Girl to Whom Every Morning Smiles* had to come up with the idea of going into a bookshop and buy me the book *The Orion Prophecy for the Year 2012*, just one of thousands of other books.

Then, I had to read this book, although the title initially did not interest me at all. After reading several sentences, I could not put the book aside. I did not know then why this was so.

Then, there had to appear in my head the thought of meeting the author of the book, Patrick. In March, in my free time, I had to receive the invitation to Brussels, to go there for an unexpected wandering. I accepted this invitation only because I had nothing else to do at that time.

Finally, and this was the most interesting "coincidence," the *Appropriate Person* had to come to my lecture, the one whose husband personally knew the author, the *Man Who Has a Black View of the Fate of the World*. Out of so many millions of inhabitants of Belgium, among the thirteen listeners of my lecture, there was one appropriate one.

That Patrick decided to come from Antwerp, where he lives, to Brussels in order to meet me, was not, I believe, due to a coincidence, but to Our Common Legend, the way, onto which we had stepped out separately, he and I, in order that our destinies would one day meet.

So that we could walk together toward Egypt.

18

THE SPHINX AND PROTECTION FOR THE EARTH

During my wanderings, I spoke more and more loudly about the *Project for Saving the Earth*, which was, of course, the ultimate goal of the *Pharaoh Project*. I was pleased that the project was developing so dynamically in Chicago. *The Lady Who Dares to Speak*, Barbara from Chicago, was creating an atmosphere of mysterious exceptionality around this subject, reaching the hearts of many Poles living in those parts. They listened to her words and were gratified with the fact that the impulse to save the world was originating from Poland. More and more often, people not only opened up their hearts and minds, but also supported the mission financially. These were not yet large sums, but financing of the first research in Egypt was now possible.

Meanwhile, Barbara more and more often asked the *Universe* to disclose various secrets, and It patiently answered her questions. People heard about issues, which had been taboo for ages, and in this way, the circle of "the fans of Cheops" grew. I thought that there was one more secret, which for so many centuries has kept many scholars and archaeologists awake at night. I decided to ask the *Universe* to tell us about the Sphinx.

Researchers, archaeologists, and scientists have been deliberating for centuries about the purpose of this *Guardian of the Great Pyramid*, with the body of a lion and the head of a human being. What does it symbolize? Why was it built? Who built it? Why with this particular form? There is no certainty about when it was built. The Priestess Ki often dreamt about it, always referring to it with great respect. Moreover, it was one of reference points to locating the tomb of Cheops. The Sphinx looked "in the direction of the tomb of the Pharaoh" and, when she dreamt about the construction of the Pyramid, the Sphinx was already there. I wondered if Ki could tell me more. When she dreamt about her times, she spoke only about what she saw as Ki. However, when we talked to the *Universe* through her, she could move through time and space; she became energy that linked up everything that had been and is. I suspected that the *Universe* also knew what will be, but did not always want to talk about this. To questions about the future, It answered, "I am not a fortune-teller, don't make one of me." It had Its own plans, Its own way of guiding us, so that we would reach what is most important: the tomb. As if there were no shortcuts.

"Do you think that we could ask the *Universe* about the Sphinx?" I once asked the *Lady Called Life*. "Few people in the world know anything about it. Someone must have built it sometime; it had to have some meaning for someone. It did not arise out of nothing. Some civilization created this body in stone, because this was important to it. Perhaps the *Universe* will tell us about the Sphinx?"

"I don't know if It will want to share this secret with us," Lucyna hesitated.

"If It does not want to, It will not tell us. What do we risk?"

"Actually nothing," She said. "I will go to sleep, and you shall ask."

I liked these "direct" talks with the *Universe*, her waking dreams. During her "normal" dreams (if one can call them "normal"), when the *Universe* talked to us through the Priestess Ki, it was more difficult. Ki spoke only about what she saw or what she heard from the Priest

Juno, in the times when she lived as his helper. Then she spoke slowly, in a manner quite different from her everyday way of speaking. During the direct talks with the *Universe*, she could move freely in time to any epoch, as if she herself were the *Universe*. She talked more slowly than normally, because she had to repeat what she heard in her thoughts from It. Her waking dreams did not have that aura of exceptionality or mysteriousness, but they were more comfortable. The entire procedure for putting her to sleep and waking her up could be skipped. Furthermore, after the waking dreams, she was not as tired end exhausted, as in the case of the guided dreams.

"Your third eye must open," Ki explained. "Then you too will be able to communicate telepathically. You will be able to focus, to open the proper channel and talk to somebody in Chicago, Australia, or even in another galaxy. Those from other dimensions, from other planets, used to communicate with people in this way. People regarded them as gods, called them gods, because they did not understand their exceptionality, their clothes, or their ability to move in space. For them, they *were* gods, and it has been so ever since."

When she made her special contact, I greeted the *Universe* and asked if It could tell us something about the Guardian of the Pyramid.

"Of course," It said, "but remember, people will not believe you, anyway, because this will not correspond with their beliefs."

"Nevertheless, tell us about the Sphinx," I asked. "Who will believe, will believe. Perhaps there will be some who will listen and start thinking. What is the story of the Sphinx? Who built it? For what purpose?"

"The entities from the Other Earth built it," the *Universe* said. "It is the Guardian of the Pyramid. Its tradition has been in existence since the time when human beings were transported to the Earth. On the other planet, the one that I call the Other Earth, the Sphinx was a favorite, a deity. When the entities from the Other Earth came here, they took it where they settled. As their main settlement was in Atlantis, it was placed there, and when they had to leave there, they took it to Egypt."

The *Lady Called Life* stopped for a while, and then, after a short pause, continued her dream.

"The wisest minds of Atlantis settled in Egypt and, already during the time of Atlantis, the history of the Earth was recorded. It was already known then that the Great Pyramid will be built, the key... the code, the gate to the universe, to the Other Earth. This had been programmed. The Sphinx is the Guardian of this Gate."

I thought that since the Sphinx had been built by entities from the Other Earth, hence by beings arriving from another planet, such contacts had been routine at some time in the past and then, for some reason, were discontinued.

"Please tell me when the Sphinx was built."

"The history of the Sphinx," the *Universe* replied, "is recorded on stone tablets located in various places. They are in the tomb of Cheops, in the Pyramid, and elsewhere. The Pyramid of Cheops and the Sphinx were built one thousand years apart."

What I have learned about the Sphinx came as a surprise. According to the *Universe*, the Sphinx was built a thousand years before the Great Pyramid, and so it is much older than estimated by official, orthodox science.

"When you behold the old Sphinx, what does it look like?" I asked the *Universe*. "Is it weathered or smooth? What does its head look like, and its body?"

"What time are you talking about?" the *Universe* asked.

"The time when the Pyramid of Cheops was built."

"It is beautiful, shining, and smooth as a mirror. It has the head of a lion."

Again, I thought that Priestess had gotten things mixed up in her head. The Sphinx does not have the head of a lion, but that of a human being. Anyone who has seen a photograph of the Sphinx or has been in Egypt knows that only the body is that of a lion.

"What are you saying?" I protested. "Look again. The Sphinx does not have the head of the lion. It has as human face."

Priestess was silent for a moment. Then she started speaking slowly and very distinctly.

"Wanderer, you asked me about the time of the construction of the Pyramid. When the Pyramid of Cheops was being built, the Sphinx had a lion's head. It was everybody's favorite. Only when the Pharaoh Chefren started to build his Pyramid, he also wanted to leave something else. Chefren had a specific sense of humor and he ordered his stonemasons to change the Sphinx's head into his own. Chefren left his likeness for our inspection."

"Was this smoothness, that you refer to, a smoothness of the stone or was the Sphinx covered with something... covered with some... I don't know... plastic substance?" I continued asking.

"That's another mystery," the Universe answered. "After it was built, it was indeed coated with special material to keep it smooth. When it was built, it had features, which are still visible today, in your time. These features were made on purpose, since the Sphinx was a true reflection of the same Sphinx that was found on that planet and on Atlantis."

I recalled reading speculations on the subject of the age of the Sphinx, on the basis of the grooves on its body, which could have been caused by rain. I did not know whether the Universe had these grooves in mind or some other features. According to some non-orthodox researchers, the Sphinx was older than the Great Pyramid not by one thousand but by *several* thousand years, and was built as a lion in the Age of the Lion. I decided to clarify this once more.

"Are you able to specify a more exact date for the building of the Sphinx? How many years before Christ was it built?"

"Wanderer," the *Universe* answered, "I would like to explain something that I already mentioned more than once. As regards the calculation of your earthly years, I — as a non-material existence — have some difficulties. Therefore, my information may contain errors. The dreams of the Priestess may also sometimes be read incorrectly. As the Priestess, a human being living during the construction of the Pyramid, Ki says what she sees, but she cannot see time. I see but I perceive it on a huge scale. Even a million years is for me sometimes a brief period, so what can I say about a thousand? It is easier for me to use the signs of the Zodiac and in this way make things more precise. Move back from Scorpio by one thousand years and you will know when the Sphinx was built."

I am not familiar with the dates of the signs of the Zodiac, so I still did not know what we were talking about and what years were involved. As a being accustomed to specific dates in history, I would prefer an answer such as "The Sphinx was built (say) 7,564 years before Christ was born, and it was officially unveiled on the fifteenth of May." Unfortunately, obtaining such precision was not possible and therefore conversations with the *Universe* were difficult in this respect. Moreover, It talked in symbols, metaphors, and parables, not like us humans, in specifics. I decided not to press It any more about dates and asked another question.

"Can you say who built the Sphinx? Were they humans?"

"I have already told you," the *Universe* continued, "the Sphinx was built a thousand earthly years before the Pyramid of Cheops. You ask how, and who built it. In the times before the Sphinx, there was a settlement named Irr, and the inhabitants of this settlement helped the Winged Brethren in the construction of the Sphinx."

"Does this mean that the Sphinx was built by those who came from Orion?"

"It is clear that people would not be able to build such a colossus all by themselves. The construction of this Guardian would have taken too long, so the Sphinx was built in the same way as the Pyramid. The blocks were brought from quarries on the other side of Nile. They were cut, polished, and shaped in the image of the Sphinx and put into place. Of course, before the construction of the figure of the Sphinx itself was started, the foundations and underground chambers on which the Sphinx stands had to be prepared. This did not require major dressing, only the placing of the blocks that had been cut to shape and size. The construction proceeded at a very fast rate. The Winged Brethren were not needed for finishing the interior of the Sphinx and the chambers.

The priests received precise directions as to what was to be placed where and they carried out the work along with the workers."

"Can you tell us what is inside the Sphinx?"

"Up to the time of the construction of the Pyramid, the Sphinx was empty! Not until the construction of the Pyramid were various pieces of equipment installed inside the Sphinx."

It was getting late, so I decided to end the Priestess's dream and return to this subject later. I wanted to find out what is inside the Sphinx, whether there are some passages, chambers, or corridors below it.

During my next visit to Wroclaw, I again asked the *Lady Called Life* for one more dream about the Sphinx. This time, Lucyna was somewhat truculent and reluctant.

"You have already heard so much. Besides, I told you that nobody will believe it anyway," she argued.

"At first, nobody believed Copernicus either," I answered.

"But Copernicus did not dream about his discoveries. He researched them." The *Lady Called Life* suddenly became very logical.

"How do you know?" I asked. "Perhaps he had dreams. It might be that his adventure with the sun and the Earth started in this way. Perhaps the *Universe* talked to him through dreams as well. *The Universe* is eternal. It was around in the time of Copernicus. For It, it is only a matter of a few hours ago, not even a whole day."

"You are right," she agreed. "I am falling asleep."

I requested that this time, as the Priestess Ki, she would look at the Sphinx, that she stand beside it, beside its paws.

"It is the time of the construction of the Pyramid, you are the Priestess Ki and you are standing beside the Sphinx. Tell me what is inside the Sphinx?" I asked.

"What is inside in the Sphinx?" Ki repeated the question. "I can only say what I know, because one cannot go into all of the rooms. The Sphinx goes down to the depth equal to its height. Rooms are located in both paws of the Sphinx. In the right paw is located the room in which the rites of embalmment of dead bodies were conducted. As to the left paw — this is shrouded in secrecy. In the room in the left paw, there are devices."

"What sort of devices?"

"I do not know about such things," Ki replied. "The Winged Brethren had a name for it. There are compartments there with equipment brought from the Other Earth, from their home planet. They often contacted their own planet or other planets such as Mars. They also contacted their base, which was located behind the Earth's Moon. The base was also on the Small Moon. No one could enter this compartment, only the Winged Brethren, Pharaoh, and Juno. Prior to this, before entering, they had to go through a cleansing. Below the head of the Sphinx, going down into its interior, there are also other compartments."

"Have you seen these compartments?"

"No, I have not seen them. Juno told me about them. The tablets concerning the construction of the Pyramid and the Pharaoh are stored there."

"But these tablets are supposed to be in the tomb," I observed.

"The tablets are in various places. There will come a time when people will start looking for this information and this multiplies the chances that they will find it."

"Interesting; where else are these tablets?" I thought. "They are in the tomb, in the Labyrinth, in the Sphinx and for sure, in the Pyramid. We are now in the twenty-first century and for so many thousands of years, people have not found them. I wonder why."

"Why has nobody found these tablets up to the Age of Aquarius?" I asked Ki and a moment later, I realized that this question was senseless. How could the Priestess know? She dreams about the time of Cheops, her dream is many thousands of years ago. To my surprise, Ki started to speak.

"I am asking Juno, I am asking Cheops, I am asking the White Brethren, and they all say the same thing. Time must pass in order that the prophecy be fulfilled. People must themselves learn to benefit from what they received from the *Owner of the Earth* — the God Yahweh. The

Pyramid and all its surroundings are protected and no one, absolutely no one, will be able to find this information without permission, until the allocated time for people passes. When the Pisces hands power over to Aquarius, the keys will appear on Earth. With these keys, one will be able to reach the places where the greatest treasures are found."

"What treasures?" I asked.

"Knowledge and the gate to the Other Earth."

There was a moment of silence. Every one of us (there were several persons in the room) was silently asking himself or herself the question: "Am I to help in finding these keys?"

The Priestess continued. "There is an underground chamber under the Great Pyramid. There is an underground passage to the Pyramid of Cheops from the side of the Sphinx, but this chamber is filled with sand. The next chamber is flooded with water. From the side of the second Pyramid, there is also a chamber, which is filled with sand, but in the center of the Pyramid, there is another. This chamber is empty, seemingly empty. In it, there is concealed information, stone tablets with inscriptions on who built the Pyramid and how it was built. There is also information about those who came from the Other Earth."

"How can one reach this chamber?" I asked.

"One can reach these rooms," the Priestess dreamt, "from the side of the Pyramid itself, but here, obstacles await the seekers. In this empty chamber, there is a device, which will effectively hinder dishonest seekers."

"What does 'dishonest' mean?"

"Those who seek only fame and gold."

"How will a device know whether someone is honest or not and what he is looking for?"

"*The Universe* knows this, and It cannot be deceived. It reads intentions, It reads thoughts. It appoints people for the mission."

"Continue," I requested.

"The device is connected with another device, which is located almost at the top of the Pyramid of Cheops. All of these protective devices are connected by a network with the tomb and with the Sphinx, and the energy flows from the constellation of Orion."

"How do you know all this?"

"Juno said so. He said that in the future, I will communicate information to people. I received permission to communicate many important pieces of information."

"Everything you say is important to those who are willing to listen."

"I will tell you now something that the *Universe* allowed me to say today," Ki continued her dream, without paying attention to what I was saying.

Her voice became very serious. She spoke slowly and I felt she was repeating words heard in her dream.

"When you find the mummy of the Pharaoh, it has a device inside. The White Brethren installed this device in it. Through this device in Cheops, there is regular connection with the Pyramid and with the Sphinx. It is the key to opening the Pyramid. Thanks to it, after the body is placed in the sarcophagus in the King's Chamber, the energy gate will open, the gate into the Cosmos; the gate to extraterrestrial communication. This is why finding the mummy of Cheops is so important. He must be laid in the Pyramid, so that the White Brethren can help, so that they mitigate the purification of the Earth and so that the Earth becomes a planet such as that imagined by its *Owner:* beautiful and heavenly, a planet that is the model for all the civilizations of the universe..."

"That is the point!" I thought. "This is the protection for the Earth about which I keep on hearing, the device installed in the mummy of the Builder of the Great Pyramid. That is why the Pharaoh MUST be found, he must 'see the sun.'" I still did not understand how this would work but, through the Priestess, the *Universe* had unveiled another piece of the secret. I thanked It for this in my thoughts and continued my questions.

"When will the secret of the Sphinx be resolved?"

"It can be resolved," Ki said, "only when people will be ready. Ready to accept the truth. If this does not happen, the secret of the Sphinx and of the Pharaoh will remain secret forever. But in this case, those who rejected this truth, because of their arrogance, will no longer be on Earth."

"Yes," I thought. "Some people treat such information in a very arrogant manner. If, in the understanding of the *Universe*, a belief in the existence of extraterrestrial civilizations is 'true,' then for many these are still fairy tales. Under such circumstances, how much of what Ki said a while ago could reach the consciousness of people, who here, on Earth, are deciding the fate of the world?"

The Universe was right. In order to have access to knowledge, Man must have faith, and meanwhile, there are still so few of those who believe...

19

THE PHILOSOPHY OF THE UNIVERSE

The year 2003 was coming to its end. I contemplated what the *Universe* had told us at the beginning of this year and what had really happened. It was to have been the year, which It had called "the beginning of purification." *The Universe* had suggested that what was starting to happen was not a series of accidental natural catastrophes or disasters caused by whims of nature or the inner tensions among people. It was an organized action of spiritual forces, a conscious communication from the levels of Higher Intelligence. Believers call such events "God's will," saying that nothing can be done about them because "God wanted it." According to the *Universe,* they are indeed God's will, but they are also information, a request from God to look within oneself and to make changes.

Looking at our world of the year 2003 much happened. It was a year of natural disasters. In the December earthquake in Iran, over thirty thousand people died. There were tornadoes, and earth slides in the United States, and floods in China. It was the year of the war in Iraq. Soldiers died and are dying every day, bombs are exploding and thousands of innocent people are being killed...

"This is just the beginning, Wanderer," the *Universe* said during the next dream of Lucyna. "This is a prelude to the Great Symphony conducted by the ***Supreme Energy***. I have already said this many times, but I will repeat it a hundred or even a thousand times, if this will be necessary. Finding the tomb, moving the mummy of Cheops into the Pyramid, and placing it in the sarcophagus will open communication between your world and other worlds, which want to help the Earth."

"I do not understand one thing," I said. "If other worlds have such a huge superiority over us, if they are so technologically advanced, as we are so far behind, why don't they help us now? Why is Cheops, in particular, needed for that?"

"You have received time from the *Owner of the Earth,* God. In this time, no one had the right to interfere with you or to help you. No alien civilization. I could only prompt, suggest thoughts, while you, having reason and free will from God, decided what you wanted to do with these thoughts."

"From what you are saying, I understand that this time has now passed, that now we can be helped?"

"The time is just now passing, but it is shrinking with the speed of lightning. Only a few years remain, and the most important for you will be 2003, 2006, 2009, and 2012. In this period, the preliminary purification will occur and either people will understand the information, which flows from me, or they will start dying *en masse,* not knowing why this is happening. The *Supreme Energy* has decided this. This is a process for bringing awareness to the necessity for change."

"Is the Earth really so 'polluted' that it is necessary to destroy us?" I asked and immediately regretted my question.

"Look at the Earth, Wanderer, look at this tortured Earth." Lucyna's voice was clearly excited. "Did the *Lord of All Times,* God, dream of such an Earth? Is this the Paradise Planet? Look at people who are living their daily life. They were created in the image and likeness of *God the Most High.* Every one of you has a divine element within, everyone has a part of perfection within, and what have you done with this perfection? God's dream is an Earth, on which every person is a good husbandman, who sees himself or herself in others, who helps others and loves others, just as he or she loves himself or herself. Man, who sends out a feeling of love into space, joyful man. Look at the Earth!" *The Universe* continued speaking. "How many people do you see who obey this one main commandment of God: 'Love thy neighbor as thyself?' See how much suffering there is in this world, how much lying, how much cheating. How much enjoyment people draw from torturing others. And you wonder why I continue speaking about purification? The Bible speaks of this. Jesus talked about it when he came to Earth, to show people how they should live. The Earth cries out for breath. It cries out for a feeling of love, for this most powerful energy in the universe. Such energy is needed by us, Spiritual Beings, is needed by God to shield the Earth, to save people from the annihilation of this planet."

"Look, Wanderer, into human thoughts. People see nothing but themselves and even if I shouted, however loudly, they will not understand what I am talking about. Those who hear me and understand are considered to be lunatics. Those who ignore me are seen as wise."

"How should people use reason, according to you?" I asked timidly.

"God the Most High told people, 'Love thy neighbor as thyself.' Do you not respect your body? Is skin color or origin important in respecting your neighbor? No. The human being is important. You need to know how to preserve national affections and, at the same time, listen to the ever-growing sound of aspirations involving all of humanity. To hear what the other is saying. This is what reason is needed for, to learn how to listen to others. To learn how to use intuition and logic, and to hear what my world, the spiritual world, is saying to you. To learn how to choose what is good for you and for other people."

"What other advice do you have for people?"

"I have a silent hope," the *Universe* said, "that people will want, even if only for a while, to slow down their pace, to think about tomorrow, about themselves, to open their eyes, and to each day, look at everything differently. That they will look at people as brothers, no matter whether they are bad or good, beautiful or ugly. That they will see them as brothers linked by the same ties of birth and death. With your imagination, you will then embrace those millions of hearts, trembling with pain, of terrified people. Human suffering is common to all. Today, your neighbors, tomorrow, you may be suffering."

I was silent, listening intently to Its words, not knowing whether I should say something or listen on.

"In human hearts," the *Universe* continued, "there is a longing to conquer space and time, but so few people admit to having this within them. People are afraid to show such feelings. The longing embraces both the simplest of minds and those that are renowned. This also links them together."

"There is more that links us," I said.

Here I had in mind the human aspiration to become perfect, the inner need to be sure of survival, the need to receive and give love, and sometimes the need to change...

"Common to all people is suffering," the *Universe* broke into my thoughts. "Therefore, let this suffering and this longing, embracing all of mankind, be the driving force for the development of spirit. Start seeing others now, today, see yourselves in them, as if in a mirror."

"Does this mean that we have to suffer and become perfect in this way?" I asked, with a slight apprehension, that the *Universe* might be taking on the tone of a priest, who was persuading us to mortify the flesh.

"Your consciousness does not like suffering. I, the *Universe*, am doing everything that is in my power, to wake you from your spiritual somnolence, to help you live in bliss; to wake all of you, regardless of class, origin, nationality, or belief. Now you are weighed down by the burden of living, materialism, and the terrible struggle for existence. You are choked by the cloak of pessimism. This is the dirt that needs to be cleansed, in order to find the beauty of life both in the physical, bodily dimension, as well as in the spiritual."

The Universe fell silent for a while and I did not know whether it would want to continue. I had not heard it previously being so critical and so full of concern.

"In the subconscious of people," the *Universe* continued Its thought, "a higher idea is now beginning to mature. The maturation, however, will take a thousand years — this has been determined by the Supreme Wisdom. But the Supreme Spirit will triumph and will absorb into itself the soul of all mankind, after a preliminary filtering."

"Do you have in mind the purification of the Earth?"

"Yes, this filtering will come by God's will. Then this present 'I,' the 'ego' of your consciousness, will disappear forever, and the divine element in every person will become more and more unified with the Supreme Spirit and your life will survive in Him. People of good will, with open hearts, without pride, will learn how to get rid of the consciousness of the sensation of time and space, which truly is a curse of everyday life."

"Does this mean that the Earth will indeed change its poles?" I asked.

"Oh, Wanderer," the *Universe* answered, "how many times do I have to repeat, that it does not need to be so, that you will get help, but you need to ask for this help. You must believe in this help and understand that you can do nothing on your own. On your own, you will lead the Earth into a catastrophe. The key... I will give you the key to the gate, because the gate must be opened."

"What are you really talking about," I asked again, "when you say that your life will survive in the spirit? Does this mean that it will be finished in the body?"

"I am talking about perfection, about the growth of the spirit. Human reason strives to attain perfection, and absolute perfection exists only in the Supreme Spirit, although fragments of it may also be found in people. There is a particle of it in every person. So I repeat once more: people, wake up from your spiritual somnolence. Give the Supreme Power a chance, let yourself be guided."

"Many people are already guided. Many are in search of spiritual growth, seeing in this a deliverance from the madness of present-day societies."

"In many people, the awakening from the lethargy of life comes too late, most often when the clock of death starts counting down the hour of departure. Then it is truly too late for repentance... Tell the people, Wanderer, that life on Earth is only a stop on the way and a preparation for another journey, so let them become good pilgrims."

"I try to talk to people about this in my wanderings, I try to write about it," I said to the *Universe*, "but how can I demonstrate this to a person who is busy with everyday matters? How do I get such a person to think about the movie of his or her life, which that person will watch after death? For such people, surviving another day, month, or year is important... Death is somewhere far away, in the future. Present-day reality is now."

"Man lives in order to learn a healthy view of the world. I call the consciousness healthy, which can see the reason for existence and consolidates itself in the conviction that it is worthwhile to live, to fall and get up, because this road leads to overcoming chaos. That is why I, the *Universe*, want to strengthen in every human being the power of the will to fight against evil. I understand suffering, so everyone who seeks liberation, who seeks help, is dear to me."

"Who are you, truly, *Universe*?" I wanted to ask but Lucyna's dream was finished and this question was left without an answer.

20

THE MAN WHO DARED TO BE WISE

This was a strong dose of philosophy. I had not previously heard such a *Universe*, neither in the dreams of Priestess Ki nor in the dreams of Lucyna. This was Its calling out to people, Its plea for attention and awakening. I felt that our time was shrinking, but little had changed in the *Cheops Project*. The big fish of this world and the businessmen were ignoring us; the *Director of the Pyramids* was silent, despite the fact that the vision of the Labyrinth and the gold hidden within it was very promising. The Labyrinth was to be the proof of the reality of the dreams of the Priestess, but for it to come into existence in the physical level, someone had to be found who would believe in it. Additional permits were needed, even if not so difficult to obtain as in case of the tomb, still, but still, somebody had to arrange this for us. I talked to archaeologists but they tried to keep aloof, afraid of losing their scientific reputation. It appeared to me that nothing was happening in this whole affair... and again, I underestimated the potentialities of the *Universe*.

In June of 2003, I was preparing for another wandering. This time, my road led again to Gdansk, a Polish city which I liked to visit and where I had many friends and listeners. I was all the more surprised when, just before leaving, I was notified that there were no people interested in coming to meet me. I had a couple of days to go, so I thought, "Well, that is the Polish nature — everything at the very last moment," hoping that many will come, as usually happened. When the time of the meeting came, I was really surprised: Not a single person was interested.

I did not know what this was all about. I was surprised with such a sudden lack of listeners.

Well, once more, it turned out that nothing in my life occurs by accident. Since I did not wander off to Gdansk, I stayed in Warsaw. This, in turn, allowed me to take another step toward the Pharaoh — at least, this was how I understood it. I met the **Man Who Does Not Fear to Be Wise**. His name is Andrzej Kaplanek; by profession, he is an engineer in mining and geology; by predilection, he is a writer, poet, and traveler. His book, *On the Trail of the Sons of the Sun,* had just been released in Poland. I met him only because I remained in the place, where he came to talk about himself.

When I told him about the *Lady Called Life*, about Cheops, the Labyrinth, and our mission, he was shocked. He did not think that information of this kind could appear in a country that is generally disregarded by the great ones of this world. We wandered together to the environs of Tomaszów Mazowiecki, in order to strengthen our unexpected acquaintance.

"Can you help us?" I asked, when we had emptied the first two bottles of wine and after we broke through the formalities between us, such as addressing one another as 'Mister Writer' or 'Mister Wanderer,'

"What you are saying is reasonable and complies with my conclusions from my own wanderings," he said. "I do not know yet how true and credible are the dreams of the Priestess Ki, but this is an adventure that many people dream of. I love adventures and if I can help, I will with all my heart."

"Good!" I was glad, "I will ask Priestess to have a dream in your presence."

The *Lady Called Life* was not surprised at this meeting.

"*The Universe* told you that It would put interesting people on your way," she said calmly.

"Yes, but see how hard the *Universe* had to work," I commented in my excitement with this situation, "in order to alter the plans and change the minds of all those who were to meet with me in Gdansk, so that nobody signed up for the meeting."

"It has its own methods, It affects our thoughts, It affects our emotions."

"And I thought that we have free will."

"We do. It did not force anybody into anything; It did not point a gun at anybody's head... It just sent out a thought. Everybody had to consider this thought consciously and make a decision whether to go to the meeting with you or not. It only has the power to send out thoughts. We have the power to decide which of the thoughts we choose."

"Like the power to do good and bad things?"

"Exactly so," she confirmed, "this is what free will comprises."

Initially, Andrzej was attentive and slightly tense. This was the first time he happened to participate in one of Lucyna's dreams, so he did not quite know what to expect and how to behave.

"You can ask questions," I reassured him. "*The Universe* will answer you."

"What universe?" he became uneasy, looking at me with suspicion.

"The one who talks to us every day, the one who made us meet."

He was not convinced, but he had no choice. *The Lady Called Life,* the Priestess Ki, was ready. She was dreaming her dream...

"Greetings, Ki," I saluted her, "where are you?"

"I am beside the third pyramid in Giza," she replied calmly, "beside the pyramid of Mykerinos. It is time zero, the time of Aquarius. I will now say what the *Universe* tells me."

I understood that the Priestess was dreaming about the present time. That for her, this was August of 2003. For the *Universe,* it was time zero. I listened with fascination.

"Greetings, Andrzej," the *Universe* addressed the *Man Who Dared to Be Wise* by his name. "There are no coincidences in our worlds, in your physical world and in my spiritual world. That you have been brought here, that you have been put on the way of the Wanderer, does not mean that you will be here forever. Like all the others, you, too, will be subjected to tests. Some of your predecessors dropped out. Their enthusiasm was immense, but in reality, it was only in words and in the wish to gain fame or gold for themselves."

I surmised that, talking about those who "dropped out," the *Universe* had in mind Roman (or the *Man Who Preferred to Doubt*) and the *Businessman*. I considered the latter as a lesson to me. I once asked the *Universe* through the Priestess why It had put him on my way, since he had contributed nothing and only delayed our project.

"*The Businessman* taught you something, Wanderer," the *Universe* answered then. "Namely — caution in looking at people. Before you open up to somebody, before you open your heart, you have to look carefully. *The Businessman* also taught you something more: an ability to listen to people, to catch small details from them, simple words, which sometimes drift away. For that, he was needed. That he was insincere, I knew from the very beginning, but you had to go through this lesson, so you would be more careful in the future. And he taught you, Wanderer, something else: not to trust as you had trusted before."

It was a powerful lesson that I received from the *Universe* and therefore, I now looked at everybody much more carefully, as if from a greater distance at the *Man Who Dared to Be Wise*.

"Greetings, *Universe*!" Andrzej's voice was trembling slightly. "I wanted to ask... because Cheops... the project..."

"You will obtain today the information for which you came," the *Universe* interrupted him, "but I expect trust from you. I see your heart; I see your doubts. Do what I ask, get rid of your pride, and I will not disappoint you. I promise."

"I wanted to ask — " Andrzej repeated.

"I know," again the *Universe* interrupted him. "You wanted to ask why the Priestess Ki pronounces the name of the Pharaoh as 'Cheops,' that was not the true name of the Pharaoh in those times. Am I right?"

"Yes," replied the *Man Who Dared to be Wise* and his eyes widened in amazement. He understood that the *Universe* was reading his thoughts through the Priestess Ki.

"Let me explain," the *Universe* continued, "People know the name 'Cheops,' The Pharaoh was really called **Khufu**, but this name is less known now, here, in the Age of Aquarius. People have heard about Cheops, but may not have heard about Khufu. That is why the Priestess received my permission to use the name 'Cheops,' this is how she calls him, how she sees him, and how she feels him."

"There will be many riddles," Ki continued in the voice of the *Universe,* "which you, with your scientific mind, will not be able to accept and understand. Some things, which seem so obvious to you scientists, are closely controlled by me and by the entities from the constellation of Orion. Believe me, only that will be shown which we want to communicate to you. Remember one thing: that scientists have examined and defined some things does not mean that they are true. Just look at how many theories there are on the subject of the construction of the Great Pyramid."

"Thank you," said the *Man Who Dared to Be Wise* in a now more assured voice, "I understand and respect your secrets. Could you please give me precise bearings for the Great Labyrinth? I want to know if I properly understand what you said to Patrick."

I knew that Andrzej had been in Egypt many times and knew the area of Giza; he had described the pyramids in his books, but from my stories, it was the Labyrinth that was of greatest interest to him. He believed that, if the pointers of the *Universe* prove to be precise, there is a good chance for a permit for the research. Now, he reverted to this subject.

"Well," said the *Universe,* "what do you want to know?"

"Several meters to the left or to the right in this rocky terrain is a considerable impediment for the probable searchers. If we take the distance, of which you spoke earlier, from the third Pyramid to the lake, am I to understand that you mean the present-day shore of the lake? Am I to halve the distance from the Pyramid to the shore of today's lake?"

"Yes, Lake Moeris today, the lake of the Age of Aquarius," the *Universe* repeated. "If you rose up into the sky, you would see the outline of the real lake, from the time of the construction of the Great Labyrinth, and then the shore would be much farther than it is now. That means closer to the third Pyramid. But a huge part of the old lake has been engulfed by the sand and we must focus on what remains."

"You see what I cannot see. Tell me, please, why nobody up to this time has found the Labyrinth? According to Herodotus, there are 3,000 chambers in this palace, is that not so?"

"It is difficult to call this a palace," the *Universe* reflected. "There are corridors, chambers, and rooms" Ki dreamed on. "It is difficult for me to say whether there are 3000 chambers there. Perhaps together with corridors, as I told Patrick. You ask why no one has found such a huge building so far. Andrzej, within the Labyrinth are located special devices, which impede your current devices, the ground-penetrating radar instruments. Those which seek out empty spaces. This happens, because the intentions of people, especially in the Age of Aquarius, are not, in the majority, pure. They are driven by a desire to enrich themselves and a desire for conquest, not only of the Earth. You should be interested in one thing only: in finding the truth. The Labyrinth is to make my words credible. To make it credible that, in order to reach Cheops, or Khufu, the Labyrinth was provided for this purpose, in order to convince you also. Archaeologists have been looking for this Labyrinth for so long, and it is so close. The simplest thing would be to go below ground level. The Pyramids and the Labyrinth have connections, but the Egyptian government will not allow such research."

We were silent for a while and the *Man Who Dared to Be Wise* considered the answer of the *Universe* and composed his next question.

"How deep is the Labyrinth? How deep do we have to dig?"

"I have indicated this place because it is the easiest to locate and to reach below the ground. You ask how deep — I will try to describe this. The layer of sand may be one or two stories. Then, there is stone, but when you dig, it will not be an obstacle for you. It is soft and you will penetrate it easily. Then, you will encounter the slab of the first level of the Labyrinth. Four stories, that is how it could appear."

"Is there a second level?"

"Yes, there is a second level. The first is completely filled with sand and one cannot walk there. Below it is the second level of the Labyrinth and this is intact. One can move freely through this. One can reach the Golden Chambers by this level."

"How does one move through it, so as not get lost?"

"Use your head, Andrzej," the *Universe* was obviously amused by this question, "use the scouting trick."

"Which means what?" despite his engineering knowledge, Andrzej did not quite understand what the point was.

"Use a string... an ordinary string."

We all laughed at this suggestion. This was how Ariadne had saved her beloved from the labyrinth.

"How precise are your indications about the depth?" Andrzej continued his questioning.

"They are not precise," Ki dreamed. "I am a spiritual world. I see time, I see space differently from you. Understand this, Andrzej: I do not measure with a centimeter tape; I do not have a clock which shows me hours and minutes. My time is eternity, my space has no limits, so I can only guess. You will have precision when the Priestess goes to Egypt. Then the place will be indicated with the accuracy which you expect, and your radar will show you the exact depth."

"I thought that you were omniscient."

"Change your thinking. I need your faith and trust. What else do you want to know about the Labyrinth?"

"Thank you, that will do me for now," answered the *Man Who Dared to Be Wise*. From the tone of his voice, I sensed that, somewhere in his subconscious, he felt uncertain.

We woke the Priestess. After she had gone home, we started discussing the whole project.

"All this is not precise enough for me," Andrzej said.

"But you are the *Man Who Dared to Be Wise,* you are an engineer and a geologist," I observed. "It is your role to make it more precise. When we go to Egypt, we will position the Priestess on the plateau and we will ask her to show the place precisely, to the nearest meter. *The Universe* will guide her."

"It will or will not... I will not risk going to Egypt when I am not sure. I have to test her here."

In this way the *Man Who Dared to Be Wise* decided to test whether the Priestess was a true priestess and whether the *Universe* was telling the truth. He decided to outwit the *Universe.*

We did not know about this, because he did not tell any of us what he wanted to do. One day, he led the *Lady Called Life* into a field and asked that the *Universe* would show the place where something was hidden. He did not take into account one tiny detail. He forgot that the *Universe* was reading his thoughts, was reading his intentions, and was asking for only one thing, a little faith. He forgot that the spiritual world is governed by different rules than the world of people. The immense knowledge shining in the words of Priestess Ki, in the words of the *Lady Called Life,* when she talked with the voice of the *Universe,* was not enough for him. He saw details, which did not fit into the whole, according to him.

The *Man Who Dared to Be Wise* proved to himself that the Priestess can be wrong, that the *Universe* does not exist, that it is only a product of imagination. He proved to himself that what was said about the Labyrinth, about the tomb, and about the world did not make sense.

The Universe looked at these tests with sadness and allowed him to prove everything that he wanted to prove to himself...

In this way, the *Man Who Dared to Be Wise,* Andrzej, the writer, withdrew from the Pharaoh group. Whether forever... I did not know at that time, but I felt that he would return. I felt some subconscious liking for him, I admired his wisdom. The *Girl to Whom Every Morning Smiles* also came to like him. However, we could do nothing but wait for what the *Universe* will think up for us. It was the boss, and It was guiding us.

21

DIRECTION SLEZA

The encounter with the *Man Who Dared to Be Wise* stimulated not only myself but also Lucyna, Łucja, and the *Girl to Whom Every Morning Smiles* to think. All who were then with us wondered what to do to get through to the consciousness of Hawass and other authorities. Because the matter concerned the Labyrinth, the financial requirements for the preliminary research were not high, and were estimated at an amount of about thirty thousand dollars. This was a question of only the trip to Egypt and the rental of a device that is called georadar. This is a device which can detect an empty space located below ground level. If the dreams of the Priestess are true, by going to the place indicated by her and using a georadar, we could find out whether there was "something there." The "something" that we were looking for comprised the underground compartments in the Labyrinth. The procedure is relatively easy and does not require digging.

Most important was a permit from the Egyptian authorities for preliminary studies and a specialist, who would perform them with suitably good equipment. For obtaining the permit, an archaeologist was needed, preferably a famous one, who would persuade the director of the Pyramids to open his mind to our project.

Our major problem was still the lack of hard arguments, the lack of faith. For a scientist, for an archaeologist, a dream is imagination and there are no proofs that this imagination is telling the truth. When I talked to the *Lady Called Life,* she defined this in an unambiguous fashion.

"You have a choice between good and evil," she stated. "You also have a choice between belief and disbelief. If you believe that God exists, you believe not because you saw Him, you touched Him, or because somebody proved His existence scientifically. You believe because you have decided to believe. When you decide to believe, all the rest is only a matter of time."

"The point here is about the belief of those who do not want to believe," I replied. "If this is so important, if we are to awaken the Pharaoh, the *Universe* should help us to find an easier way of confirming your dreams. In the world of a man of science, specifics are needed, and we will not obtain these through dreams but by digging. The Labyrinth is good, but the gate to Egypt will not be opened for us, until at least the slightest trace of your dreams is translated into the physical level. Then there will be faith, which will be supported by knowledge."

Lucyna asked, "What do you suggest?"

"I suggest talking to the *Universe* about Poland. *The Man Who Dared to Be Wise* had a good idea but he put it into effect in a bad way. I want to ask the *Universe* to point out to us something in our own country; something which would make your dreams credible beyond any discussion."

I knew that archaeological findings must be located in various places of Poland, about which the *Universe* knows, but about which we do not know. If It tells us about even only one of them and we find what he tells us, we will have the proofs that we are seeking.

"I have a request for you," I turned to the *Universe* when the Priestess was sleeping her waking dream. "In order to get to the Labyrinth, we need something closer and easier to find than the Labyrinth. Could you point to something in Poland?"

"I can," the *Universe* said, "That is a good idea... Since this is your request, Wanderer, I will indicate to you a place, which will make the dreams of Priestess credible once and for all. Have you heard about Mount **Sleza**?"

"Yes, I have. Could you tell me something more about this mountain?"

Sleza is a sacred mountain with immense energy. On its summit, there now stands a church and also the ruins of a castle. Under these ruins there are dungeons, underground passages, and corridors from old mines. One can enter the dungeons under the castle on Sleza, though nobody has managed to do it until now. With my help, we will try to enter there, because very precious findings are hidden there."

"Fantastic," I said. "I hope that you will tell us where we should enter."

"The easiest entrance to the Sleza dungeons is through the small church standing on the top of the mountain."

"How do we do it?"

"First, the Priestess Ki will go there and carry out her examination. I will guide her hand and show where one has to dig. I will show the easiest entrance to the underground and I will let her feel energy of this place. In your language, it is called dowsing, and a simple pendulum is the tool."

"Can you say exactly what is there? What will we be looking for?"

"The Sleza dungeons run in several directions and they have an exit to the outside. You ask what is hidden there? At the times of King Boleslaw Chrobry (the first king of Poland living in the eleventh century), people believed in **Swiatowid**. He was the sun god. During ceremonial occasions, offerings were made to the god... Most often, these consisted of gold and precious stones. These offerings were stored under the castle. In the vicinity of the mountain, there prowled bands of robbers, who knew about the dungeons. This was their hiding place. There were passages between the dungeons, and the robbers from these dungeons attacked merchants who passed that way. It was difficult to find them, because they disappeared 'under the mountain.' Finally,

King Boleslaw Chrobry managed to deal with them and annihilated the whole band. The robber chief knew that he could not remove from the dungeons all of the loot that had been hidden there. He covered up the tracks and concealed the entrances to the underground, so that nobody could find them. The secret chambers and the entrance were known only to the band. This particular entrance is located close to the **two bears**, halfway up the mountain, where the stone cross stands. Here I want to say that this entrance cannot be forced. However one looks at this, a thousand years have passed since then."

"Will the entrance through the small church be therefore better?"

"Yes, this is the easiest entrance. After you enter the dungeons, the underground, I will guide you toward the hidden chamber."

"What sort of chamber is it? Where is it?"

"After entering the dungeons, go in the direction of the two bears, and in that section is found the chamber, within which is the treasure."

"What are these 'two bears?'" I asked, having no idea what the *Universe* was talking about.

"These are two very old stone sculptures on the slope of Slea. Archaeologists will know what this is about."

"Are there any traps or dangers there, in these dungeons? What should we watch out for? What should we avoid?"

"Here also you are right, Wanderer. Therefore, when you open the entrance, lead Lucyna in there first. I will protect her and she will show you a safe way."

"What way?"

"The direction to the two bears is the safe way," the *Universe* said. "If you went toward the first bear, the one at the foot of Mount Sleza, on the side of Sobótka, you could come across traps. They are simple traps but very effective. After going several meters and touching particular stones, the whole structure would collapse on your heads."

I thought about the unusual nature of this information. Not so long ago, we were worrying about Egypt, the Labyrinth, and the director of the Pyramids, and here, there was opening before us a completely new prospect, a new vision, a new project. In my thoughts, I thanked

Andrzej, the *Man Who Dared to Be Wise,* for the idea. Apparently, this was to be his role. If what the *Universe* is saying proves to be true, if we find the underground dungeons and the treasure, do we need a better way of making Lucyna's dreams credible? I was more and more excited by this, so I continued asking.

"Is the passage to this treasure, to the chamber or chambers, bricked up? Closed? Secured?"

"Yes, it is filled with stones. But they are easier to remove than the stone cross or the boulder on which a cross is engraved on the slope of Sleza. I give you my guarantee, nothing will collapse on your heads."

"I understand that, after entering the underground and reaching the proper corridor, you will show Lucyna which wall is to be dismantled in order to get to the chamber with the treasures?"

"If you remove the stones protecting the passage, you will reach the chamber without obstacles. There are no safeguards there now. It is simply a room, an open room."

The matter seemed to be simple. Having such information, there was nothing left for us but to find someone willing to dig. I was curious, however, how the *Universe* came up with the idea of Sleza and if the mountain itself had some connection with Egypt."

"Do Sleza and its surroundings have any connection with the pyramids in Egypt?" I asked.

"Sleza is a place of special power, because the energies on solstice days, in autumn and in spring, flow down from above, that is from Mars or from the moon. Sleza additionally also possesses the power of the energy of the moon, especially when the first day begins of the full moon. The entire mountain emanates immense energy then. Just be there, on the summit, on the first day of the full moon, and you will feel the power of the energy of this unusual mountain. You ask what the Giza plateau has in common with Sleza? There was a landing ground in Sleza, even in the times of Boleslaw Chrobry and much earlier. The local people, who saw this phenomenon, believed that gods were sending down punishment or reward."

It was astonishing news to me. Sleza was a former landing ground for spaceships? I began to understand why the *Universe* chose it for the test area.

"Does this mean that Mount Sleza was artificially created by extraterrestrial entities?" I asked.

"No, Wanderer, this mountain is a work of nature. That is why it was selected, because it has a strong energy connection with the moon. Moreover, it was rich in minerals which were mined from it for a long time."

"Is there something special among these treasures, which could gain world renown?" I asked, thinking about the permit for research in Egypt,

"Yes, Wanderer, there is. When, during the times of Boleslaw Chrobry, the people made offerings to the sun god, they found fragments of a spaceship. Exactly 1,000 years before the Age of the Pisces, there was an accident of such a spaceship. The sensation will not be gold, Wanderer, but showing the fragments of this wrecked spaceship to scientists. The people in those times did not understand this. They believed that God himself came down to Earth in his heavenly ship, then left it and flew away. Some parts, which were not completely destroyed by fire, are found among these treasures. And this treasure is most important."

I did not want to ask more. I decided to find out some more about Sleza and its history. I was interested whether anything of what the *Universe* had told was recorded in old documents, chronicles and legends. I thanked the *Lady Called Life* and I told her about the conversation.

"Yes," she said, "we have a task close to home. Mount Slea lies forty kilometers from Wroclaw."

22

THE FIRST TRIPS TO SLEZA

It seemed that arranging a permit for excavations on Sleza would be child's play, the more so that we already had money in Chicago for this research. The **Man Who Prefers to Remain in the Shadows** had given this. When I was in Chicago on one of my trips, he approached me and asked quietly if he could be the sole sponsor for the Sleza excavations. "Of course," I said. In this way, Sleza found a sponsor, while the entire **"Cheops Project"** was divided into three stages.

The first, seemingly the simplest one, was the **"Sleza Project"** (so it was named by the *Universe*). This was the project to penetrate the underground in Mount Sleza and excavate that, which the Priestess had dreamt about. Only a permit from the appropriate authorities was needed to start digging.

The second stage, more complex, was the **"Labyrinth Project."** More money was needed for this and permission from the Egyptian authorities, first for the georadar examination, and then, if the georadar readings confirm the indications of the Priestess, for the excavations. The finding of even a single chamber of the Great Labyrinth would be the archaeological sensation of the millennium. Money for this purpose was being collected by the *Lady Who Dares to Speak,* Barbara in Chicago.

Third, the most important, stage was the **"Cheops Project."** Its objective was to dig up the tomb of Cheops, the Pharaoh Khufu. Because the tomb, according to dreams of the Priestess, was located close to the Great Pyramid, obtaining a permit for excavations would be almost a miracle. I thought to myself that this was a job for the *Universe,* with its unlimited energy, to carry out such trifles as miracles. It would suffice for the Director of the Pyramids to think just one thought; to think "yes" instead of "no." So simple and yet so difficult.

The plan was prepared in detail and the implementation of the first stage of the research was initiated. I decided to seek advice from the *Universe* on what we were to do in turn, with regard to Sleza, in order to reach the goal as quickly as possible.

I asked the *Lady Called Life* for another dream, "What moves would you suggest? What should we say?"

"The threshold here is a bit lower than the Pharaoh threshold, as only the local Wroclaw authorities need to be contacted." the *Universe* answered. "You have to speak the truth, Wanderer. Every lie, even disguised in the most beautiful clothes, or painted in the most beautiful fashion, must come to light at some point and burst. This matter has to be presented just as it is."

"That means how? Am I to say that we have information from You, through the dreams of the Priestess, and that is how we know what is inside Sleza?"

"The investigation can be conducted in the small church, and therefore, the first permit for the preliminary measurements has to be obtained from the custodians of the church, from the priests. For the time being, you should keep silent about my involvement, since the priests will be irritated and may throw you out when they hear that the information comes from another dimension."

"So what are we to say?"

"Use the words 'dowsing examination.' It will be the most appropriate solution and it will be true."

I understood that the first step would be to contact the priest who supervises the small church and to request permission to conduct a dowsing examination.

"Are there any obstacles waiting for us before climbing up Sleza?" I asked.

"Yes, there are some waiting. I would prefer that, for the time being, this not be divulged too broadly. It will surprise you, but the Germans may be an obstacle, because during the war, they hid something in the dungeons that may be of interest to the Polish government. All the entrances were effectively filled up and mined. They left themselves only one way in and that is through the church on the summit of Sleza. When the Germans learn that such an expedition or such excavations are to be carried out, they may interfere considerably. I, Wanderer, am only a spiritual world. I do everything that is in my power to help you, but if you do something beyond my control, I cannot vouch for the consequences. It may come to some unnecessary clashes."

This information did not surprise me. I had already heard stories about treasures hidden in Sleza by the Germans just before the end of the Second World War. I heard about several unsuccessful attempts to reach these treasures. Our objective, however, was not to look for German gold, but to provide credibility to the dreams of the Priestess, so I was not particularly worried about this.

"What do you advise in this situation?" I asked. "Shall we make this matter public just before going in to Sleza or not divulge it to the public at all?"

"I would suggest getting some publicity but 'not till five minutes to twelve,' so that those who would want to put up obstacles were in no position to do so. Remember that those who put in that thing during German times knew what they were doing. The hidey-hole is unworldly and in an ideal place. No one would think about getting into the dungeons by entering through the church. The Germans have their contacts and may make trouble. That is why we will make the matter public shortly before the first insertion of a spade."

I liked this plan, all the more so because, as the Russian saying goes, "The more quietly you move, the farther you will reach." In our situation, this was the best solution.

Thus, one September afternoon 2003, we went with the *Lady Called Life* to Sleza. The small church, in which we were interested, was open only during the summer. On Sundays, masses were held there, while on the other days of the week it was closed, and we did not know whether one could even go inside without permission from the priest.

It turned out that entering the church was simpler than we had expected. We were given the key from the supervisor in the hostel on the summit of Sleza, and we had the whole church all to ourselves. Lucyna immediately started her work and, guided by the *Universe,* made the measurements with a pendulum, which performed the weirdest pirouettes in her hands, sometimes so abrupt that it fell out of her hands and landed on the floor.

"Why is it spinning so fast?" I was surprised, as I have seen several dowsers in my life, but none of them had the pendulum whirling so fast. Their pendulums rotated slowly and gracefully, corresponding with the dignity of the person who held the pendulum in their hand.

"The pendulum is my talk with the *Universe,*" Lucyna answered. "I ask It in my thoughts to show me something and It, by means of this whirling, lets me know, responds to my questions."

"But why does it spin so fast? Is the *Universe* angry with you, when it rips it out of your hand?" I still wanted an answer.

"How do I know?" Lucyna smiled warmly. "Perhaps in this way, It is making sure that I am properly hearing its words."

The *Lady Called Life* found several places for digging, but two of these were the most interesting. Both were on the right side of the small church, facing the altar. One was under the pulpit, the other was closer to the entrance, about half a meter from the side wall.

"Digging should start here," Lucyna said, and with this, her investigation was completed.

I recalled that the *Universe* had asked — almost ordered — that the same tests be repeated by three independent persons, three dowsers who did not know what we were looking for.

"Now we have to find *Three Specialists* to check it out for us once more," I said to Lucyna.

"Of course,' she answered. "You will find them in Wroclaw, for sure."

I did indeed find them, and not only in Wroclaw. For the next trip, three new people came with us: Józef, Mietek, and Robert. Józef and Mietek were *Dowsers of Considerable Reputation*. One used a dowsing rod, the other used a pendulum. Robert was a journalist who used to look for treasures. It is true that he found no treasures, but he knew how to do this and he had special equipment for this, some kind of a metal detector.

Each one of them conducted their investigation independently. The two dowsers established the places in the small church that were active spots, and these corresponded quite closely with what Lucyna had detected. Robert was most excited, because his device emitted some mysterious sounds, which none of us understood. Robert claimed that his device was squeaking because "something" was there. Everybody was very happy. In the hostel, each of us drank a couple of glasses of mulled wine, because it was getting cold and we considered this stage of our research completed.

Dowsing is recognized by many archaeologists as a research method, but it is a subjective method and does not comprise a so-called "hard proof." It does not provide a basis for applying for permission for investigations. Now we needed a **Truly Scientific Proof** that indeed "something is present" under the floor of the small church and that excavations were worthwhile. Examinations that comprise such a Truly Scientific Proof are those conducted with georadar, that is, a device which "peeks" deep into the ground with electromagnetic waves and shows what is there on a screen. Whether it is solid rock, whether there are some empty spaces, or whether there are other anomalies, which may be interpreted as prospective archaeological finds.

There are only a few georadars (GPR) in Poland. One of them was located in Wroclaw, in the department of geology of the University of Wroclaw. Another coincidence? Maybe. The person in charge of it was Adam, a Ph.D. in geological sciences. I called him the **Man Who Understands the Language of the Earth**. His wisdom lay in the immense knowledge, which he possessed, in the field of the application and interpretation of georadar. Moreover, having an artist's soul, he was capable of perceiving the beauty of the women around him and he treated his profession as his passion.

Georadar investigations cannot be done in secret; permits are needed. This went surprisingly smoothly. The extremely kind priest who was in charge of the small church gave permission for us to enter there "officially" and the Office of the Provincial Warden of Historical Objects had no objections to the investigations being carried out.

I was happy that the *Girl to Whom Every Morning Smiles* was with us. She came back to the Cheops Project with passion and commitment. Her smile stimulated the male portion of the group to a high level of motivation and energy. Iwona proved to be invaluable as a link between myself, Lucyna, Adam, and those with whom I could not always make contact, while wandering all around the world. For me, she became once again the morning smile of the sun, which signified that the road, onto which we had stepped out together at the moment of her first smile, became again Our Shared Legend.

The georadar measurements inside the small church were carried out in February of 2004. They showed disturbances and anomalies, which the *Man Who Understands the Language of the Earth* interpreted as possible burial places, underground passages, and cellars.

We were very proud and happy that Official Science finally started coming close to the dreams of Priestess Ki, that for the first time what the *Universe* communicated through her was beginning to take shape not only in thoughts, but also on the tangible, physical level.

This was the first step in the direction of giving credibility to the dreams of the *Lady Called Life*. Now the second step awaited us, the real one: the excavations.

23

BONIFACY,
THE GUARDIAN OF SLEZA

Everything seemed to be so simple: We only had to enter the small church on Sleza and start the excavations. It turned out, however, that appearances are sometimes deceptive. Despite the consent of the priest, despite our sponsor from Chicago, despite the georadar readings, the small church was still beyond our reach. This was the decision of the *Very Important Office Which Allows or Does Not Allow Digging.* In this case, it did not allow.

Sleza is an exceptional mountain. It is surrounded by legend and mystery, which create around it an aura of extraordinariness and even a fear of the unknown. Long ago, it was a center of the proto-Slavonic cult of Swiatowid. It was always something unknown and very interesting. One of legends said that Sleza has a guardian, a spirit which makes sure that no unauthorized person enters its inner parts.

Archaeological examinations have been conducted on Sea for many years, both on its slopes and also in the small church. The reason for the refusal was the fact that drilling had been carried out many times in the small church, which unequivocally showed that the small church is located on solid rock and that there is nothing under its floor.

Every time drilling was carried out in some area of the floor, the drill encountered solid rock. The scientists decided that rock was all there was and their interest in the small church evaporated.

Obviously, breaking up the rock under the church does not make sense and therefore the *Very Important Office,* taking pity on the money of our sponsor from Chicago (why should that poor man unnecessarily throw away dollars, hard earned in the U.S.?), decided to prohibit digging. That the georadar showed "something" was assessed as an error in the interpretation of the test results.

I began to suspect that perhaps there really was some spirit, who was impeding our activities. With regard to spirits, the *Universe* was our best interpreter of the unknown. So I decided to clear up this matter directly "with the management" and to seek advice on what we should do next. I asked Lucyna for another dream.

"What are we to do now?" I asked the *Universe* in a plaintive tone, "They do not want to let us dig."

"Do you have a mind?" the *Universe* responded.

I was taken aback and did not really know what to say.

"I sometimes think I have," I finally sputtered.

"So why do you not use it sometimes?"

"What do you mean by 'not use it'?" I retorted, not knowing what the *Universe* had in mind.

"Allow me to help you," the *Universe* explained, as if to a child. "I will pose you some questions and you try to answer them."

"All right. Please ask."

"Does the church on Sleza have something like a floor?"

"It does." The question seemed strange to me. How can a church not have a floor?

"And what does it look like?"

My mind was empty. As a typical representative of the male gender, I had little recollection of the appearance of the floor in the small church. Men in general pay little attention to such details. They are created for much more important issues. Women have been placed on the world to be responsible for details. Fortunately, the *Girl to Whom*

Every Morning Smiles was a participant in this conversation and she, as a woman, takes notice of every detail of every place and immediately formulates a plan in her mind on how she would rearrange the place, if she was its owner.

"The floor is in a terrible state," she answered immediately. "The stone tiles are grey and ugly, many are broken, they are not flat, and do not fit each other."

"Bravo, Iwona!" the *Universe* was pleased. "Now another question to the Wanderer. Do you have a good relationship with the priest who takes care of the small church?"

"Very good," I answered.

"Do you think that the priest would be happy if you proposed to him a restoration of this floor, or even its replacement?"

I understood what It had in mind. *The Universe*, the spiritual world, was teaching me, the Wanderer, to think like a human being. "If you cannot enter by the front door, go in by the back door."

"You see, Wanderer," the *Universe* said, "sometimes one has to take the roundabout road, if one cannot take the shortest. This *Very Important Office* of yours will certainly not oppose repairing the floor in the church. If it did have any objections, this would be very strange to me. Priests have a lot to say in your country and in this case, you have the enormous support of the priests. When you dismantle the old floor, who will prevent you from looking what is deeper? I, the *Universe*, guarantee to you that the small church does not stand on solid rock, and that there is an entrance to the underground by that way."

I was taken unawares and put to shame by the logic of the *Universe*. It was so obvious. Why did I not think of this idea?

"I have one more question," I said. "It is said that Mount Sleza is guarded by some spirit, which puts obstacles in the way of people making investigations. Could you talk to this spirit, so that it would help us?"

"Wanderer!" I felt the smile of the *Universe* in Lucyna's voice. "Of course, Sleza has a guardian. His name is **Bonifacy**. He is a very wise spirit and keeps away people with bad hearts, those who only seek gold and fame. He will help you, because Sleza is a part of the Pharaoh mission. It is a stage, which is to open for us the road to Egypt. This is my project, it is under my direct charge, and I will ask Bonifacy to help the chosen group. Even more, I will arrange it that you will be able to talk directly with this spirit. When the time comes, I will invite it to one of the dreams of our Link."

I was delighted and I asked the *Lady Called Life* to arrange a "meeting" with Bonifacy. From that time on, things started to arrange themselves into a beautiful mosaic of permits lined with roses. Our invaluable priest arranged a permit in the *Very Important Office* to have the floor repaired. From Chicago, there came a task force, headed by Barbara, the *Lady Who Dares to Speak. The Man Who Prefers to Remain in the Shadows*, the main sponsor of the project, also came, as did the *Lady Called Fame*. The American group immediately started a frontal attack on the Institute of Archaeology in the University of Wroclaw, which up until then, was unyielding in its conviction that "the small church stands on solid rock, so digging is pointless." The personal charm of Barbara and Slawa was irresistible, the cash of the *Man Who Prefers to Remain in* the *Shadows* was available, and the hearts of archaeologists are not made of stone, so there could be only one outcome. We could start digging, which means "replacing the floor."

One day, the *Lady Called Life* came with interesting news.

"*The Universe* said that Bonifacy is ready to talk to you."

We all gathered in Iwona's apartment, together with the American group, and an interesting and strange conversation commenced by way of another dream of Lucyna. First, the *Universe* greeted us.

"Before I give way to the spirit of the mountain, Bonifacy, I would like to welcome you. I promised to help you and bring to you the spirit of Sleza. The spirit of the mountain, Bonifacy, because this was his name, is a real figure, not conjured up only to frighten people. This spiritual entity is now here with you and now I let it speak."

There was a moment of silence and I wondered about what to ask the *Spirit of the Mountain.*

"Greetings! I am the spirit of Mount Sleza, the magical, sacred mountain," Bonifacy spoke in Lucyna's voice. Her voice was quite normal, just the same as in other dreams.

I listened to this dream with some trepidation, because talking to spirits was something mysterious and unknown to me. The Universe was something else. It was for me a Higher Intelligence, the Wisdom of All Times. Thanks to the *Lady Called Life*, it talked to us like friends talk to each other. It had a sense of humor, It was able to joke, to soothe, and to scold. I felt relaxed during these dreams, especially when the Priestess Ki was traveling in time. On this occasion, it was a different dream. A dream about a spirit, and I have been afraid of spirits since my childhood. I have heard so many strange stories about them...

"I lived at the foot of the mountain about 500 years ago," Lucyna dreamed on, "and I was a shepherd, who was considered as the local idiot. This idiot mastered the art of healing, because in my times, the mountain was, to use your earthly language, a pharmacy. I prepared various kinds of infusions. I treated people with various ailments. I knew the mountain like nobody else; I knew its energy and its history. I also knew the strangers, the entities who came here. The local people considered them to be gods."

"Why did they think so?" Barbara asked.

"They were not gods, Barbara. They were strangers from beyond the Earth. They flew in onto the mountain to obtain minerals. The last time they were here was shortly before I died. The local people also saw them and said that the gods had sent down punishment. Punishment, because they had destroyed the castle, which was still there. They destroyed it because they did not understand one essential thing... The Mountain speaks all the time."

"What does 'speaks' mean?" This time it was Slawa who plucked up the courage to ask a question.

"These were phenomena and manifestations of spiritual entities. Now these phenomena have ceased, but in my times, these entities were visible and the people from neighboring villages were terrified. Because of this, the local priests announced that the castle was a 'devils' conglomeration' and this abode of Satan had to be destroyed. Nothing could be farther from the truth, but it happened. I, as a healer, was spared, since I was considered as an idiot anyway. When I died alone on the mountain, after leaving my body, I promised God that I would be the *Guardian of the Mountain* until the time when the secret of the mountain is revealed. For all these years, I have been closely tied to the mountain, to the ruins of the castle and to the dungeons. That I was an idiot," Bonifacy continued, "meant nothing. I was respected anyway, although the people were afraid of me. The priests said that the body of Bonifacy was to be thrown into the 'devils' dungeons' and now a church stands on these dungeons."

"Please continue," Iwona said, "this is a fascinating story. Did you have to wait long?"

"Yes, long... I would choose the appropriate people by appearing to them as a human being. When I met a person on the trail, I always asked for bread. It rarely happened that the ragamuffin gets a piece of bread. These were tests, until the time came... the time of Aquarius, when the *Universe* was preparing the Link, who now has the name Lucyna. Several years ago, she was invited by a group to the May mass and I also was there. I sat beside her, as a poor, dirty ragamuffin. When she received some food to eat, I asked her for bread. I saw that she was very hungry herself. Without a word, she gave me her bread and sausage. She said, 'Eat.' When she went to buy me something to drink, I left. How amazed she was when, a moment later, she turned around and the bench was empty. She looked for me but did not find me. This bread connected us and I communicated the news to God: 'This is an appropriate person.'"

I was curious if Lucyna remembered that event. I could not really understand how a spirit could suddenly become a physical body and ask for bread. I did not know the world of spirits well enough. Actually, I had never seen any in my life (or so I thought).

"I will tell you also," Bonifacy said, "that Lucyna was being observed. We already had some influence on her mind. She was strangely attracted to the small church, and I knew that I had chosen appropriately. Listen, I am the *Guardian of the Mountain* and I watch over not only the treasures but also the bones. The mountain is surrounded by energy and God said that only a chosen person can break this protection and connection. The local people still say up to the present time that the ruins and the small church itself are under a curse and that whoever dares to disturb the peace of the bones lying in these tombs will be damned. This has indeed been so. The energy and the curse have effectively deterred prospective robbers. The time had come and, when the friendship evolved between Lucyna and myself, I said to her thoughts, 'You will be guided to the ruins.' She was not aware of the protection or of the curse. She was completely unconscious of these. Now there is a group and it is strong. All those who are needed have been chosen. Beyond Lucyna's consciousness, the curse has been removed and now I can cooperate only with you. I am the spirit of the mountain, Bonifacy."

"How can you help us?" I asked

"Wanderer, since the very beginning, when Lucyna, you, and Iwona crossed the threshold of the church, I have been watching you. Had the group not been chosen, it would not yet be the time to enter the dungeons. That not the whole group is fully committed to what will be done is irrelevant. It is important that several persons are committed and these people will lead to revealing the secret, to showing the history to the people. Those who do not believe in the power of spiritual entities will have to fall into line. I can say this now. Any attempts at outwitting you will be futile, as I will have custody over the excavations. This is my mission. When everything is finished, my bones will be laid in the ground and I will finally go to where my place is. My dears, this is not about my bones, which are still lying in the subterranean regions of the castle on Sleza. What is shown to the eyes of scientists is more important. The road to the Pharaoh will open up. This is the main goal and I am proud that I can participate in this immense event."

Silence ensued and none of us asked any more questions. Lucyna broke off her dream and we were still silent, moved and staring in space. Somewhere above our heads, Bonifacy was with us, the *Spirit and Guardian of Sleza,* and now our guardian.

Nothing strange in things going so well, I thought, since Bonifacy is helping us.

In the second half of August in 2004, the archaeologist, together with Lucyna, entered the small church and the work started.

"I give you a one percent chance that there is something other than just rock under the floor of this small church," said Olek, the *Chief Archaeologist of the University*, the head of the investigation, to Lucyna.

How quickly he had to change his opinion.

24

THE SECRETS OF THE SACRED MOUNTAIN

O lek, the Archaeologist, the **Man Who Was a Total Skeptic**, started looking at Lucyna in a completely different way immediately after the first days of the Sleza excavations: with immense respect and admiration. It turned out that under the floor of the church, close to the pulpit, in the place indicated by Lucyna, there was no rock. Digging down deeper, the astounded archaeologists discovered galleries and a courtyard of the castle, unable to fathom how it happened that in all of the previous drillings rock was encountered every single time and that at a depth of sixty centimeters under the floor.

"But we drilled in various places, and every single time, it was the same," Olek said.

How was I to tell him that it was Bonifacy mixing things up, playing tricks and guiding them astray? He influenced their thoughts and the conclusions, which they drew from their investigations. Could something like this be explained logically? I preferred, at this time, not to tell the scientists the story and legend of the Sleza spirit who was watching over his sacred mountain and who allowed only that which he wanted to allow.

When the archaeologists became acclimatized to the sensation, when they looked deeper under the floor and their eyes confirmed that Lucyna's dreams were right, while they were wrong, there was a shower of questions: "How did she know that?" And again, how were we to explain to a doctor of science that it was the Universe talking through her? That our task and objective was not only Sleza, but also something more important, something greater? Sleza was only a prelude, a first stage, which was to create physical reality from the dreams of the Priestess.

I surmised that sooner or later, it would be necessary to explain to Olek that it was not by chance that he came to Sleza and to us. For the time being, Olek, the *Archaeologist,* changed from the *Man Who Was a Total Skeptic* into the **Man Who Was Lost in Admiration**. He was clearly thrilled. Sleza was his life, his archaeological passion. Now he had both the funds for research and the support of a world, about whose existence he may have known, but he had not expected that this world could so tangibly affect his archaeological reality.

I asked the *Lady Called Life* if she could have another dream about Sleza. I wanted to find out how Lucyna, Basia, Slawa, and the *Man Who Prefers to Remain in the Shadows* were to guide Olek, so that he could work safely and find that which would open up Egypt for us.

She immediately agreed, and after a while, was ready to dream her waking dream.

"The archaeologists have started to dig in the place You indicated in the small church, near the pulpit. What will they come across in their way? What should they expect?" I asked the *Universe.*

"Wanderer," Lucyna dreamt, "there are two levels under the castle: the cellar and the dungeons. How deep does the first way down go? I am not sure, but I believe that five meters should suffice. Then we will reach the first level of the dungeons. The small church itself has no such dungeons, since it stands on the courtyard of the castle ruins. The castle had the dungeons."

"What will happen next, when archaeologists reach the dungeons?"

"After entering the dungeons," the *Universe* explained, "go toward the two bears. This is the safest corridor in the dungeons, but only this one."

"Does this mean that there are also other directions?"

"The second direction is the dungeons which lead toward the way down or the road along which the cars come up the mountain. Toward the village of Tapadlo. There is also a third direction, toward the village of Sulistrowiczki, but there a part of the dungeons is filled in. The Germans did this, Wanderer, because what is the best way to hide something? By cutting off the way to it."

"Is this way mined?" I asked, having in mind the stories told about post-German treasures.

"The only safe way is that leading in the direction of the two bears. Part of the dungeons is filled in there but, after the stones are removed, there will be free space and one can move freely."

"Could you tell us the secret of what the Germans hid in Slea?"

"Certainly not human bones, Wanderer. Precious things were taken from Wroclaw, which had been looted and hidden there. As you know, Mount Sleza evokes fear and respect. The Germans knew this very well, so they used it to hide their precious loot. In addition, they cut off all the roads at the foot of the mountain, leaving only the emergency entrance, the one indicated by Lucyna. The Germans knew well what they were doing. Why do you think that I told you not to publicize anything before the first spade was driven into the ground? If the publicity had been much earlier, then even I would not have been able to help you. There would have been found people, who would have effectively made this mission more difficult."

"Could you be more precise about layout of these dungeons?" I asked.

"When you dig down, you will enter one large compartment and it is from this that the corridors branch off in the three directions, which I mentioned."

"What is the height of the dungeons under the small church? Can an adult stand there upright?"

"Oh, yes... A prison was located in these dungeons in the times of King Boleslaw Chrobry. It is difficult to imagine not only the convicts but also their guards walking on all fours. Of course, it is not the height of the chamber in the Pyramid of Cheops, but a man can stand there upright easily."

"Is Sleza hiding any more secrets?"

"Sleza has many secrets, which will be revealed and communicated in turn, if science itself opens up to this."

"Could you say something more?"

"On the first level of the cellars, you will find a sarcophagus. It will disclose the first secret. The second will be disclosed when you dig through from the outside — if it comes to this. The third secret is hidden half way up the road to the summit of Sleza. The sculpture will indicate the place, the one that you call 'Maiden with a Fish' and 'The Bear,' The secret of the sculpture with the fish will also be revealed, because in reality it is not a 'Maiden with a Fish,' Here we will place the triangle, which will indicate the cave. As the work progresses, the secrets of this sacred mountain will be progressively disclosed."

"Whose bones are hidden in the sarcophagus?"

"I cannot say this now. However I will tell you that very long ago, for more than 4,000 years, back to the times of Piast, Sleza was a gold mine and within the mountain, there are still shafts and the remains of those mines. I cannot disclose anything more..."

This was quite a bit of information as for one dream. I recalled a story told by the priest, who was in charge of the small church on Sleza, about several attacks on the small church that had occurred at the time of the equinox by a group of Satanists. They destroyed the wooden pulpit and tried to burn the huge wooden cross. Strangely enough, the cross did not want to burn, despite several attempts. This was a sort of a miracle and the priest's voice suggested that some higher powers were at work here. I was curious what the *Universe* would say on this subject.

"Who are the people who devastated the small church on Sleza?" I asked. "The priest suggested that they were Satanists."

"That is a mistaken understanding of the *Spiritual Entity Named Satan*. These people call themselves Satanists. Believe me, Wanderer, the spiritual entity named Satan will not acknowledge this group or any other such groups scattered throughout the whole world and may calmly say, "I don't know these people,' They act in contravention of all principles, in contravention of any standards of the universe. They and similar groups will be the first to be removed from the Earth. For them, there is no longer any possibility or chance of correction."

"It is said that the cross in the church, which they tried to burn several times, did not want to burn even once. Whose help was this? Did the Supreme Deity involve himself in this?"

"God has his messengers, Wanderer, including Bonifacy, the holy, the wonderful spirit, Bonifacy. Of course, he could not prevent these people from devastating the small church. Furthermore, this was not about the church, but about the cult, the cult of **Swiatowid**. Destroying is not allowed, no. It was Bonifacy who, when they exceeded the bounds, frightened them severely. He gave them a sign in this way that raising one's hand too high is not allowed. The 'Satanists' fled in fear, without completing their mass."

I thought how very warped must be the need for exceptionality in some people, that they would suddenly form a group of fanatics, whose aim was to destroy good, to destroy symbols... to destroy traditions.

"Could you say something more about Swiatowid? What sort of god was it?" I asked last of all.

"A god-spirit, Wanderer. The gods took on names, which were needed for the time of the given years, for the given century. The sun god himself is behind Swiatowid. His true name, known from the very earliest times, is **EN-KI**.

This was the second time that the *Universe* mentioned the name of the *One Who Created* the *Human Race*. But how could EN-KI be the same god as Swiatowid? Gods are eternal, that I know. They may take on different names in different cultures. But how did EN-KI find himself in this area? He had to come here to be called Swiatowid. When did this happen and what did he do here? What did the proto-Slavonic people have in common with the Sumerians?

Many questions came to my head, so I thought that sometime I would ask the *Universe* to say a few some words on the history of the Earth. Now, when the Sleza investigation was underway, when it was already clear that Lucyna's dreams, her talks with the *Universe*, were not the hallucinations of a sick woman but true, verifiable knowledge, our eyes turned back again toward Egypt, toward the *One Who Decides about Everything: the Great Zahi.*

25

THE GUARDIAN OF GIZA

When, during my wanderings, I talked about Sleza, the tomb, the Great Labyrinth, our plans for digging up Pharaoh Cheops, opening the Pyramid, and activating the channel connecting the Earth with the extraterrestrial dimension, I kept on hearing the same comments: "You will never get by the *Director of the Pyramids,*" "He does not give permits to anybody," "More than one archaeologist has broken his teeth on him." I was curious myself as to why he was painted by so many in such black colors. Some said, "He's an egotist," "He will steal your idea and put his name on it, because of his greed for fame." Still others said, "He's a patriot. He wants all the glory to go to Egypt and Egyptians." The general opinion about the *Director of the Pyramids,* was unanimous: He does not believe in any extraterrestrial civilizations. He opposes all non-orthodox theories on the construction of the Pyramid of Cheops and other pyramids. There is no chance of obtaining any permit, especially a permit for digging close to the Great Pyramid...

I thought that within every person, there generally exist a number of identities... Perhaps in reality, this *Guardian of Giza* is not at all that bad. He is fulfilling the role designated by the *Universe* in this time, when interest in Egypt is increasing, when many archaeologists are more and more aggressively trying to learn what is inside the Great Pyramid. I knew that he identifies himself with someone who does not believe in anything but the official version, according to which the Great Pyramid was built by people from the Stone Age, who had no knowledge yet of the wheel. I knew that he tries to ignore or torpedo every attempt at proving anything different. I also knew that he must be a very intelligent person, who is able to think clearly. In such case, what is his true visage? His true identity? It may be that the one he presents now is needed to fill the time given to people for digging up the Pharaoh. It may be that, without him, some rich lunatics would have long ago have rummaged through everything around the Pyramid in search of gold and fame.

I knew that there are various madmen, who would love to break down the Great Pyramid into small pieces with dynamite, as was tried once by some English colonel. An idiot like that could even now come to the conclusion that explosives are the best way for looking into the Great Pyramid and the Sphinx.

I also knew that the *Universe* was very anxious about excavating the Pharaoh during the Age of Aquarius. Since this is so important, it is also important to learn what the *Director of the Pyramids* really thinks and who he is. He has already made an appearance in several of the dreams of the Priestess, but none of these dreams concerned exclusively his person. He was simply mentioned as a very important link in the chain of causes and effects, which will lead to the excavation, first of the Labyrinth and then of the Pharaoh. He is the *Guardian* and without his permission, no one would drive his spade into Egyptian sand... I decided to ask Lucyna for a "Dream about the *Guardian of Giza.*" I thought that the *Universe* would tell me what the *Man Who Decides about Everything* is thinking, what he feels and what his role is in the mission...

This time, the *Universe* itself asked for a meeting. I came to Wroclaw and when the *Lady Called Life* went to sleep, I greeted the *Universe.*

"Sleza provides you with arguments," the *Universe* began, "the proofs which you asked for. The next objective is the Labyrinth, Egypt. Time is getting short, Wanderer... "

"You are right," I answered, "Sleza allows us to talk with archaeologists, it is providing facts, but this is just the beginning of the investigation. The excavations in the small church are proceeding slowly, the archaeologists dig slowly, layer by layer. For the present, the excavation goes down to a depth of four meters and the archaeologists will not go deeper before the winter. We have not reached the cellars yet and we have found no treasures. If we are to go to Egypt, we need permits, and we still do not have any contact with the *Guardian of Giza*, Dr. Zahi Hawass. You place people on our way and regulate the speed of our activities. If time is getting short, how are we to speed up these activities?"

"Your 'train' is still running slowly and new 'swallows' are still coming aboard... What is to happen, must happen. People should begin to understand some dependent relationships, so that more and more of them could start seeing with their eyes."

I noticed that the *Universe* was starting to sing Its favorite philosophical song, which it sometimes lavished on us. This time, however, I wanted to obtain specific information about the *Director of the Pyramids*. Since it was necessary to hurry, we should know how to talk to him.

"Tell me something more about the *Guardian*," I asked.

"Why do you want me to repeat myself, Wanderer?" The *Universe* was not happy with my question.

I thought that perhaps this might be a difficult subject for It. Still, I asked again.

"I remember that you talked about him, but I would like to learn more. Since we are to go to Egypt, tell us something about his heart, his character."

"He is a person standing very firmly on the ground," Lucyna dreamed. "Concrete facts and gold are important to him. But I am already giving him signs; I am trying to reach his consciousness. These signs consist of all the misfortunes which are happening now and will be happening in the years to come. Not a single day will be peaceful. Every day, people will be dying."

"What is his heart really like? What is his role?"

"A very important role, Wanderer. But for him, the whole world would throw itself into digging up treasures in Egypt. It is not by accident that this *Guardian* has been placed in this post. He was sent to the Earth to be the *Guardian of Giza*. Human envy and greed for profits is huge. But for this man, believe me, people would be reaching into the Pyramid of Cheops like barbarians, with the help of explosives. He is the *Guardian* and my messenger. He is not liked, because his behavior is far from standard, but he must behave like this."

"He appears not to have scruples," I noted.

"That is what they say about him," the *Universe* said, "but he is needed. His lack of scruples produces the result that not everyone obtains a permit for digging. He holds to his convictions, although in the depth of his heart, he feels that some elements of this logical pattern, which he created for himself, do not fit each other. For now, he is ignoring this. At this moment, he is still a proud Egyptian, guarding the message of his ancestors, a scientist investigating reality only with those senses which he knows. The day will come when his intuition will also start to wake up and he will ask himself other questions. He is a wise man, very necessary to me and to you on Earth."

"If he is needed, why is he slandered so?"

"Because people do not see the deeper sense in the history of the Earth. The knowledge of Atlantis is placed in the category of legends. So-called 'serious scientists' forejudge that it is nonsense. I, the *Universe,* with my whole spiritual message, am also ignored by science. That which I say through the dreams of the Priestess, I am saying not only to her alone. Thousands of people in the world have similar dreams. But let any of them try to speak about them and they will be laughed at and, in the best case, completely ignored."

"What do you have in mind by the 'history of the Earth'?"

"The history of the Earth, Wanderer, is the history of the cooperation of your earthly physical world with the world of extraterrestrial civilizations and with my spiritual world... I am energy. The God Yahweh, the *Owner of the Earth,* is also energy, the *Supreme Energy.* It was our world, which decided about your history and your human existence. This history did not start, as your scientists claim, just a few thousand years ago. This history started many millions of years ago on other planets... We were creating you, people, with the help of other civilizations. We were moving human beings from other planets, even from the planet, which once existed between Jupiter and Mars. It is only now that man, in his arrogance, has started to consider himself as the only inhabitant of the Cosmos. All the signs which present-day people have received and are constantly receiving on Earth are ignored and diligently hidden from other people. At one time, in the times of Atlantis, in the times of the construction of the pyramid, such contacts were a daily routine."

"What signs are you talking about?"

"For example the signs pressed out in crops. In your country, in Poland, in the locality of Wylatowo, there are many such signs. In England, in Italy, and in other countries, there are plenty of them, and so what? They are neglected. All the spaceships that you call UFOs and appear to you now and then, are signs of the existence of extraterrestrial civilizations. Look at the architecture of your ancestors in Peru, Mexico, Bolivia, Egypt, and in so many other places in the world. The civilizations of those times were in no state to erect such buildings with their own hands and the technology, which they had at their disposal then. Am I to continue?"

"I understand this; you do not have to convince me. I only want to persuade the *Director of the Pyramids,* and he does not believe in you or in the signs about which you are speaking."

"He is not the only one who does not believe. His mind would have to open up to another history of the Earth, than that which he was taught in school. He would have to understand that nothing on Earth happens without a reason and that it is no accident that he finds himself in that post. He would have to understand WHY he is so exceptional and important. It is due to him that the Labyrinth and the Tomb are waiting for the proper day and for the proper people. They are waiting for those whom I have chosen and am constantly choosing."

I was silent for a while. I could not imagine how I was to communicate this knowledge to the *Director of the Pyramids* and the people, whose only worry are to earn plenty and to entertain themselves on what they earned.

"How do we penetrate this veil of indifference?" I asked.

"There is something that will move the heart of every person," the *Universe* answered. "Sometimes it is fear, sometimes gold, sometimes love, sometimes passion, and sometimes pride. If you find the proper key, you will open every soul and, through this chink, you will help it to see that something that it was unable to see before. Don't worry. The soul and heart of the *Guardian of Giza* will also open up. When this happens, he and his Egypt will take their rightful place in the history of mankind and in the new history of the Earth."

I bowed my head to these words. I now knew that, when the proper time comes, the doors of Egypt will open to us, for our investigation on the Labyrinth and for digging up the Pharaoh. When this will be... the *Universe* will decide.

26

THE LABYRINTH:
A DREAM ABOUT THE FUTURE

Dreams about the future are called precognition. With their help, the gate of time may be opened for a short while. Such dreams may be a way of communication between the world of human beings and the world of spiritual beings. These are worlds so distant and at the same time, so interconnected. From the dreams of the Priestess, it was evident that the spiritual entities, having no matter, need us, humans, to make changes on the physical level. We, in turn, need their guidance to achieve our way to becoming perfect, our Mission in Life, with which everyone comes to the Earth.

I asked the *Lady Called Life* to have a dream about how the future of the Earth will look when the Labyrinth is found, when we dig up the Pharaoh, and we open the Great Pyramid. I asked that the *Universe* would give me an opportunity to look at what will be.

"Dream a new, different dream," I asked her, when she fell asleep. "A dream about finding the Labyrinth. Move forward in time, to Egypt, and tell us what you are dreaming about. What future do you see?"

"I can dream," Ki answered, "only one of the possible futures. Whether this one will come true, I do not know, because it depends on the people. The *Universe* will guide me in this dream. It will speak to you with my voice."

"What has to be done, so that people would create the best future, so that we would find what we are looking for?" I asked the *Universe*.

"Penetrating the energy of human ignorance and stupidity," It answered with sadness in its voice, "is like attacking an enormously thick concrete wall with a pneumatic drill. Sometimes the wall will crack, but only sometimes."

"The goal in front of us is Egypt and the excavation of at least one chamber in the Labyrinth. Will the *Guardian of the Pyramids* permit us to make this investigation?"

"Wanderer, I am trying to influence the *Guardian* and his thoughts. Remember, however, he is a scientist and, like every human being, he has free will. He will decide whether to listen to me or to continue holding onto his beliefs."

"I believe in the wisdom of his free will and in your help," I said. "Show us what will happen when the Guardian of Giza takes the decision that is good for us, when we start to dig, and when we find the Labyrinth. I want to see such a future, so that I can create it in my imagination and in the imagination of those who are with us. In this way, I will best help your world and mine."

"All right," said the *Universe*. "I will allow the Priestess to have such a dream."

"Dream and speak about what you are dreaming," I turned again to Ki.

We were alone in the room. One could hear the loud ticking of the clock and her tranquil breathing. The Priestess was waiting for the voice, which would start talking to her. She was waiting for the image, which the special dream would create in her imagination. She was waiting for a signal from the *Universe*, that she could start talking to me, the Wanderer, to fulfill my request.

"I see the image," Ki started the dream. "We are in Egypt with the whole group, there are many of us. There are people I know, but there are also people whom I have not seen yet and I do not know who they are. I know, I feel that they are helping us, that they have been with us for some time, that they are part of our mission, but I cannot recall their names. Now we are in a room. There are five persons. You are there, Wanderer; there is an Egyptian man, there is myself, and there is Iwona. The **Guardian of Giza** is sitting in front of us, the *Man Who Decides about Everything*. He is looking at us calmly and is going through some papers. He looks at Iwona and I feel that everything is well. The *Guardian* smiles. Iwona also smiles her Morning Smile and this is something that he needs now. A normal, human smile... I do not see his thoughts yet."

"Dream on," I asked the Priestess, "this is another important dream. You are showing the way, you are dreaming what will happen."

"Now I hear what the *Guardian of Giza* is saying," Ki dreamt on. "He is telling us about his life, his dreams, and the successes he achieved as an archaeologist."

"Do you see the time?" I asked. "Do you see time when you are dreaming? What year is it? What month?

"I do not see time... I do not see...," she answered.

"All right, keep on dreaming," I requested. "What is the *Guardian of Giza* talking about now? Is he saying anything about the Labyrinth?"

"He says that he had a dream... A very strange dream..."

In my thoughts, I thanked the *Universe*. Indeed I did not know yet what the *Guardian of Giza*, the *Director of the Pyramids* dreamt about, but the Priestess was talking about the dreams of a scientist who does not believe in dreams. The archaeologist who, up to that time, saw only one reality. The one that was tangible, real, not subject to any visions of clairvoyants, dreamers, and all those who had the audacity to claim that the pyramids were built by somebody other than people.

"What did the *Guardian of Giza* dream about?" I asked. "Ask him to tell you about his dream."

"I don't have to ask him," she answered, "he is telling it all by himself. He dreamed about a great catastrophe, about the extinction of the Earth. He saw floods, he looked at the terror of the people, and then he saw silence and emptiness."

"But this is already happening," I thought, "The terrible tsunami in Asia was a sign, a warning for people."

"Why did he see this? Why did he dream about this?" I continued my questions.

"He says that his dream was for him to understand that the time for change had come. He said," Ki continued speaking, "that the dream was a signal that it was time to look differently at everything that he had been guarding up to that time. He says that..." here she suddenly stopped and fell silent.

"What else did the *Guardian* dream?" I urged her on.

"He says... he says..." the Priestess hesitated.

Silence. I did not know whether to ask about the rest of the dream or to wait until the *Universe* discloses to us the secret of the *Guardian*, the one who once did not believe in dreams.

"He says..." Ki very slowly measured out each word, "that we can go ahead with the investigation... and if the investigation confirms what we are saying... the digging may start... he says that he will be watching... he will be with us... that he will help us. He says... that the world needs change... and he understands this now... He says... he requests... not to tell anyone... about his dream..."

I listened to the voice of the Priestess and I felt immense emotion. She had never yet had such a dream. Suddenly, the great *Guardian of Giza* had become an approachable human being, who also has his fears. In my thoughts, he became the **Man Who Wants to Help**.

"I want now to talk to the *Universe*," I requested.

"I am listening," the *Universe* answered in the voice of the Priestess.

"How am I to understand this dream... the dream of the *Guardian*?"

"The dream is a trip into the future," It answered. "You know this. If such is the destiny, it will happen."

"But you create the destiny."

"But you, people, make it happen and only then, the destiny becomes the reality."

Until now, nobody with whom I talked believed that the *Director of the Pyramids*, the one who was so uncompromising and so difficult to talk to, could suddenly change his mind. "Could it be that his mission as *Guardian* is coming to its end and that the *Universe* is leading him toward an altogether different mission?" I asked myself. I fearfully hoped that the dream of the Priestess would not turn out to be only a dream.

"Dream on," I urged her, "and ask the *Universe* if It can show us further stages of this future."

"I can," the *Universe* answered. "The first step will be Lucyna's investigations. With her help, I will show precisely the place where it is easiest to get into the Labyrinth. I will show you one of the entrances. Lucyna must go with the pendulum to the place, which I will show her. My energy and her energy will link up. I will disable the protection and she will receive the signal."

"What protection?" I was surprised.

"Wanderer, I have told you many times," the *Universe* patiently explained, "that the Labyrinth and the Pyramid are protected by the energy which flows from the belt of Orion. Nobody, no one at all will find anything without my permission. The Labyrinth is huge, science knows of its existence, and so far, nobody has found it. I can disrupt every one of your devices, I can cause erroneous readings."

The Universe was right. Neither the tomb nor the Labyrinth has been found up to this time. Herodotus described the Labyrinth, he described its huge treasures and the gold hidden there, and he described its location. Despite this, the Labyrinth still remains a Great Secret.

"What will happen after Lucyna — with your help — indicates that place?"

"Her investigation must be confirmed by your wise device, which you call georadar. In my opinion, Lucyna's measurements are sufficient and more accurate, but you people need 'scientific proof' all the time. Science does not regard the pendulum as proof, so a group of scientists with a georadar will go to Egypt after Lucyna, to carry out tests in the places indicated by her. The georadar will confirm her measurements, just as it happened in Sleza."

I thought to myself that the dream of the Priestess is only a fulfillment of what the *Universe* had decided long ago. It is creation of a work, which is already formed in space. We only remove the unnecessary pieces from a mould that exists in the cosmos. Destiny is the final sculpture.

"How can one reach the Golden Chambers?" I continued asking. I thought that the prospect of finding large amounts of gold will be especially attractive to the archaeologists and to the *Guardian of Giza*.

"When you dig down into the place designated by Lucyna, you will find the entrance to the Labyrinth. There, you will find the first level of the above-ground Labyrinth. This level has been covered over. You will keep digging and in this way, you will get through to the second, deeper level, and there you can move freely, going in the direction of the Pyramid. Along this section, there will be several such precious chambers, which you call the Golden Circle."

"You speak of two levels of the Labyrinth. Do I understand this correctly?"

"Yes, there are two levels," the *Universe* explained, "perhaps not along the whole length, but in this section, which I have indicated, there are two. One level is the above-ground level. At the time when the Great Pyramid was being built, this section was visible above the desert to a height of about half a meter. The rest was in the ground. Time did its work. Over thousands of years, the sand covered this above-ground section. The underground part of the Labyrinth is the most important. The above-ground sections were there only to mislead treasure huntress."

"And what about the pyramids beside Lake Moeris, about which you once spoke?"

"One of them is now a stack of used-up stones and seemingly there is nothing interesting there. No one knows that there was an entrance there. In the times of its glory, when the pyramid was still intact, it was a special gateway into the Labyrinth. Only priests entered through this gateway. Only they had the plan of the Labyrinth and could freely move around it. Reckless adventurers did not dare to enter there, since such entry would be equivalent to death."

"Is digging beside this pyramid also possible?" I asked.

"It is. If you insisted and got a permit, you could dig down and you will then find yourself in the first corridor of the Labyrinth. But I consider that such effort is unnecessary."

I thought to myself that the *Universe* had said a lot, so the session should be finished to let Lucyna rest.

"What will happen next?" I asked. "You promised to show me the future of the Earth after finding the Labyrinth."

"The Earth will not change at that moment," It answered. "People will change. The Earth will change only after finding the tomb."

I did not want to give in, however. That was not what I had in mind.

"I know what you had in mind," the *Universe* said. "I read your thoughts, but be patient. In her next dreams, the Priestess will see more."

Lucyna opened her eyes and breathed deeply.

"What did I dream about?" she asked.

"You dreamt about destiny, about one of the probable futures."

"How probable?"

"That depends on us, on you, on me, on the people who will believe us or not..."

27

THE MISSION OF SAVING THE EARTH

We had put a great deal, a very great deal of effort into our activities related both to Sleza and to the Labyrinth, to the way in the direction of Egypt. The question that kept on recurring in my thoughts, in the conversations with the Priestess and with the *Lady Called Life*, was: "What does it really mean to open the Great Pyramid?" For a long time, the *Universe* has been mentioning in the dreams of the Priestess that opening the Pyramid will save the Earth and the people, and will change the world. It said that the White Brethren will come, the entities from Ashun, from the Other Earth, and that they will help people live a better life. Human consciousness will change. The process of purification of the Earth will be gentle. So far, none of us understood exactly how this would be, what this "gentleness" would involve. The vision of Patrick from Belgium was very pessimistic. It is true that the *Universe* mentioned several times that "it did not have to be so bad" but It did not say what would happen instead. How will opening the Pyramid protect the Earth against pole reversal? What is the true meaning of our mission? What effect will be caused by moving the mummy of Cheops out of the tomb and placing it into the Pyramid? Why is this so important that the whole universe and the Supreme Energies are assisting in this process?

I asked the Priestess for a special dream; a dream which would answer our questions and give us a better insight into that which we are pursuing and which we should avoid. It seemed to me that we had much faith but we also needed more knowledge.

"I have been wandering over the world for a long time," I turned to the *Universe* through Ki, "telling people about You, about the Priestess, about Sleza, the Labyrinth, the Pyramid, and about Cheops. Many listen to me, but I still do not know how to answer some important questions. Please help me. I myself want to better understand some issues."

"Ask," the *Universe* answered, "I am listening..."

"We talk so much about the changes on Earth which are to occur in the year 2012. Patrick claims that they will be caused by cyclic changes in the sun, others talk about a mysterious **Planet X**. Tell us, please, what is the greatest danger?"

"There is danger both from the sun as well as from that Planet X. That is why the shield is needed around the Earth, Wanderer. I repeat, the shield. If it is not there, the gloomiest forecasts of Patrick and all the others will come true."

"What shield are you talking about and what is this Planet X?"

"Let me start with the planet. Planet X, also called the Tenth Planet, the Twelfth or Nibiru (that is the same planet) is huge. Not several, but several dozen times larger than the Earth. If the tail of this planet, made of meteors, touches the Earth, devastation will result. The planet itself will not touch the Earth. It would be an unimaginable catastrophe, and I cannot allow it. The tail will touch. Speaking in the language of the beings from the Other Earth, it will sweep the North Pole or the South Pole with its tail. Then what Patrick was talking about will happen: melting of the ice and almost immediate flooding of great tracts of the Earth."

"A vision as in Noah's flood... How can we protect ourselves against this?"

"The Supreme Deity has said: 'I shall not punish the people with water...' provided that the people will help God himself. If they do not help, then there will be extermination. If energy protection around the Earth is created, something in the form of a bell-glass, then the planet passing by the Earth will not cause harm and the sun also will not cause harm. All this is in your hands. If my words reach people, if they understand what is being said, then the Earth and the people may be saved. To all people, I want to say: human beings remember. The energy of love is the highest energy on Earth. Initiate... Initiate this energy. Then all the bad things that are now happening on Earth will turn around."

"Again, You speak about the energy of love. If all the people on Earth started sending such energy out toward the cosmos, toward God, will the Earth be saved?"

"Yes, Wanderer, then it will be so. This energy is so immense that it could protect the Earth. Then purification would not be needed."

"Is this possible?"

"Look at the world, Wanderer, at what is happening among people and answer your own question."

"So why do you continuously talk about it, constantly remind us about it?"

"Because it is needed as a balance between good and evil. Between those who will have to go and those who will stay. The more people will find it in their hearts, the more people will be saved."

In my heart, I admitted the *Universe* was right. Various other thoughts flowed in to my head. I started to understand what role "the help of Mother Nature" could play in the purification of the Earth. The flood caused by the approach of the unknown planet. This was what the *Universe* had in mind.

"You say that the only salvation for people," I continued asking, "in the face of the oncoming changes is digging up the Pharaoh and opening the Pyramid, the gate of Time? How will we be saved? What will happen?"

"Listen, Wanderer, listen carefully and tell this to all who want to listen. That the Priestess Ki is transmitting information is a fact. For the time of the Age of Aquarius she chose this body for herself. I can also tell you something that the present-day Lucyna does not know. The Priestess Ki took over Lucyna's body after her clinical death. The Priestess Ki, living in the times of the construction of the Pyramid, has the task of communicating to people that which may happen. Whether people will take advantage of this help, of the hand extended from the Other Earth and of our hand, that all depends on the human beings themselves. We will do everything that is possible to save you. The Pyramid, Wanderer, is the last link that needs to be connected. There is no... There is no other way."

"What will happen when we dig up the Pharaoh? Will mankind be saved then and will it change the course of what we are talking about?"

"The Pyramid is the gate, the Pyramid is immense energy. The Pyramid, which stands in the central point of the axis of the Earth, was not built as a whim of the pharaoh. Human beings, I give you a message: Do not reject the proffered hand. You alone, without assistance, will do nothing. By yourselves, you will bring extermination to the entire Earth. Human beings, I continue to give you this message: The Earth will remain, and you, through your stubbornness, will lead to everybody leaving the Earth. What else am I to say in what manner? I can only contact people telepathically, plead, shout, and say: 'People, this is the only way. Set in motion the protection,' the **energy and magnetic protection**, which is scattered all over the Earth. The opening of the Pyramid, this main gateway, will result in the merger of the energies in all the places of power. They will create the protection. There is no need for the catastrophe, for the huge tragedy in the year 2012."

In the voice of Priestess, one felt an intensity of emotion that was rarely encountered in her dreams. This was an appeal to all the people on Earth, to the governments of states, to businessmen, to the real and hidden elites governing our planet. A cry to open the mind, to come to one's senses. I was silent... Ki also was silent. I did not know if the *Universe* was waiting for another question or if it would continue speaking. Finally, I asked a question.

"How will the planet, which is endangering the Earth, behave after the opening of the Pyramid of Cheops?"

"When the *Gate of Time* opens, there will be a release of energy, which is called energo-magnetic energy. This is energy contained not only in the Pyramid of Cheops. It also flows from the Pyramid to the planet Ashun, so it has a connection with the Other Earth. There will arise a giant chain of energy, connected with the axis of the Earth and the belt of Orion. The central axis of the Earth is located in the place where the Great Pyramid stands. When the *Gate of Time* is opened, all the energo-magnetic points on Earth will be activated. The energy will shoot upwards, into the cosmos, and will create something like a shield. The Earth will be shielded and when Planet X flies by close to it, it will not do any harm."

"What do you have in mind, when you say 'all other energo-magnetic points?' What is this?"

"I have in mind all the pyramids scattered all around the Earth and the chakras or points of power."

"So the displacement of the Earth's axis and the reversal of the poles need not occur? Does this mean that it is not some regular cosmic cycle, which affects our planet, despite there having been several such cataclysms in the history of the Earth?"

"They need not occur. There have been such cycles, it is true, but, Wanderer, remember Atlantis, when the gods managing the Earth said, 'There will be no more such cataclysms. The Earth is to remain the jewel.' This was said in a session of the Council of Gods. It was decided that the Earth would have protection. It is known that the cosmos, the stars, and the planets are continuously in motion and it is difficult to stop them, but there is another possibility for protection. Through the Other Earth, an energy protection has been established. The two planets have been connected with one another, so that, in case of need, this force could be activated to protect the Earth and the people. This protection will be activated when the mummy of the Pharaoh is placed in the sarcophagus in the Great Pyramid. This is your true mission: to save the people and to protect the Earth."

The Priestess stopped speaking. I was aware that Sleza, the Labyrinth and all of the archaeology connected with this are only a cover, beyond which there is concealed something so great, that my mind embraced the colossal magnitude of this task with great difficulty. I did not want to believe that these few people gathered around Lucyna carried on their shoulders the fate of the entire world, of the entire Earth... None of us possessed big money, fame, or wide contacts. At this time, such a task was beyond my imagination. The *Universe* continued to be silent, so I shook off my momentary musings and again interrupted the silence.

"How will placing the mummy of Cheops into the sarcophagus 'open' the Pyramid?"

"Very simply, Wanderer. A special device is mounted within the mummy of the Pharaoh. The White Brethren installed it just before placing the mummy in the tomb. At the moment when the mummy of Cheops finds itself in the sarcophagus, the device in the mummy will be connected with a device located in the Great Pyramid. This, in turn, will activate the energy connection with the Other Earth, with the other energy points on the Earth, and will create the shield of protection, about which I have spoken."

At last, everything became clear. This was a simple answer, why the tomb, why the mummy, why the Great Pyramid, and why this had to be done now, in the Age of Aquarius.

"What should be communicated to our earthly scientists about the coming changes? What should they know?" I continued asking.

"It is difficult to convince scientists; it is difficult to make them aware of something. That was why we chose Lucyna, a simple mind, as the tool, so that information could be communicated. The minds of scholars are closed, limited. These people think only about themselves. They cannot see small people, but I see everyone. Both the smallest and the great ones. The learned scholars do not speak about the coming danger, about the year 2012. There was talk not only of the twelfth year, but also of the third, sixth, ninth, and twelfth. The twelfth year may be the most tragic in the history of mankind, but people will decide how it will really be."

Again, I thought about the recent natural disasters and the forecast effects of global warming.

"Are the changes which are beginning to happen the effect of the global warming that is occurring on our planet?" I asked.

"This is just the beginning, Wanderer. When the tail of Planet X sweeps the Earth, it will be happening instantly, within hours."

"Is this the catastrophe which the Mayan people forecast in their calendar for the year 2012? Is this really so precisely calculated?"

"There may be fluctuations of a few years, but this is unavoidable, unless that energy shield around the Earth is created."

I thanked the *Universe* and woke up Lucyna.

"What did I dream about?" she asked, as usual.

"About the flowers in the Earth being always beautiful, the sky being always blue, and the sun shining and smiling to us and to all the people in the world."

"It was a beautiful dream."

"Yes," I thought. "Beautiful, but how difficult to make it happen."

28

THE DREAM ABOUT THE LABYRINTH

The present, associated with the investigations on Sleza, was so promising that the time had come for planning future events — the investigation of the Labyrinth. This was the next stage in our activities before approaching the tomb of Cheops. I knew that the most important issue was to obtain the permit for research in Egypt. In order for this to happen, the *Universe* through Lucyna must first indicate the place. Then, her indications need to be confirmed by georadar and, finally, an application must be made to the *Guardian of Giza*, the Director of the Supreme Council of Antiquities, Dr. Zahi Hawass for a permit for the excavations, on the basis of the results obtained. I needed a vision for this plan; a vision of the future or of one of the possible futures; the one which we wanted which would lead us first to the Labyrinth and then to the Pharaoh.

Until now, the dreams of the Priestess included everything I could ever imagine. The *Universe* responded through her to every question, which was important and advanced the whole issue. I also felt that what was occurring was really happening at the appropriate moment, in the best possible time for this very event. I wondered if I could once again ask the *Universe* to look again into such a future, as we had in mind.

I asked Lucyna for another dream about the future.

"Could you show me what our activities and excavations of the Labyrinth will look like?" I asked the *Universe*.

"Do you know, Wanderer, why we are looking for the Labyrinth?" It asked in response.

I was surprised. *The Universe* did not answer my question but was again initiating another philosophical discussion. I have known why for a long time: The Labyrinth was to pave our way to Cheops.

"You told me more than once," I answered. "We are digging because digging into the Labyrinth is much easier than to the Pharaoh, because it will give credibility once and for all to the communications from the Priestess, because there is gold there, which motivates people, because this is a stage which we have to complete in order to obtain the permit for digging up the tomb…"

"All this is true," the *Universe* answered, "but there is another truth as well."

"What truth?"

"The purification of the Earth has already started," It explained. "There are people who are beginning to notice this, who see what is happening, that 'something is wrong.'"

"What do you have in mind?"

"Those who make the decisions see only their own interests, they see gold, authority, popularity, their own power… Just imagine what will happen if the population of the Earth doubles. Think how much the requirement for energy will grow."

"But there is much energy on the Earth." I noted.

"Yes, but people use the expensive, least effective sources like coal and oil, because profits are made from these. Science has long known very cheap sources, but those who make the decisions do not allow this information to get through. Gold… omnipresent and omnipotent gold… As if no one of those who fight so eagerly for it was aware that here on my side, I do not accept gold as payment for life."

"Yes, you have said that already," I commented.

"I have, and I will repeat it until there are found such who will start to hear me."

"Maybe you need a louder megaphone..."

"So you see," the *Universe* was pleased, "you have worked it out yourself as to why we are digging up the Labyrinth... It will be the megaphone. People need to be shaken up. Shaking by means of wars, floods or other natural disasters has already started. Not many notice this connection yet, not many understand that these signs are from me. Not many hear my call: 'People, come to your senses, start thinking in a different way.'"

"Do you think that the Labyrinth will change them?"

"Wanderer, I, the *Universe,* am the *Guardian of the Earth* and I will not allow it to be destroyed... I will cry out with a voice that will get stronger and stronger, louder and louder, because I want to save as many people as possible. Yes, the Labyrinth will change thinking, will open the eyes of all those who will want to see. The truths in which they used to believe and which they considered to be absolute will prove to be clay tablets, which break when a stone falls on them. Balloons blown up with air, which disappear when pricked with a pin. The gold of the Labyrinth is a minute part of its treasure... The true treasure is knowledge, which will see the light of day. This knowledge will be a shock and a megaphone so loud that even the blind and the deaf should notice it."

"How are you so certain that after the excavation of the Golden Chambers or any other part of the Labyrinth, anybody will find out about it?" I asked. "There have been so many discoveries, which do not fit into present-day dogmas, beliefs, and opinions, that have been moved into the shadow, hidden from the world, ridiculed and concealed so meticulously that no one can find them."

"You are forgetting, Wanderer, that the *Labyrinth Project* and the *Tomb Project* are my projects," the *Universe* answered. "I am taking care of them, I am guiding you, I am choosing the people and I will take care that this news reaches wherever necessary... People are easy to cheat. You are naive, you believe in authorities, in words. I cannot be cheated. I can see who has love in his heart and who is full of greed."

I did not quite know what love has to do with the Labyrinth, but it was an oft-repeated refrain of the *Universe*. It evidently talked about this whenever It could, so as to drum into our heads the thoughts that will help to feel love and send it into space.

I reminded myself that with me also, everything had started with a smile. When I first saw the smile on the face of the *Girl to Whom Every Morning Smiles,* that was the start of this never-ending dance to the extreme limits of love, the dance which is to save the people and the Earth.

"Please, show me what will happen with the Labyrinth project," I returned to our main issue.

"I will, Wanderer," It answered. "But this time, I will show it to you without the mediation of the Priestess. I will show it to you directly. As you know, my language is images that I can create in human imagination. As you call such images 'a vision,' I will show you one of the futures awaiting you, if everything goes according to my thought."

"What am I to do?" I asked.

"Just relax, close your eyes, and look deep within yourself..."

I did what It asked for and for a while I saw nothing, only darkness... Slowly, an unclear image started to emerge, the outline of something unspecified. "Maybe that is the Labyrinth," I thought.

Suddenly, I saw the *Lady Called Life.* She was walking slowly with a **pendulum** in her hand. All around was sand. I understood that we were in the desert. Suddenly, her pendulum started rotating so quickly, that she had to hold her elbow to stabilize the hand. It was rotating like an airplane propeller and I wondered how she was able to keep it in her hand. Finally, her hand dropped inertly and Lucyna sat down on a stone. "It is here," I heard her voice in my imagination. "One must dig here."

After a while, another image appeared, another vision. In place of Lucyna, I saw men with a georadar. They were bending over it and discussing something. I noticed that the georadar was going crazy and they did not know if it was indicating anomalies in the ground or had been affected by some technical bug, as sometimes happens with electronic equipment. At last, they shrugged their shoulders, closed the computer, and went away.

Then I saw the excavation. I saw how it was expanding from day to day, becoming ever deeper, and as it got deeper, it seemed to become narrower. None of those digging knew exactly how deep it would be necessary to dig. It was known only that many, many thousands of years had passed since the entrance to the Labyrinth, which we were seeking, was last used. "The labyrinth is as deep as the height of the Sphinx." I recalled a fragment of a dream of the Priestess.

In my imagination, I saw an excavation, which already seemed very deep to me. "How many meters down has been dug?" I asked one of the Egyptians working in the excavation. "More than fifteen meters already and nothing," he answered, with a mixture of fear and hope in his face. I saw that Patrick from Belgium was also there, walking back and forth around the excavation and muttering under his nose, that the Labyrinth is to the south of Lake Moeris and not here, in the middle of the desert, and that all of this did not make any sense. I saw Lucyna. She was calm and smiling. At this moment, my vision disappeared.

"Why did you interrupt my vision?" I asked with some resentment in my voice. "I want to see what will happen next."

"Remember, Wanderer," the *Universe* said in my thoughts, "everything is going well. These words have effective power. Not 'will go well' but 'is going well.'"

"Is going well," I repeated in my mind. We will reach the Golden Chambers and the tomb. I thanked the *Universe*, I thanked Lucyna, and I felt a pleasant peace in my heart. "Is going well," I thought once more. Everything has its time and is developing as it should.

29

THE DREAM ABOUT FUTURES

U p to this time, there have been many prophets of doom in the world, who predicted various versions of "ends of the world" and none of these have yet happened. People have become immunized to warnings of danger, to admonishments and prophecies. Those who regard themselves as normal, when they hear about a "danger to the world," smile with compassion and go their way. I also heard talk about the end of the world in my childhood, about the Last Judgment and the Apocalypse. My grandmother talked about it, as did priests in religion classes, although they did not explain what this meant. I also smiled ironically then, believing that the priest was simply trying to frighten us. Are these really only fairy tales for naughty children?

"Looking at the modern world," I once asked the *Girl to Whom Every Morning Smiles,* "don't you have the impression that people need a good shaking, because so many strange, unexplainable things are happening? More and more aggression, stress, and tension. They search you in airports, as if you were a terrorist. Special government agencies want to know everything that you do; soon they will implant special chips into your fingers, 'for your safety' and for control over you. You barely know your neighbors. The world is becoming more and more nervous, more and more dangerous."

"To this, I would add also," she answered, "the way the majority of people and the official world of science close themselves off from the world around them and ignore all the signals which come to us from the outside..."

I asked the Priestess for an explanation. The changes on the Earth are self-evident. The theory of Patrick from Belgium is convincing. We are under the threat of polar reversal, the mysterious Planet X, hyperactivity of the sun, global warming, and God knows what else... *The Universe* claims that opening the Great Pyramid may prevent this, but how do we explain to people that a real danger truly exists?

"I can see that you want to have another talk with the *Universe*. You want me to fall asleep." Lucyna said.

"You are reading my thoughts," I answered.

"Well, that is not so difficult. Ask."

"How can I convince people that the danger is real? The newspapers don't write about it. Television is silent and if anyone says so, they label him an esoteric or a madman."

"It was the same in the time of Noah," the *Universe* answered. "Noah explained and pleaded. He did not shout, did not warn but pleaded, until the very end. People did not believe. Tragic events will come one after another and if this does not bring results, the twelfth year will put an end to it. Then will start a raging storm throughout the world. Then the people will awaken and become terrified. They will recall that there were some who tried to explain, warn, and tell them, but it will be too late."

"Why are the press and television silent now?"

"Wanderer, science already knows that something is going to happen. The Pentagon and NASA have their reports and are conducting preparations in secret. They don't talk about it, because they do not want to cause panic. They want to retain control and save themselves."

I realized that the *Universe* was right. If the BBC, CNN, or any other television station suddenly broadcast a message that a global flood would come in 2012, that entire continents will be flooded, it is not difficult to imagine the panic that would erupt among people.

Some would consider whether to start drinking away their money right away or to wait a few years. Others would fall into depression and do nothing. Still others would probably start building bunkers or boats like Noah's Ark. However, there is a huge gap between what the prophets of doom say and what the *Universe* is saying. It points to a specific physical solution: to dig up the Pharaoh. How to make people aware that there is a solution?

"I would like to ask you," I said to the *Universe*, "to move the Priestess once more into the future and show her the world after the year 2012. Is this possible?"

"It is possible, but not today. The Priestess must fall asleep for a different dream. The images may be too difficult for her to view during a waking dream. You must help her fall asleep into a special, deep sleep, as it was in the beginning. Then and only then will I be able to move her forward in time, to when the year 2012 comes to its end."

So, I made an arrangement with Lucyna to do this later. It was time for my wandering around Poland and America. Everywhere I talked about Cheops and, as usually, after listening to my story, the people went back to their homes and sat down in front of their television sets with a feeling of complete safety. Earthquakes, tsunamis, and other catastrophes remained somewhere far away. They were already an old echo and an opportunity to send a few dollars to assist the flood victims.

At last, I was back in Wroclaw again and I met with Lucyna. She was ready.

"Fall asleep," I asked her, "and have a dream which will show you how it may be some time... Ask your Angels for help, ask the *Universe* to help you in this journey... Ask it for a vision after the year 2012..."

The Priestess was silent for a while, breathing calmly and falling into a deeper and deeper sleep. It seemed to us that this took a very long time, but it was just a moment... There were two of us beside her, myself and the *Girl to Whom Every Morning Smiles*. We listened to her breath and we waited for the dream, uncertain if it would come to her...

After a moment, she started to dream the dream of the *Universe*...

"I will show Ki two images," the *Universe* said in her slow and sleepy voice. "I will show the time of the twelfth year... I will show the image when Khufu, Cheops, does not open the gate. Then I will show the image when the Pharaoh sees the sun, the Pyramid is opened, and protection is activated."

Ki started to breathe more and more quickly, more uneasily. It was clear that her dream was different, that the images were more unusual. Her chest rose and fell more and more violently. Her face twisted with pain and worry... After a while she began to talk in a halting, tense voice.

"I am... I am... I see the year... I don't know which... Twelfth, perhaps fourteenth... Silence, horrifying silence... I am coming out of some cellar... Oh, no... Only ruins... God... What silence... There is nobody, there are no people. I see... Please... why is it so silent?... Not a single person... There are even no birds... What is this..? Silence... Such deafening silence... Where are the people...? None... there is nobody..."

Ki curled up and wept... she sobbed ever more loudly... in a more and more horrifying way...

I tried to calm her, "This is only a vision... only a vision... It does not have to be so."

"Get me out of here..." the Priestess pleaded, "Nobody here... nobody..."

"This is only a vision of the future," Iwona spoke to her in a calming voice, "just an illusion... not the reality... This does not have to happen... This is not the reality. In a while, you will move and you will see what will be in another time. You will see a different future..."

Iwona's voice was warm and calming. The Priestess's breath slowly calmed down. Her body relaxed. After a moment, she again started to talk.

"Yes... I am ready... I see... images... Other images... Still... there will still be diseases... They will still decimate people. I have an image of the twelfth year. I see beautiful houses... I see smiling people... They greet each other... They smile to one another. Love can be felt all around... peace. People are happy... There are so many of them....

How pleasant it is to see this image... People will still die, but death will not be terrible any more. People will have the hope of returning. The world will change from year to year. I see the beautiful Earth. The people respect it... love it. I would like to be here... I feel so much goodness... So much love..."

The smile on Ki's face said everything. Her face shone, her body was relaxed and her voice was calm... Her dream was not a nightmare any more and became a beautiful, colorful vision of a perfect world... a world of dreams. I decided to move Ki back to the present. I wondered how many futures still await the Earth and us. Only two?

"How many futures are there for people, for the world and for each one of us?" I asked the Priestess.

"Two," the *Universe* answered through her. "Those that I showed. The free will of human beings, the free will of mankind will decide which one will come true."

"What does this depend on?"

"It depends on the thoughts, decisions, and activities of every human being, and, in case of the world, on the sum total of the thoughts, decisions, and activities of all of mankind, all the people on Earth."

"What should people think, so that the future is the best possible one?"

"Believe... believe in the existence of the spiritual world, which wants to help. Think good thoughts; send out love in my direction... in the direction of the Creator. I will repeat once more: the scale of good and evil is now tilted toward evil. That is why the future of the world depends on how many people will believe, that something has to be changed, and how many people will open up their hearts to my cry."

"What will happen to people who won't change?"

"They will have to go... Purification will happen, in one way or another... God created a perfect planet and will not allow its destruction... If the Pharaoh does not see the sun, cataclysms will follow. The planet will remain, but the people will die..."

A moment of silence followed. As no other questions came to my mind, I decided to wake the Priestess.

When she opened her eyes, we were silent for a long time. Lucyna did not understand why there was such solemnity and such silence around her.

"Have I dreamt something bad? She asked.

"No, you just dreamt a few words of truth," I answered.

30

THE FUTURE ONCE MORE

The dream of Priestess Ki about the two possibilities for the world after year 2012 was both terrifying and comforting. I thought for a long time about what she had dreamed and about what will really happen. I dreamt hopefully about the future from her second dream. This vision was beautiful; in it, one felt the aspirations of every single person to live in a world full of love, harmony, happiness, and goodness. In a world where there are no stresses, where everyone has everything needed to feel fulfilled.

One day, I decided to talk to the *Universe* myself. I wanted to ask that It show me these futures, so that I could see them. For some time already, I had the feeling that I knew how to do this myself. I closed my eyes, relaxed my body, I greeted the *Universe* in my thoughts as warmly as I could and our conversation started.

"You state," I said, "that the Great Pyramid is the *Gate, the Great Passage, the Contact with You,* and *the Channel Through Which Entities from Other Dimensions Will Contact Us* and that this channel must be opened now. Since it is to be opened, it must have been closed some time ago. When?"

"You have reproached me," the *Universe* told me in my thoughts, "that my answers are not precise enough. You, people, like being given everything laid out on a tray. Everything must be in accord with mathematical accuracy, 'from - to,' If something is not in accord, it is rejected. Will I explain precisely with mathematical accuracy? No, for the simple reason that I also am bound by a law of silence and some facts cannot be released to you. Sometimes, I can slightly raise the veil to show a little of the secret."

"If you cannot unveil the whole window, let it be a chink, through which knowledge slips in," I consented.

"I have to make a reference to the birth of **Jesus**," the *Universe* said slowly, as if deliberating about every single word. "The connection existed before he was born. The decision to break it was made and the time was set. This time was the date of his birth. At the moment when he was conceived, when Jesus — the *Word* (because that is his name in my dimension) entered the newborn baby — then the connection between this and the Other Earth was broken."

I was astonished. In truth, I was not sure if what was appearing in my thoughts was the *Universe* speaking or only my imagination, but whatever it was, the information was interesting. *The Universe* often referred to Jesus in Lucyna's dreams. It always spoke about him with great love and respect, calling him the *Prince of Peace*. Now he linked the birth of Jesus with the channel of extraterrestrial communication.

"In the **Old Testament**," the *Universe* continued, "it was said many times that there is a channel linking the Earth with the other world. People could not understand this. What does it mean 'with the other world'? What 'other world'? Why was this channel closed? The reason was the fact that preliminary purification truly started from the moment of the coming of Jesus into the world. Jesus was to announce the message and speak about it, teaching people how to live. That was why this direct connection was closed. For a period of 2,000 years, people were left all to themselves, so that nobody, but nobody would disturb them in creating their own destiny. When it is to be opened, you already know."

"Does this mean that there is no communication between our dimensions?" I asked.

"The channel is closed, but there is communication. When needed, I can make contact with you. Your dreams and your thoughts are an example, when you relax and direct your attention in my direction. Then it is I talking to you and not your imagination. The dreams of the Priestess and our conversations, with her intermediation, are examples. You know that she can hear me not only in dreams. She hears me when she is awake and is able to perceive me at any time. There are many people on Earth who perceive me, and there will be more. The time will come when we will be able to communicate telepathically whenever we wish and without any restrictions."

Thousands of questions crowded into my head but I knew that every piece of information from the *Universe* had its time and that I would not learn anything either earlier or later than had been decided and allowed somewhere on high.

"Tell me something more about the future of the Earth," I finally asked.

At that moment, instead of hearing words, I saw an image. My imagination offered me a vision. I felt that I was not standing on solid ground but was somewhere in space, above our planet and was looking at it from above. I see clouds below me and I have a feeling of exceptional power. I feel that I can move in time and space. I need only to form a thought and it becomes a fact.

I decided to move forward in time and see the Earth in the future. My thought answered: "The future is not yet determined."

"Show me these most probable futures," I requested.

"There are only two futures," my knowledge answered me, which, at this moment, was not restricted by anything.

"I want to see both," I sent the order to my thoughts.

Suddenly, I saw an image, which looked as if it were taken from the surrealism of Salvador Dali, but seen as if at the time of its painting Salvador was in the deepest depression and with a major hangover. I did not know what year this was but I knew that in the place where I was time was an unknown notion... The image presented complete destruction. The Earth was a huge, lifeless skull, detached from the skeleton; a cemetery with no end and with no beginning. I was standing somewhere, where probably once had been a city but now resembled a garbage dump, of muddy, deformed shapes scattered over an enormous area, which once were buildings, automobiles and something else that I was unable to identify. I was gliding several or several tens of meters above the ground and gazed with horror at this twisted, battered, and putrid image of a complete annihilation of the traces of human existence.

I felt as if I were Superman, returning to the Earth from his planet Krypton after many years, in search of any life. I was circling the Earth and could find nobody and nothing. Wherever I glided, I saw an image of emptiness and had a sensation of terrifying silence. It was an icy emptiness, which spoke to me in the silence of a dead world without people, without animals, without birds, without insects... There were no cities, only their shadows remained; there were no houses, only outlines of their ruins. I was gliding above this dead world faster and faster, not knowing in which direction to go, to find even a trace of life. It was as if the *Universe* had shown me a supplement to the first dream or precognition of the Priestess; even more horrifying... even more depressing.

"What is this?" I asked my thoughts. "What planet am I on? This cannot be Earth."

"You are on Earth," My thoughts answered. "I showed you the image of the world which may exist after the year 2012, if the energy of love is not sent to the Supreme God. Such will be the world, if Cheops does not see the sun, if the tomb is not found, and the protection of the Earth is not activated in time."

"Will everybody perish?" I asked.

"Not everybody. The human race must survive; it cannot die out completely. In this future that I showed to you, both good and bad will perish."

"But you said that it did not have to be so," I reminded the *Universe* about Its promise.

"Purification must occur," It answered. "Surely, I do not ask for much. I do not want to create a new religion, new sects or to ordain new priests, so that they would pray to me or compose hymns and new liturgies to honor me. I only plead, shouting with the facts of natural phenomena. I indicate that it is necessary to dig up a few meters of ground near the Great Pyramid. Is this too much to save the people? It is not yet too late. There is still time but this time is shrinking from day to day. If people do not understand my message, even I will not be able to help."

"People have been threatened with the end of the world many times, although this has not occurred so far," I thought. "There are religious groups who have been talking about this for a long time."

"Those who speak about the 'end of the world' are right, although, as you know, it may be the end of the old world and the beginning of a new one. However, the solutions offered by these groups appeal to the imagination of only a small group of people. Moreover, some of them seek uniqueness, while some seek fame, and others gold, because you, human beings, are so fond of applause and the spotlight shining on you. That is why various sects and religions arise, which claim to have 'the only' solution, of a form such as 'if you join us, you will be saved' or 'pray with us and we will protect you,' I am showing a simple solution, the simplest possible."

"You have shown me one future," I said, after a while of emptiness in my mind, "but I know that it is not the future that you want to create for us."

"It is not I who creates your future," my thoughts flowed by one after another. "You create this future yourselves. You create your destiny. I can only show you choices, suggest thoughts, and speak through events and coincidences. I love you human beings. But for my love for you, the human race would have been gone from the Earth long ago."

"Show me another future, the one that is the choice of the Supreme," I asked the *Universe*.

Again, I felt that I was gliding high above the Earth and this time below me, I saw the entire globe, wonderfully blue and peaceful. I again had this strange and rare feeling of inner power: the possibility of moving freely in time and in space, being where I wanted and when I wanted. Every thought was creative. Whatever I thought happened immediately.

"I want to see another possible future," I instructed my thoughts, remembering the previous horrifying visions.

This time, I was standing on a street in an unknown city. The houses were tall, white, with beautifully sculptured balconies. It was evening and music was playing. It was a mixture of small bells, flute, and female voices, which immediately brought to mind the voices of angels. In truth, I have never heard Angels singing but I thought to myself that, if Angels sing, this is how their music must sound. I knew that the music was bidding farewell to the day, which was just ending. People were standing on the balconies. On some, there was only one person, on others — couples, while sometimes, there were groups of people.

The people smiled to one another and conveyed the sign of peace, the sign of love to one another. This was a warm "good night," mutually expressed among the people. I had the impression that everything was happening without words, although words appeared now and then in my head. When my attention was directed to a specific person or group of persons, I heard their greetings and wishes of good dreams... I felt their smiles and the harmony flowing from every person. Even when I looked toward two elderly people, looking like a married couple, standing on a distant balcony at the end of the street, I clearly heard their words.

"Sleep in peace, may love be with you. Have beautiful dreams." I thought the same about them and I noticed them sending me a greeting with a wave of their hands.

"How can I hear them?" I wondered. "They are at least 400 meters away from me."

"This is a different kind of communication," I heard the voice of the *Universe* in my head. "All people now communicate in this way, as

I do with you. This is **telepathic communication**. There are no more language barriers. There are only flying thoughts, which reach to where you send them."

"What year is this?" I asked.

"This is a view of the Earth after the purification, the possible future after the year 2012," the *Universe* answered.

"Is it like this everywhere? You have showed me a part of an unknown city, in an unknown country. What about the poor countries in Africa? Asia? What about the tension in Iraq? What about terrorism? How did this end? I am sure that you don't want to tell me, that all over the world will live people, who say a telepathic loving 'good night' to each other and go to sleep comfortably in their bedrooms in white houses costing a million dollars each with furniture for another million. Who could afford that? Why did you not show Indians from Peru or black people from Ethiopia, who now starve to death when there is a drought?"

"Your imagination, Wanderer, is still limited," the *Universe* noted sarcastically. "You are conditioned by your current experience on Earth. I showed you the world after purification. I showed you the possible future, assuming that the Pharaoh will see the sun before the year 2012 and that the tomb will be opened by the chosen group: by the people with pure hearts and pure intentions.

"I showed you the state of the spirit and the mind of people after the year 2012, and you ask me about material things. Wanderer, ornaments such as houses, apartments, balconies, streets, and automobiles — these are accessories. These are not the elements of harmony; these do not decide what a person feels in his heart. Yes, there will be poor people and rich people, but both the one and the other will have the same smile of life in their hearts. Even now, in your present time, there are people who have nothing and are happy. There are people who have everything and move from depression to alcohol, from suicidal thoughts to drugs. When the *Angel of Death* stands beside a person, what counts is how much good he did in his life and how much love he has in his heart. For a person who gave and received love in his life, death is not terrible. It is just a passage to me, a release from the prison of the body. Therefore, after the purification, there will be nothing to fear... The Earth will become more and more like the planet, which we call the Other Earth... It will become the Paradise Planet..."

In my imagination, I looked once more at the image, which was still in front of my eyes. "I want to be in Ethiopia," I thought and right away I saw happily playing black children and their smiling parents. "I want to be in Iraq," I thought and I saw mosques full of peacefully praying people, women and men in the streets, smiling to each other. "I want to be in Poland," and I saw the huge tower near Wylatowo, built to commemorate the contacts between people and visitors from other dimensions...

Everywhere, I felt unusually good thoughts, and I perceived the harmony and the high vibrations of the entire Earth.

"Yes," I thought to myself, "I also would like to live in such future," and I woke up from my dream.

31

AWAKENING THE PHARAOH

What I now relate is a shared dream, the dream of all of us who are taking part in the *Cheops Project,* in the mission of saving the people and the Earth. This dream was dreamed by us at the same time, by all of us simultaneously, and for all it was the same. All the details were in agreement. It was dreamt both by those who deeply believed in the mission and by those with doubts and vacillations. It was dreamt by Patrick from Belgium and by Barbara from Chicago. It was dreamt by the *Man Who Prefers to Stay in the Shadows* and by Andrzej, the *Man Who Dared to Be Wise.* It was dreamt by Lucyna, Iwona,) and many, many others. I, the Wanderer, dreamt it, and therefore I can describe it. It was a dream about the opening of the tomb of Pharaoh Cheops.

We were on Egyptian land, in our hearts feeling joy, excitement, curiosity, and a sensation of fulfillment... This, for which we had been waiting for so many years, was now a fact. The dream in our dream had become reality. That, which had been decided above, was being fulfilled down here. The spiritual world had combined with the physical world in the gigantic task of saving the people and the Earth. What seemed impossible for so many, turned out to be solely the barrier of Free Will. It was a miracle, which in the extraterrestrial dimension was the fulfillment of a prophecy, the execution of a decision, which we humans are not yet capable of understanding. Everything became so simple, that it seems strange. I recalled the sentence so often repeated by the *Universe:* "That, which is simple, is so difficult for you people."

We were standing not far away from the Great Pyramid, in the place where years after the last farewell to *the Builder*, the excavation of his tomb was to commence. Lucyna, the *Lady Called Life*, the Priestess Ki, who first indicated the place and opened the way to his awakening, was now the central figure in this unusual ceremony. She was surrounded by a group of scientists, archaeologists, and representatives of the Egyptian authorities and the Pentagon. There were delegations from Russia, Israel, Japan, China, Korea, and many other countries. There were several important businessmen and *All Other Very Important and Even More Important Persons...* Just beside Lucyna stood Don Severiano Olivarez, a humble shaman from Peru, the guardian of the Sacred Mountain Markahuasi, whom the *Universe* had designated as the incarnation of the Priest Juno himself.

His meeting with the Priestess Ki was an extraordinary event. It was a meeting of two loving spiritual entities, living in different bodies, which immediately recognized each other and fell in love again.

"And everything began with a smile," I thought, remembering the sequence of unusual coincidences initiated by the *Girl to Whom Every Morning Smiles;* the chain, which led to this day, to the place of the burial of the Pharaoh.

The Priestess, the *Girl to Whom Every Morning Smiles*, and I were standing at some distance from the rest, observing the people, who had initially been so skeptical and even hostile to the whole enterprise, and now were listening so intently and attentively to the words of the Priestess, a simple woman from a far away Poland, from the city of Wroclaw — a masseuse, without scientific degrees or titles but with a big heart. She had convinced everybody, first by Sleza, then by the revelation of the Labyrinth and the discovery of the Golden Chambers... The events, which started happening all around the world, convinced them.

Even the blind had to notice that the issue of global warming was not only a theory of a few mad scientists but a real problem, which could not be shrugged away. People started to notice that the increasing catastrophes were not just coincidences, but a repeating pattern of successive events. They began to understand that the theory of Patrick from Belgium, concerning the writings of the Mayas and the year 2012, was not only a vision of a madman but a real danger of extinction. At last, wise people in governments of this world understood that something had to be done to save themselves and the planet Earth.

The simplest, the most logical, and what was most important — the *only* — solution, which had no risk attached to it, was reaching the tomb of the Pharaoh. The *Director of the Pyramids*, understood this and the Egyptian government understood this and influential people from the Pentagon understood this. Thanks to this, the formalities, which had seemed to be an iron curtain, turned out to be a wooden fence, which collapsed under the weight of one wise thought.

I thought that this was the moment from which the new future was to start. The good future from my dream, from the dreams of the Priestess...

The Universe had very precisely described the procedures, which must be followed in digging up the tomb. The location of the tomb had been indicated by the Priestess with a precision of within one meter. It was confirmed by a dowsing survey and by georadar. Now it was clear that "something" was there, under the ground, close to the Great Pyramid.

The entire **Very Important Group** was now standing close to the designated place, waiting for Lucyna's words. She was in contact with the *Universe* all the time, she could talk with It telepathically, she could take advice and ask for pointers. Thanks to her skills, the *Universe* indicated the entrance to the Labyrinth. All eyes were on her.

"The tomb has several active energy safeguards, which need to be interrupted and neutralized in turn," Lucyna said. "To interrupt the first safeguard, three people must form a triangle."

We had known all this for a long time, but until now, we did not know who will be the people to break the first energy safeguard. We knew that they must place themselves in a triangle in strictly defined places. The first person must stand above the place where the tomb was located. The second must stand between the paws of the Sphinx. The third was to be in the middle, in front of the wall of the Great Pyramid, on the side of the Nile. The triangle formed in this way was to neutralize the protection flowing from the Other Earth. I knew that the *Universe* would choose people, to form this triangle, from among those who had come to Egypt for the ceremony of starting the excavations and were now gathered around the Priestess. It must make the choice; It was the only one who sees the hearts of the people gathered around Ki, who reads their intentions and sees what is invisible for us. Who will be first? "Anyone can stand on the corners of the triangle, but the chosen persons must have courage and pure hearts." the *Universe* had said once.

"Why would a person be afraid?" I asked then.

"All of you, Wanderer, are afraid of dying."

"But you said it yourself, that this mission is safe."

"For the chosen people, yes. But if inappropriate persons enter the tomb, who desire only profit and fame, they will all die."

"In that case," I asked, out of curiosity, "could these places be taken by, let's say, Lucyna, Iwona, and me?"

"Yes, they could. But when I feel even a trace of fear, the person will be changed."

"How will you make it known that a person will be changed?"

"The person will eliminate himself or herself. By fear."

I understood then that the *Universe* will assess fear of the unknown. Even the smallest trace of this will be amplified by It to such a magnitude that the person will simply run away and so exclude himself or herself... I checked the level of fear in myself. At this moment, I did not feel any; there was only joy from the choices made, the joy of reaching all the way to here, curiosity about what will happen, and what will be next, and pride; immense pride that we have succeeded and that we are participating in a moment of such importance to all mankind. I thought that perhaps the *Universe* will choose one of us. Perhaps Lucyna... Iwona... me? On the other hand, I knew that we had already done so much, that we have been very greatly favored, and that this special honor would be appropriate for someone else. For someone who was in the shadow until now..."There is a principle, Wanderer," the *Universe* said once. "Who humbles himself will be elevated."

"On the first point, at the top of the triangle, will stand the Priest Juno," Lucyna said quietly, "now Don Severiano."

She spoke in Polish, and so the interpreter, named Anibal, a friend of Severiano, a Polish-speaking Peruvian, who was standing beside the shaman, told him that he was to stand at the top of the triangle, in the place where the tomb was located. I was not surprised with this choice. I expected it. He, as priest Juno, had buried the *Builder*, protected the Tomb and now his energy was to disable this protection.

Severiano walked toward the designated place. Meanwhile the Priestess remained silent, focusing on her thoughts. Perhaps she was talking telepathically with the *Universe*, perhaps she was only waiting for his words.

"Between the paws of the Sphinx will stand the *Guardian of Giza*," Ki said at last. Her voice was now more expressive, stronger and there was no hesitation in it.

Zahi Hawass's eyes sparkled with joy. He immediately walked toward the majestic Sphinx to stand in the designated place. In my mind, I was happy with this decision of the *Universe*. For a long time, Dr. Zahi did not believe in the dreams of the Priestess and, just like multitudes of well-known scientists, he did not agree to the search for the Great Labyrinth in the place indicated by her. But it was he, however, who made the decision to support our preliminary survey secretly. He was the first of the whole series of *Very Important Persons*, who not only heard the voice of the *Universe* and listened to its advice. So many others for such a long time could not distinguish the words of Lucyna, a woman living on Earth in the twenty-first century, from the dreams of the Priestess, who was receiving direct information from the Other Dimension.

"Yes," I thought, "the *Universe* really does see our hearts..."

Two corners of the triangle were already occupied. We continued to wait. Lucyna was silent for a minute... two... three... This time seemed an eternity to us. We knew that she, as Ki, was listening to the Voice of the *Universe* and waiting for his instruction, but in the group around her, common human curiosity was the dominating factor... Who will be "the third"? Looking at her face, I saw her concentration, though, at one moment I noticed a strange smile, as if she was bantering with the *Universe* in her thoughts.

"Beside the Great Pyramid," Lucyna said at last, "will stand Geza Kisteleki."

I think that many of those standing around Lucyna felt some disappointment at this moment, perhaps envy, perhaps sadness, that "it is not me." For me, this choice was the biggest surprise. Geza, a Hungarian scientist, who had only recently joined our group, seemed to be so distant from my imagined list of candidates for this distinction, that, even in my boldest speculations, I did not take him into consideration. Sure, it was through him that we became acquainted with his Egyptian friend, who helped us to make direct contact with the Egyptian authorities, but so many others seemed more "worthy." I thought that perhaps this choice was a bow by the *Universe* to Sirius. Geza was convinced that spiritual entities from Sirius were also helping us in this work, that they were adding their energy to the task of saving the Earth.

I felt sad for Lucyna. I thought about the whole road, which she had to travel from her clinical death to her first dreams with Łucja, with me, and with Iwona. The humiliation, the mockery, the accusations of psychological disturbance, the black visions of many *Very Well-Known Clairvoyants* (I called them "prophets of doom"); she had to accept everything with humility, without losing her faith in the wisdom and guidance of the *Universe*. It seemed to me that the *Universe* should reward her for her faith and determination, for walking along this "thorny road" and leading us to the Pharaoh. It should place her, as Priestess Ki, in one of the corners.

"She will be the first to enter the tomb," my thoughts told me at that moment. "Nobody else can have this honor. I smiled in my soul to myself and to the *Universe*. "Of course, she is the chosen one."

The triangle was formed. None of us knew what we were to expect at this moment. How this will be "manifested." What will happen? I thought that perhaps some sparks would fly from the persons placed at the three apices and that this would indicate that something was happening. Perhaps some visible energy will flow through them and suddenly all three will shake and this will be the sign.

I was sure that each one of the chosen was the best, the most appropriate person at this moment to perform the task. I saw that Don Severiano had slightly vacant eyes. Perhaps before he was chosen, his spirit moved back in time to become the *Great Priest* again, the friend of the Pharaoh. He was experiencing the moment when he had to bury in the sand of the temple the mummy of His Master, knowing that it would only be excavated after so many years had passed. He was one of the few people who were aware at that time of the true meaning of the tomb, of the message of the whole Pyramid.

We were now waiting for some sign, a word, some information that it had happened, that the energies protecting the tomb were neutralized. It was late afternoon and the sun was lengthening our shadows. Suddenly, a light refreshing wind blew in from the Nile. "Perhaps this is it?" I thought. I closed my eyes and imagined that I was looking at the whole scene from above, that I was seeing the triangle made by Severiano, Hawass, and Kisteleki from a bird's-eye view. In my imagination, I saw their energies connecting them, the lines of energy, which were undulating, changing colors, filling in the center of the triangle with vibrating air, sometimes of a greenish color, sometimes violet. The vision became more and more clear and the colors more and more vivid... I tried to hold onto this image as long as I could.

I remembered the experiment of the Italian professor Ferlini, back in 1980s, who moved pairs of huge electromagnets up to a model of the Great Pyramid, constructed at a scale of 1:100. At a certain moment, a strange field of energy was generated and the professor, who bent down over the pyramid out of curiosity, disappeared for a while from the field of vision of his assistants. He appeared again when, in panic, the field was disconnected. The visions that he had during his "absence," which lasted several seconds, were so extraordinary that a veil of complete silence was drawn over this incident and it did not come to the attention of the public. "I wonder if any one of us will disappear," I thought and quickly opened my eyes to check that everybody was there.

They were. Nobody disappeared and nothing unusual was happening. For a while, it appeared to me only that within the region of the formed triangle I saw some slight refractions of the light in the air, rising upwards, toward the sky. I wanted to ask Patrick from Belgium, if he could see anything, but his eyes were closed and he was probably creating his own visions. Perhaps he was rejoicing at the fact that December of the year 2012 does not have to be the end of human existence, as the Mayas had predicted.

"Digging can start," suddenly Lucyna spoke, "the way is open."

We looked at one another. No thunderclaps, no energy storms that is it? Just "the digging can start..." I was curious if anyone felt disappointed with this lack of something unusual.

"Well," I thought, "we have completed the ritual from the dream of the *Priestess*. That will do."

★ ★ ★

The Director of the Pyramids drove the first spade into the sand. This honor fell to him, because for so many years, he had been the faithful *Guardian of Giza*. Thanks to him, no unauthorized person even came close to "our" place. No one had the right to dig on the Giza plateau, although there were many who wanted to dig. He did not know why he prohibited this, he did not know that the *Universe* had appointed him to perform this ungrateful role. With his stubbornness, he constantly exposed himself to the wrath and envy of archaeologists and various other prospectors, who had an appetite for the pyramids, the Sphinx, and the treasures, which could be hidden there. This time, he was the *Person Who Initiated the Most Important of all the Excavations that Man Has Ever Conducted Throughout His Existence.*

We knew exactly what we were to expect in the process of digging up the Pharaoh. I recalled the dream of the Priestess when, in the year 2002, we were talking about the tomb.

"What will we find when we dig toward the tomb of the Pharaoh?" I had asked the *Universe* then.

"Wanderer, I will tell you what is awaiting you, what surprises," It answered, "Protection is awaiting the appointed persons, the chosen ones, because, as you know, the area and the tomb have protection. This is the protection which flows in waves directly from Orion."

The first protection was neutralized and we knew that our group is the one which should dig. We are the group selected and accepted by the *Universe.*

"After penetrating the layers of stones and hard sand," the Priestess dreamt at that time, "you will reach the graves. People unknowingly made a cemetery there. You will encounter skeletons. Some of them will be of little importance, but there will also be dignitaries. This will not be what we need, so you have to go on digging. After removing the cemetery layer, you may encounter tunnels made by insects. This is another trap. For safety reasons, you must have fire with you, in order to burn this. It may happen that, when you are digging down, the insects will move away, since my energy will kill them. When you remove this obstacle, only digging will remain. Then only sand will be found down to the tomb of the Pharaoh. "

And this is what happened. The excavation became deeper and deeper from day to day. We knew that the tomb was hidden at a depth of about fifteen meters, so from the beginning the excavation was wide enough to be gradually narrowed in steps, as the digging and construction of the appropriate safeguards progressed. At a depth of ten meters the archaeologists encountered the predicted cemetery. This gave rise to huge enthusiasm in everyone. This was another proof of how precise were the indications of the *Universe*.

Finding the cemetery delayed the excavation work. Archaeology has its rights and archaeologists have their procedures. Every bone had to be cleaned with a brush and catalogued. Every grave was thoroughly checked and every vessel found was carefully described.

We waited patiently, knowing that just a moment more was needed, that in a few days, or perhaps weeks, would be revealed to mankind the biggest secret of all times. In this way, we will save the Earth from something unknown. The cosmic destiny predicted by the gods. That the protection offered to people will be activated and many, many millions of human beings will avoid death, and the Earth will avoid another cataclysm. These were extraordinary moments; moments of hope, tension, and uncertainty. Many asked themselves the question, "What if there is nothing there?" Perhaps all of this is some political game, a cover-up to hide the real problems of the world? There were some who predicted that opening the Pyramid of Cheops will be "the end of the world." They warned against "the black forces, which will take over the Earth..." The answer was now only a few meters below the ground.

Gradually, the excavation deepened to the required depth. The georadar, probes, and vertical drilling all showed the existence of a specific, large formation, which, in our minds, could be nothing else but the tomb we were looking for; a compartment built of stone blocks similar to those in the Great Pyramid. What was hidden in it was to be more precious than all the gold in the world. It contained the history of mankind inscribed on tablets by the Egyptian priests during the twenty years of construction of the Great Pyramid. It contained the mummy of the Pharaoh, the *Great Builder*, the *Son of the Sun*, who was waiting impatiently to look again, after so many centuries, at the face of his father. It contained the key to the Gate of Time.

I wondered if the spiritual entities feel excitement just like us, this special kind of excitement before an event for which they have been waiting for a long time. I knew indeed that time passes in a different way in the dimension of the *Universe,* but the very fact of a change, of the fulfillment of the prophecy, of the fulfillment of the Will of the Supreme, of the fulfillment of destiny, has to be something exceptional even for them. I knew that the spirit of Khufu was among us and was also waiting for this moment. I imagined that, if he were a physical entity, he would surely be stamping his feet now and rubbing its hands from time to time.

"What can spiritual entities do in such moments?" I wondered. "Perhaps they feel some special kind of emotion, unknown to us mortals. Maybe these are the emotions known to only a few humans, close to that which the chosen call "enlightenment."

The digging advanced slowly, as caution was imposed on account of the trap with insects, which had been predicted. The diggers had flame-throwers, in case the insects had to be incinerated. At a depth of fourteen meters, something was encountered resembling pipes or holes formed in the soil. They were empty. *The Universe* had kept its word. If any insects had ever been there, the energy had killed them. Just in case, the workers threw the flames along one side and then the other, and the digging continued.

The expected moment arrived in the evening on one of the following days of the excavation. A spade struck against a stone.

The next days were dedicated to uncovering the tomb. Everyone was aware that after the uncovering of the entrance, the last energy protection would have to be neutralized. The energy of the Priestess Ki, our contemporary Lucyna, was needed for this.

"What should we do after opening the tomb?" I asked the *Universe* during one of her first dreams about Cheops.

"This is a very significant question," It answered in a serious tone. "Only those will enter who have truly pure intentions. The first to enter will be Priestess Ki, who is devoted to the Pharaoh. She will break open the last blockade of energy protection and then there will no longer be any danger."

The pit leading to the Tomb looked huge. On the side of the Great Pyramid, there was also found a filled-in part of the labyrinth, a corridor, which probably led to the Pyramid itself and along which the priests walked in the funeral procession, to lay the Pharaoh in the place of his rest. Now, from the surface to the uncovered but still-closed tomb, there led a whole series of ladders, creating a sort of stairway, down which one had to go to reach the level of the entrance itself.

"The wall of the tomb on the side of the Pyramid has to be cleared," Lucyna said, when the whole structure was uncovered,

It was obvious to us that the stone on the side of the Pyramid was the one forming the entrance. The archaeologists considered how to move it. Should it be lifted with a crane or drilled through its structure? The stone had not been moved for many thousands of years. It was feared that careless action could damage the inside of the tomb. Finally, it was decided to drill very slowly through the stone, in order to penetrate into the inside.

The workers were amazed when it turned out that, soon after the first drilling was started, the external layer became loose and was easily removed by the workers from the proper wall, revealing the entrance, a niche obstructed by a stone block. Removing this block was now child's play. The entrance to the tomb was open. We were standing beside the end of the old and the beginning of the new age in the development of mankind...

"Is there any further procedure after removing the Pharaoh from the tomb?" was another question from the dreams of the Priestess.

"Yes, Wanderer, there is a procedure," the *Universe* had answered then. "The mummy of the Pharaoh with the procession (that is, with all of you) will proceed to the Sphinx. There, you will bow to it. Then, you will move to the Pyramid and lay the body in its sarcophagus."

"I understand that this whole procedure is to serve to open the Pyramid, to open the way for extraterrestrial communication. What will happen next?" I had asked then.

"That is so. You are right, but what will happen next, Wanderer, you will learn later. I am not allowed to tell you everything. And what will happen after waking the Pharaoh will then directly concern all of you."

"All the people living on Earth? Is that what you have in mind?"

"On Earth, yes, the people living on Earth..."

This was a dream the *Priestess* had long ago, but it was strongly imprinted in my memory. At that time, I did not understand its true meaning; it seemed to me distant and unreal. Now, when her dreams had started becoming fulfilled, the centuries-old prophecies took on the meaning of an order. "This is how it is to happen," the Gods said then and everybody knew that this must happen so.

Lucyna went down the ladders and stood in front of the dark, still unlit entrance. She closed her eyes, as if for a while giving herself up to prayer or meditation. I knew that in her thoughts she was talking to the *Universe,* which was reassuring her and perhaps explaining the further procedures.

After a while of hesitation, she took a step forward. She entered the dark opening of the entrance and stopped inside. At this moment, the last protection was disabled. The key to the Great Pyramid, the *Gate of Time*, was in the reach of human hands... It was shortly after noon. The sun shone brightly, waiting for the appearance of its son.

EPILOGUE

In April of 2005, Pope John Paul II died and people suddenly started to change, the world looked at itself with the eyes of love, with the eyes of understanding.

"Look at the world in the days of mourning for the pope," I asked the *Universe* through the Priestess. "Are you not talking about such energy? Is this not what you are asking the people for and what you have received? People are capable of it. If such a need arises, they can save both the Earth and themselves without Cheops."

The *Lady Called Life* was silent for a while and then started repeating the words of the *Universe* with sadness in her voice.

"I never concealed the fact that the pope was for us, the spiritual beings, a swallow, a precursor, a herald of the coming of the symbolic spring. He flew everywhere and proclaimed the message. But tell me, Wanderer, how much of this message did the people understand? The pope, or your White Father, was the last link in the chain; the chain, which still restrained the heavenly army, waiting for the sign given from the *Great Commander*, to descend onto the Earth. The last link breaks and the chain is released."

I thought to myself that the *Universe* was not answering my question, but I knew that this was his style of talking, and that sooner or later, It would get down to specific details. Apparently, It had to say everything that lay in Its heart and concerned the late pope.

"Oh, human beings," the *Universe* continued Its thought, "do not weep after the departure of this last swallow. Weep for yourselves. Now weep for yourselves. So that the *Great Prince*, the *Great Chief* can come down to the Earth and start life in the new order, this order must first be made and purified. The people have already made the pope a saint. He will be a saint, but he will be able to intervene only when the Earth is cleaned and purified. Now he is with me and he will be able only to watch. Today, sadness appears in your faces, human beings, and I ask where were you for all those years, when this swallow was proclaiming, talking, pleading for a turning to God and for being good to your neighbor? Here, I can count on my fingers those people who understood the words of this swallow. Now weeping is not needed but rather a wise analysis of the current situation."

"But I am thinking of the energy," I interrupted diffidently, "the energy, which the people were sending up to the heavens, during the memorable April days when John Paul II departed. Then all the televisions of the world described his life; millions of people came to Rome to pay him homage. It was an immense dose of the energy of love."

The Universe continued to remain with his thought.

"People do not want to admit into their consciousness that there exists something more than their conceit. It is necessary to convince enlightened people, who consider themselves to be wise and omniscient. These people have to be informed how important saving the Earth is, not only their own skin. Those who want to be saved are few, and the whole great mass of people would have to leave. Wanderer, people are dear to me. One may say that every human being carries a particle of me, a divine element. Along the way, people have lost only their instinct, the instinct of love. This was why the energy of love alone will not suffice. All of the devices which are located around the entire Earth have to be activated and only then, can we speak about saving the people."

"I really am thinking of the energy of love. The energy, which the *White Father* released with his passing."

"The Earth, Wanderer, shall remain," the *Universe* continued, once again ignoring my question. "If the people could see with the eyes of their imagination this empty Earth, then surely their way of thinking would change. You are asking about the *White Father...*"

"At last," I thought.

"Some people do not believe that love is energy. It is immense energy. At the time when your *White Father* was taken, when he returned home, human beings managed to unite. They were able to be kind to each other and to show love. But this lasted briefly. When the *White Father* was buried, everything returned to its place and the energy sent out into the space is as it was before. Can such energy save people? Here I will repeat what I have said: the Earth... the Earth will survive, but inhabitants of the Earth may not. The Earth will heal its wounds and then, already healed, it will be fit for settlement by another civilization. I will say that I would have to look with pain in my heart if my entities had to leave the Earth and this because of their own stubbornness, because of stupidity. What did the *White Father* preach when he was traveling all around the Earth? What did he preach, I ask? What did he preach? He preached love, love of one's neighbor; he pleaded for conversion. Before he left, he managed to tell you not to fear. *Nie lękajcie się* – that means in Polish: "Do not fear". The *White Father* knew about saving for the Earth. That was why he was so reluctant to leave."

"The prayers for the intention of John Paul II created energy. Is this energy protecting the Earth?" I made my question more specific,

"This is an indisputable fact," the *Universe* acknowledged. "Energy was created, but it should persist all the time. At this moment, this beautiful energy, which was created by the people, is again frayed. It needs to be consolidated, to be repaired. Can you people create all by yourself such strong energy, which could protect the Earth when another planet flies by close to it? Believe me, Wanderer, people alone are not able to do this. That was why the entities from the belt of Orion built the message that is the *Pyramid* or the *Gate of Time*. This message is also scattered all around the Earth and everywhere there are hidden secured energies, which must be activated prior to the year 2012. In other words, one must catch up in the time available."

I received my answer and in my mind, I knew the *Universe* was right. Indeed. Already, just a few days after the pope's burial, the world returned to its commonplace routine, to conflicts, quarrels, and all that makes up our daily life. The energy, this beautiful energy, was again frayed.

One other question had been on my mind for a long time and I came to the conclusion that this was a good opportunity to pose it.

"You have used the phrase," I addressed the *Universe,* 'we, spiritual entities.' If you were given the Earth into your care, who are you really? What is your true name? Can you answer this question?"

I was not sure if the *Universe* will want to talk on this subject. It had already avoided answering several times but I risked nothing. In the worst case, I will hear that "It is not yet the time." To my joy, the answer was very specific.

"So this is what is worrying you, Wanderer," I felt a smile in the words of the Priestess. "Now I can answer you. Now you are ready, but the answer is not simple."

"Why?" I was surprised.

"My time is *Eternity.* My name has changed along with your earthly time."

"So what was it in the beginning?"

"My true name is *EA*. Then people gave me different names, depending on the time in which they were living. I am the *One Which Created the Human Race*, I am ENKI. When I came to the Earth, human beings were still very primitive. My role was to lead you to perfection, and therefore my element, the divine element, is present within every human being; the element which I myself received from the Supreme Deity. In the old difficult times, I fought to preserve the human race; I protected it against destruction and therefore you are so very dear to me. I also had other names. I was called **Ptah, Oanes, Ra**. I had many other names in different periods and civilizations. You in the Slavonic land called me **Swiatowid**. The proto-Slavonic people used to worship me as a god, just like many other civilizations. I stand at the highest levels of the spiritual hierarchy; I am one of the first sons of the Supreme God. That was why I received the Earth into my care."

I was silent; the Priestess was silent. Ea, Enki, was evidently waiting for another question, but nothing wise was coming to my mind. Although I had expected this, I was dazed by the importance of the Spiritual Entity with which I talked almost daily. Another question came to my mind, "What is your name now, in our civilization?" but I was subconsciously afraid of asking it

"How am I to call you now?" I finally asked.

"Keep on calling me the *Universe*. I like this name. Nobody up till now has addressed me in this way."

"I do not know what else to ask you about," I admitted honestly. "Is there anything else that I should know, which could help in the *Cheops Project*?"

"Yes, there is," the *Universe* answered. "The scholars will admonish you that Cheops could not have built the Great Pyramid 10,500 years ago, because he lived in a different time, much later."

"I know. Many have spoken to me about this. Andrzej talked about it, the *Man Who Dared to Be Wise*."

"You have to know that, in fact, Cheops and Khufu are not the same person, not the same Pharaoh. "

Again, I fell silent, hearing these words with amazement. Indeed, ever since I learned through Lucyna that the date of the construction of the Great Pyramid was many thousands years older than the official date, this did not fit into the dynasty of the pharaohs, as determined by science. Pharaoh Khufu, the one commonly called Cheops, was a pharaoh of the fourth dynasty and, according to history, lived in about 2500 BC (about 4,500 years ago). So he could not have built the Great Pyramid. The Priestess Ki was always calling him "Cheops." Why?

"If Khufu and Cheops are not the same person, why does Ki call this pharaoh Cheops?" I asked.

"I have already spoken about this. People have difficulty understanding very complex things. That is why I allowed the mind of the Priestess to accept the pharaoh as Cheops."

"So who built the Great Pyramid?"

"Science claims that Cheops built the Pyramid two and a half thousand years before the Era of the Pisces," the *Universe* answered. "That is inaccurate, because the Pyramid was already standing at that time. It was heavily damaged, and therefore Cheops (for the sake of simplicity, let us call him **Cheops Number Two**) was given the task of repairing it. He accomplished this and, indeed, on this repair only people did the work."

"So who built it?" I repeated my question.

"What I will tell you will astonish you. The building of the Great Pyramid was supervised by the **One Who Came from the Sky**. That is how he was named. Let me explain why the inconsistencies in the name arose. Well, as you know, the outstanding beings, who were to teach the primitive population, came from Atlantis. After the evacuation, those who survived dispersed all over the Earth. The same language, habits, and beliefs existed over the entire Earth. There were no divisions into countries or continents. Changes came only after the second flood."

"The name of Khufu," the *Universe* continued, "was already known on Atlantis. *The One Who Came from the Sky* was exceptionally skillful. The people thought that the gods had sent him. When the construction of the Pyramid started, the chief supervisor had to have a name. The memory of Atlantis was very much alive, so he was named Khufu. It is also true that Cheops the Second lived many years later and that it was he who repaired the damaged Pyramid. It is also true that Cheops Number Two did not enter into the Pyramid. He was sure that the bones of the one who built it were inside. He respected the Pyramid."

"It is also true," the *Universe* spoke on through the Priestess, "that the bones of both the one and the other pharaoh have not been found. When you open the tomb of Khufu, you will see who is resting in this tomb. The burial place of Cheops Number Two will also be revealed to you. Neither of them rests in the Valley of Kings."

I thought to myself that any archaeologist or somebody engaged in the history of Egypt would have hundreds of questions, if he were in my place. My formal knowledge in this field was too scanty to allow me to drag out this subject.

"That the name of Cheops was borrowed for the time of the messages, was done deliberately," the *Universe* Itself returned to the question of names. "This happened in this way, so that it would be easier to reach human minds, and in order to awaken the curiosity of men of science. The name Khufu means 'great.' Open the Labyrinth or the tomb and you will learn the name of the one that rests there. You will learn the secret of the universe and the future of the Earth. Who would believe if you spoke about the Pharaoh who supervised the construction of the Great Pyramid, the *Gate of Time*, the *Code of Mankind*, '*The One Who Came from the Sky*'? And so, when the name 'Cheops' was uttered, it awoke both curiosity and antagonistic opinions. And so it succeeded."

"In that case, why did Cheops Number Two appropriate the same name? Why did he call himself Khufu?" I asked.

"Doesn't it happen today, in your time, that the name Jesus is given to people? Aren't there people with the name of Washington? Cheops was a descendant of Khufu in the direct line. The names, dates, and important information were all inscribed on stones. Cheops ordered all of this to be removed. The truth may be found only after digging up the tomb."

THE MYSTERY OF THE GREAT PYRAMID

In June of 2005, a team of six persons traveled to Egypt for the first survey. Besides Lucyna, there was Andrzej (the *Man Who Dared to Be Wise*); there was a georadar specialist, Adam (the *Man Who Understands the Language of the Earth*); there was Iwona (the *Girl to Whom Every Morning Smiles*); there was Patrick from Belgium (the *Man Who Sees the Fate of the World in Black*); and there was myself (the Wanderer).

Lucyna precisely marked the place of Khufu's burial and two entrances to the Great Labyrinth; one beside the mud brick pyramid in Hawara and the other beside the third pyramid in Giza. *The Universe* guided her also to the burial place of Cheops Number Two. Both tombs are close to the Great Pyramid.

In January of 2006, the Supreme Council of Antiquity in Egypt granted an official permission to the Institute of Geophysical Sciences in Cairo for deep ground penetration radar (GPR) research in Giza area, by the pyramids. The research was done in February 2006 at several sites, also those indicated by Lucyna to the depth of twelve to about sixty meters. The Polish Foundation for Supporting Archeological Research *Dar Swiatowida* and the American Foundation *The Mysteries of the World* in Chicago provided the funds. The data was analyzed by the scientists at the National Institute of Astronomy and Geophysics in Cairo, and by the Institute of Geological Sciences at the University of Wroclaw in Poland. The results are known by now. They confirmed one undisputable fact. Deeper, under the pyramids of Giza complex there is a whole system of man made structures: open spaces, chambers, corridors, tombs, etc.

The data analysis also confirmed the indications of Lucyna Lobos. Will this pave the way to excavating the *One Who Came from the Sky*, the *Son of the Sun*, Pharaoh Khufu? The answer to this question depends on us, humans.

* * *

In February 2008 the University of Cairo in Egypt and the University of Wrocław in Poland signed official agreement of mutual scientific cooperation in order to start archaeological research at the Hawara Necropolis area. The goal: looking for the labyrinth described by Herodotus 500 years BC. The Foundation *Dar Swiatowida* provided the funds for this project through the University of Wrocław.

In March 2008 the Supreme Council of Antiquity granted the permission for this research to the Department of Archaeology of the Cairo University. Works started in April by making GPR tests supervised by Dr. Adam Szynkiewicz, geologist from the University of Wrocław under the supervision of the Dean of the Faculty of Archaeology, Prof. Dr. Alaa Shaheen as the General Manager, and Dr. Reda Abdel Haleem as on site manager.

In April 2009 Dr. Zahi Hawass stopped this project on the ground that the Polish Foundation is not allowed to pay or such research since dowsing and channelings are "not scientific". The book *In Search of the Great Labyrinth* by Andrzej Wojcikiewicz describes the whole project.

In November 2009 Lucyna Łobos, *The Lady Called Life*, withdrew from the *Cheops Project*. She was replaced by other medium: Anna Dolinska.

On November 11, 2011, at 11:00 am and 11:00 pm the Foundation *Dar Swiatowida* organized in Cairo two Ceremonies called 11.11.11. One inside of the King's Chamber of the Great Pyramid (at 11:00 am) and another outside the Pyramid on Giza Plateau, (at 11:00 pm) together with a worldwide meditation for peace and protection of Mother Earth. The Ceremony inside involved only 4 specially selected people. For the evening Ceremony everybody was invited, regardless of nationality and faith. However both Ceremonies were performed from outside the Giza Plateau (in spite of all permissions from Egyptian Government were granted). Reason: some unknown group of very powerful people had spread a gossip that "1200 Jews came to Cairo, they want to surround the Great Pyramid, place the Star of David on its top and meditate in order to move the Pyramid to Israel".

In January 2013 Foundation *Dar Swiatowida* ceased to exist. On its place the *Foundation for the Support of Research to Disclose Ancient and Modern Knowledge "Wisdom of Nations"* was crated. Name in Polish: *Fundacja Wspierania Badań Nad Ujawnianiem Wiedzy Starożytnej i Współczesnej "Mądrość Narodów"*. The same task: financially support excavations in Egypt (to uncover hidden treasures buried there under sands – especially in areas of the Three Pyramids of Giza and at the Hawara Necropolis area), in addition to promote research of free energy such as Zero Point Energy, energy hidden in water (Brown's Gas), wind energy, etc.

Symbolic "mummy of Cheops" seems to be a completely different archaeological object and its energy is still available to activate the Great Pyramid. The sarcophagus in the King's Chamber is still waiting to fulfill its role; nevertheless, it should never be called a „sarcophagus". It was never intended to contain a mummy of any pharaoh.

The mystery of the three pyramids on Giza Plateau and all other pyramids in the world suggest, that we are NOT alone in the Universe. It looks like the awakening of Cheops should be moved to present times and re-named as The Awakening of World Pyramids, especially the Great Pyramid. Planet Earth and its people are still in danger.

Andrzej Wojcikiewicz, Ottawa, Canada, August 2019.

Website: HYPERLINK "http://www.wisdomofnations.com"
      www.wisdomofnations.com
Contact: fundacja@projektujawnianiawiedzy.com

THOSE WHOM I WOULD LIKE TO THANK AND SAVE IN MEMORY

The world is changing every minute and every second, just like human memory. For this reason, I would like to pay tribute to all those, who, as the forerunners, initiated the *Cheops Project* and started traveling toward the new, unknown destiny. This "unknown" is still a *Great Secret,* but it poses stronger and stronger proofs of its existence.

Therefore, I would like to save in memory the Priestess Ki, **Lucyna Łobos**, to whom this Project owes its existence. One has to have incredible courage not to fear being different from everybody else. Thank you, **Lucyna**, for your humility, patience, and inner strength, and for making all of us aware that we can do something important for the people and for the Earth.

I would like to save in memory the *Girl to Whom Every Morning Smiles,* **Iwona Stankiewicz**. Thanks to her, the meeting of the Priestess with the Wanderer became possible. **Iwona** became the spark which ignited the lamp illuminating the way to Egypt, and the thread which connected individual elements of this puzzle. Thank you for appearing on my way.

I would like to save in memory the *Lady Who Can Go Back in Time,* **Łucja Szajda**. As a clinical psychologist, she was able to assess the condition of Lucyna's mind and did not hesitate to move her back into times about which she knew nothing. Thank you, **Łucja**, for putting at stake your authority as a psychologist and for giving credibility to the hypnosis sessions with Lucyna.

I would like to save in memory the *Lady Who Dares to Speak,* **Barbara Choroszy** from Chicago, who amazed us with her courage to speak on radio about things strange, difficult, and so different from official theories. Thank you, **Barbara**, for your courage and help.

I would like to save in memory the *Man Who Saw the Fate of the World in Black,* **Patrick Geryl** from Belgium. Thanks to his passion, the *Labyrinth Project* originated as a step to discovering the tomb of the pharaoh. Thank you, **Patrick**, that you did not hesitate to come to Brussels for the first meeting with me, and that you have been patiently helping us through your contacts.

I would like to save in memory the *Man Who Dared to be Wise*, the engineer and geologist, **Andrzej Kaplanek**. The *Sleza Project* owes its existence to him, as the first step toward the discovery of the tomb of the pharaoh. Thank you, **Andrzej**, for your inquisitiveness and knowledge, so helpful in our project.

I would like to save in memory the *Man Who Was a Total Skeptic* and who turned into the *Man Who Was Lost In Admiration*, the Ph.D. in archaeological sciences, **Aleksander Limisiewicz**. Thanks to him, the excavations on Sleza were started and are continuing, and this most mysterious mountain in Poland has been revealing its secrets. Thank you, **Aleksander**, that, despite immense doubts, you started the investigations on Sleza.

I would like to save in memory the *Man Who Understands the Language of the Earth*, the Ph.D. in geological sciences, the georadar specialist, **Adam Szynkiewicz**, thanks to whom the *Cheops Project* has become not only a dream but also a scientific reality. Thank you, **Adam**, for your love of the Earth and the commitment to a project about which you knew so little.

I would like to thank all who have been and are helping in the *Cheops Project*, physically, financially and spiritually, through sending good thoughts and giving us words of hope, reassurance and understanding.

I would like also to thank **Lidia and Cezary Tousty** from Darlowo, the founders of the *DAR SWIATOWIDA* Foundation for Supporting Archaeological Research, the first organization in Poland whose objective is to reach the tomb of the Pharaoh Cheops.

I thank you and I bow my head to your commitment and courage on stepping out on a road, sometimes covered with potholes, but oh, how interesting!

9 781951 461737